Differentiated Instruction:
English Language Learning Support

Grade 7

EMC School

PART OF CARNEGIE LEARNING

PITTSBURGH, PA — ST. PAUL, MN

English Language Learning Consultants and Reviewers

Robert Leos
Senior Director, Textbook
Administration, Retired
Texas Education Agency
Austin, Texas

Rebecca Rodriguez
Bilingual/ELL/Reading/ELA
Instructional Specialist, Retired
Davila Elementary/Middle School
Houston ISD
Houston, Texas

Caroline Castillo De La O
Secondary ESL Teacher
Katy ISD
Katy, Texas

Annie Arredondo
District Secondary ESL Specialist
Ector County ISD
Odessa, Texas

Monica Velarde-Ruiz
Instructional Officer, Bilingual
and ELL
San Elizario ISD
San Elizario, Texas

Stacy Courtright
English Language Learning Specialist
Tucson, Arizona

Differentiated Instruction: English Language Learning Support, Grade 7

Care has been taken to verify the accuracy of information presented in this book. However, the authors, editors, and publisher cannot accept responsibility for Web, e-mail, or newsgroup subject matter or content, or for consequences from application of the information in this book, and make no warranty, expressed or implied, with respect to its content.

Trademarks: Some of the product names and company names included in this book have been used for identification purposes only and may be trademarks or registered trade names of their respective manufacturers and sellers. The authors, editors, and publisher disclaim any affiliation, association, or connection with, or sponsorship or endorsement by, such owners.

ISBN 978-1-53384-153-7

©2020 by Carnegie Learning, Inc.
875 Montreal Way
St. Paul, MN 55102
E-mail: info@carnegielearning.com
Web site: www.emcschool.com

Printed in the United States of America

27 26 25 24 23 22 21 20 19   3 4 5 6 7 8 9 10

CONTENTS

Literacy & Reading Skills

English Language Development

Foundational Literacy Skills

Literacy & Reading Skills

Name: _____   Date: _____

page 7

After Twenty Years

A Short Story by O. Henry

ABOUT THE STORY

"After Twenty Years" tells the story of two old friends who made an appointment twenty years ago to see each other again in New York City. They have lived very different lives since their days together. What happens and how they meet will surprise you.

MAKE CONNECTIONS

Do you have any friends that you have not seen for a long time? Do you think they have stayed the same or do you think they have changed? Explain your answer.

_____

_____

_____

_____

ANALYZE LITERATURE: Plot

The **plot** is the series of events that happen in a story. Different pieces of the plot show the exposition, or introduction to the story; the climax, or highest point of interest in the story; and the resolution, or conclusion, of the story.

USE READING SKILLS: Analyze Cause and Effect

A **cause** is the event that makes something else happen. An **effect** is what changes after the cause. For example, if the cause is a beautiful, sunny day, the effect could be many people in the park. If the cause is rain, the effect could be wet, empty streets. As you read, look for cause and effect details in the story. Fill out the chart below.

Cause	Effect
The weather is chilly, rainy, and windy.	The streets are nearly empty.

PREVIEW VOCABULARY

Key Words and Phrases Read each key word and rate it using this scale: ①I don't know this word or phrase at all. ②I've seen this word or phrase before. ③I know this word or phrase and use it.	Words and Phrases in Context Read to see how the key word or phrase can be used in a sentence.	Definition Write down what you think the word or phrase means. Then use a dictionary to check your definition.	Practice Practice using the key words and phrases by completing the following sentences.
habitual hab • it • u • al (hə´ bi ch [ə] wel) *adjective* ①　②　③	Each day, he takes his **habitual** morning run around the track.		In literature class, I habitually sit…
intricate in • tri • cate (in´ tri kət) *adjective* ①　②　③	The needlework on that fabric is very complicated and **intricate.**		An example of something intricate is…
swagger swag • ger (swa´ gər) *noun* ①　②　③	Students are so full of confidence after the test, they **swagger** down the hallway.		An arrogant person might swagger because…
staunchest staunch • est (stônch´ est) *adjective* ①　②　③	He loves politics. He is actually the **staunchest** republican that I know.		I am a staunch believer in…
egotism e • go • tism (ē´ gə' ti zəm) *noun* ①　②　③	Jane thinks she is so perfect; her **egotism** is out of control.		Egotism shows a lack of consideration for…

After Twenty Years

A Short Story by O. Henry

The policeman on the beat[1] moved up the avenue impressively. The impressiveness was **habitual** and not for show, for spectators were few. The time was barely ten o'clock at night, but chilly gusts of wind with a taste of rain in them had well nigh
5 depeopled[2] the streets.

Trying doors as he went, twirling his club with many **intricate** and artful movements, turning now and then to cast his watchful eye down the pacific thoroughfare, the officer, with his stalwart form and slight **swagger,** made a fine picture
10 of a guardian of the peace. The vicinity was one that kept early hours. Now and then you might see the lights of a cigar store or of an all-night lunch counter, but the majority of the doors belonged to business places that had long since been closed.

When about midway of a certain block, the policeman
15 suddenly slowed his walk. In the doorway of a darkened hardware store a man leaned with an unlighted cigar in his mouth. As the policeman walked up to him, the man spoke up quickly.

"It's all right, officer," he said reassuringly. "I'm just waiting
20 for a friend. It's an appointment made twenty years ago. Sounds a little funny to you, doesn't it? Well, I'll explain if you'd like to make certain it's all straight. About that long ago there used to be a restaurant where this store stands—'Big Joe' Brady's restaurant."

25 "Until five years ago," said the policeman. "It was torn down then."

The man in the doorway struck a match and lit his cigar. The light showed a pale, square-jawed face with keen eyes and a little white scar near his right eyebrow. His scarf pin was a large
30 diamond, oddly set.

"Twenty years ago tonight," said the man, "I dined here at 'Big Joe' Brady's with Jimmy Wells, my best chum[3] and the finest chap in the world. He and I were raised here in New York, just like two brothers, together. I was eighteen and Jimmy was
35 twenty. The next morning I was to start for the West to make my fortune. You couldn't have dragged Jimmy out of New York; he thought it was the only place on earth. Well, we

---

1. **beat.** Area regularly patrolled by a policeman
2. **well nigh depeopled.** Almost emptied
3. **chum.** Friend

agreed that night that we would meet here again exactly twenty years from that date and time, no matter what our conditions
40 might be or from what distance we might have to come. We figured that in twenty years each of us ought to have our destiny worked out and our fortunes made, whatever they were going to be."

"It sounds pretty interesting," said the policeman. "Rather a
45 long time between meets, though, it seems to me. Haven't you heard from your friend since you left?"

"Well, yes, for a time we corresponded,"⁴ said the other. "But after a year or two we lost track of each other. You see, the West is a pretty big proposition,
50 and I kept hustling around over it pretty lively. But I know Jimmy will meet me here if he's alive, for he always was the truest, **staunchest** old chap in the world. He'll never forget. I came a thousand miles to stand in this door tonight,
55 and it's worth it if my old partner turns up⁵."

The waiting man pulled out a handsome watch, the lids of it set with small diamonds.

"Three minutes to ten," he
60 announced. "It was exactly ten o'clock when we parted here at the restaurant door."

"Did pretty well out West, didn't you?" asked the
65 policeman.

"You bet! I hope Jimmy has done half as well. He was a kind of plodder,⁶ though, good fellow as he was. I've had to compete with some of the sharpest wits going to get my pile. A man gets
70 in a groove⁷ in New York. It takes the West to put a razor edge on him."

The policeman twirled his club and took a step or two.

"I'll be on my way. Hope your friend comes around all right. Going to call time on him sharp?"⁸
75 "I should say not!" said the other. "I'll give him half an hour at least. If Jimmy is alive on earth, he'll be here by that time. So long, officer."

---

4. **corresponded.** Communicated by letter
5. **turns up.** Comes or appears
6. **plodder.** One who works slowly and monotonously; a drudge
7. **gets in a groove.** Gets in a routine
8. **call time on him sharp.** Leave if he doesn't arrive exactly on time

staunch‧est (stônch′ est) *adj.,* most loyal or committed

Build Vocabulary

These two friends *lost track* (line 48) of each other. Name something or someone you have lost track of.

_____

_____

Think and Reflect

Do you think Jimmy will keep his promise and show up to the appointment with his friend?

"Good night sir," said the policeman, passing on along his beat, trying doors as he went.

80 There was now a fine, cold drizzle falling, and the wind had risen from its uncertain puffs into a steady blow. The few foot passengers astir[9] in that quarter hurried dismally and silently along with coat collars turned high and pocketed hands. And in the door of the hardware store the man who had come a

85 thousand miles to fill an appointment, uncertain almost to absurdity, with the friend of his youth, smoked his cigar and waited.

About twenty minutes he waited, and then a tall man in a long overcoat, with collar turned up to his ears, hurried across

90 from the opposite side of the street. He went directly to the waiting man.

"Is that you, Bob?" he asked, doubtfully.

"Is that you, Jimmy Wells?" cried the man in the door.

"Bless my heart!" exclaimed the new arrival,

95 grasping both the other's hands with his own. "It's Bob, sure as fate. I was certain I'd find you here if you were still in existence. Well, well, well!—twenty years is a long time. The old restaurant's gone, Bob; I wish it had lasted,

100 so we could have had another dinner there. How has the West treated you, old man?"

"Bully; it has given me everything I asked it for. You've changed lots, Jimmy. I never thought you were so

105 tall by two or three inches."

"Oh, I grew a bit after I was twenty."

"Doing well in New York, Jimmy?"

110 "Moderately. I have a position in one of the city departments. Come on, Bob; we'll go around to a place I know of and have a good long talk about old times."

115 The two men started up the street, arm in arm. The man from the West, his **egotism** enlarged by success, was beginning to outline the history of his

Analyze Literature

Look at lines 82–87. What words or phrases in this section create suspense for the reader?

Read Aloud

Read aloud the dialogue between the two men in lines 92–115, starting with "Is that you Bob?" and ending with "talk about old times." How does Bob feel about seeing his old friend again?

_____

_____

_____

e·go·tism (ē´ gə' ti zəm) *n.*, large sense of self-importance; conceit

9. **astir.** Walking around

career. The other, submerged in his overcoat, listened with
120 interest.

At the corner stood a drugstore, brilliant with electric lights. When they came into this glare, each of them turned simultaneously[10] to gaze upon the other's face.

The man from the West stopped suddenly and released his
125 arm.

"You're not Jimmy Wells," he snapped. "Twenty years is a long time, but not long enough to change a man's nose from a Roman to a pug."[11]

"It sometimes changes a good man into a bad one," said the
130 tall man. "You've been under arrest for ten minutes, 'Silky' Bob. Chicago thinks you may have dropped over our way and wires[12] us she wants to have a chat with you. Going quietly, are you? That's sensible. Now, before we go to the station, here's a note I was asked to hand to you. You may read it here at the window.
135 It's from Patrolman Wells."

The man from the West unfolded the little piece of paper handed him. His hand was steady when he began to read, but it **trembled** a little by the time he had finished. The note was rather short.

140 *Bob: I was at the appointed place on time. When you struck the match to light your cigar, I saw it was the face of the man wanted in Chicago. Somehow I couldn't do it myself, so I went around and got a plainclothes man to do the job.*

Jimmy   ❖

---

10. **simultaneously.** At the same time
11. **Roman to a pug.** Two distinctly shaped noses
12. **wires.** Communicates by telegram

 **MIRRORS & WINDOWS** Do you think that Jimmy Wells did the right thing by having his old friend arrested? Would you have done the same thing? Why or why not?

_____

_____

Use Reading Skills

Cause and Effect
Find the cause and effect described in lines 136–138. Record them here.

_____

_____

_____

trem·bled (trem´ bəld) *verb*, shook from fear

Note the Facts

Who is the man that was talking to Bob?

_____

How do you think Bob feels now that he has been caught?

_____

_____

READING CHECK

Circle the letter of the correct answer.

1. Why is the policeman walking down the street?
   A. He is searching for a criminal.
   B. It is his regular job to patrol the street.
   C. He is on his way home.

2. Which of the following best describes the man waiting in the doorway?
   A. friendly and cooperative
   B. shy and nervous
   C. angry and rude

3. Why is the man waiting in the doorway?
   A. He is waiting for the restaurant to open.
   B. He wants to talk to a police officer.
   C. He is waiting to see a friend.

4. Where does Jimmy live?
   A. Jimmy lives in New York.
   B. Jimmy lives in the West.
   C. The story doesn't say.

5. How does Bob realize that the man he is talking to at the end of the story is not Jimmy Wells?
   A. He is shorter than he remembers.
   B. His nose is different.
   C. He has a different voice.

VOCABULARY CHECK

Circle the letter of the correct answer.

1. Bob calls his Jimmy his best chum. What does *chum* mean?
   A. supervisor
   B. friend or pal
   C. older person

2. Bob says Jimmy was the *"staunchest old chap in the world"*. What does this description mean?
   A. Jimmy was really old.
   B. Jimmy was a very loyal friend.
   C. Jimmy did not like to spend a lot of money.

3. Bob is waiting for his friend to turn up. What does *turn up* mean?
   A. arrive or appear
   B. turn around
   C. walk faster

4. Bob says, "A man gets in a groove in New York." What does *gets in a groove* mean?
   A. gets rich
   B. gets in trouble
   C. gets in a routine

5. The story says that the man from the West had "egotism enlarged by success." What does this phrase mean?
   A. All of his worry about money gave him health problems.
   B. He thought he was very important and was not modest about his success.
   C. He was very nervous about getting caught.

ANALYZE LITERATURE: Plot

Write a paragraph summarizing the plot of the story. Remember to include the exposition, the climax, and the resolution.

_____

_____

_____

_____

USE READING SKILLS: Analyze Cause and Effect

1. What might have been the cause of the scar on Bob's face?

   _____

2. Look at your cause and effect diagram. Which cause and effect detail is the most important to the story? Why is it important?

   _____

3. Bob did something in his past that gets him arrested. What do you think the cause for the arrest might have been?

   _____

BUILDING LANGUAGE SKILLS: Superlative Adjectives

An adjective is a word that describes a noun. A superlative adjective is made by adding -est. It describes a noun to the extreme or to the highest level. Fill in the columns below for some of the adjectives found in the story. The first one is done for you.

Adjective	Superlative Adjective	Use It in a Sentence
staunch	staunchest	Robert is the congressman's staunchest supporter.
long		
near		
straight		
sharp		
high		

SPEAKING AND LISTENING: Listening skills

Your teacher will read or play the first paragraph of the story. Fill in the missing words as you listen, without turning back to the story.

The (1) _____ on the beat (2) _____ up the avenue impressively. The

impressiveness was (3) _____ and not (4) _____ show, for spectators (5)

_____ few. The time was (6) _____ ten o'clock at night, but

(7) _____ gusts of wind with a(n) (8) _____ of rain in (9) _____

had well nigh depeopled (10) _____ streets.

BEFORE READING

page 53

A Day's Wait

A Short Story by Ernest Hemingway

ABOUT THE STORY

"A Day's Wait" tells the story of a young boy who has a fever. The doctor comes to see the boy at home and says that he has a fever of 102°. The sick child has a horrible day in bed, but not only because of the fever.

MAKE CONNECTIONS

What things make you scared or worried? Give a few examples.

_____

_____

_____

_____

ANALYZE LITERATURE: Conflict

Conflict is the struggle or the problem that the character has in the story. The conflict can be an internal conflict or an external conflict. An internal conflict is a struggle with feelings within you. An external conflict is a problem with something else, like another person, nature, or something in society. As you read, try to determine what type of conflict the character in the story is experiencing.

USE READING SKILLS: Draw Conclusions

When you **draw conclusions**, you are gathering pieces of information and then deciding what that information means. As you read, look for ideas and words that are repeated. Put them in the details column of the chart below. Then tell why you think the author repeated these words in the conclusions column.

CONCLUSIONS CHART	
Details	**Conclusions**
sick	Author wanted the reader to understand how the boy looked, acted, and felt

PREVIEW VOCABULARY

Key Words and Phrases Read each key word and rate it using this scale: ①I don't know this word or phrase at all. ②I've seen this word or phrase before. ③I know this word or phrase and use it.	Words and Phrases in Context Read to see how the key word or phrase can be used in a sentence.	Definition Write down what you think the word or phrase means. Then use a dictionary to check your definition.	Practice Practice using the key words and phrases by completing the following sentences.
capsules cap · sules (cặp sulz) *noun* ① ② ③	There were fifty **capsules** in the bottle of prescription medicine.		Something that is available in the form of a **capsule** is . . .
influenza in · flu · en · za (in' flu['] en´ zə) *noun* ① ② ③	The **influenza** virus gave her a fever and a headache.		A person with **influenza** should . . .
epidemic ep · i · dem · ic (e' pə de´ mik) *noun* ① ② ③	The AIDS **epidemic** affects many people around the world.		A county-wide **epidemic** would cause . . .
lightheaded light · head · ed (līt hed ed) *adjective* ① ② ③	He felt **lightheaded** after smelling the chemicals in the laboratory.		A person might feel **lightheaded** when . . .
flush (flʉsh) *adjective* ① ② ③	His cheeks looked pink and **flushed** with embarrassment.		A person might look **flush** when . . .

Differentiated Instruction: Literacy & Reading Skills   © Carnegie Learning, Inc.

A Day's Wait

A Short Story by Ernest Hemingway

He came into the room to shut the windows while we were still in bed and I saw he looked ill. He was shivering, his face was white, and he walked slowly as though it ached to move.

"What's the matter, Schatz?"

5 "I've got a headache."

"You better go back to bed."

"No. I'm all right."

"You go to bed. I'll see you when I'm dressed."

But when I came downstairs he was dressed, sitting by the

10 fire, looking a very sick and miserable boy of nine years. When I put my hand on his forehead I knew he had a fever.

"You go up to bed," I said, "you're sick."

"I'm all right," he said.

When the doctor came he took the boy's temperature.

15 "What is it?" I asked him.

"One hundred and two."

Downstairs, the doctor left three different medicines in different colored capsules with instructions for giving them. One was to bring down the fever, another a purgative, the third

20 to overcome an acid condition. The germs of **influenza** can only exist in an acid condition, he explained. He seemed to know all about influenza and said there was nothing to worry about if the fever did not go above one hundred and four degrees. This was a light **epidemic** of flu and there was no danger if you avoided

25 pneumonia.[1]

Back in the room I wrote the boy's temperature down and made a note of the time to give the various capsules.

"Do you want me to read to you?"

"All right. If you want to," said the boy. His face was very

30 white and there were dark areas under his eyes. He lay still in the bed and seemed very detached from what was going on.

I read aloud from Howard Pyle's *Book of Pirates*; but I could see he was not following what I was reading.

"How do you feel, Schatz?" I asked him.

Note the Facts

How did Schatz look when he came downstairs?

_____

_____

Build Vocabulary

The author has described Schatz many times throughout the story. What are some of the words to describe how he looks today?

_____

_____

in·flu·en·za (in' flu['] en´ zə) *n.*, viral disease characterized by fever, muscular aches, and respiratory distress

ep·i·dem·ic (e' pə de´ mik) *n.*, outbreak of contagious disease that spreads rapidly

---

1. **pneumonia.** Disease marked by inflammation of the lungs

Use Reading Skills

Draw Conclusions

Does Schatz want his father to stay or leave? Why might it bother him to stay?

_____

_____

Note the Facts

Was the boy's father alone on his walk?

_____

_____

Build Vocabulary

The author uses many words to describe the setting where the father is taking his walk. What are some of the words used to describe the nature around him?

_____

_____

flush (flŭsh) *adj.*, having a red color to the skin

35   "Just the same, so far," he said.

I sat at the foot of the bed and read to myself while I waited for it to be time to give another capsule. It would have been natural for him to go to sleep, but when I looked up he was looking at the foot of the bed, looking very strangely.

40   "Why don't you try to go to sleep? I'll wake you up for the medicine."

"I'd rather stay awake."

After a while he said to me, "You don't have to stay in here with me, Papa, if it bothers you."

45   "It doesn't bother me."

"No, I mean you don't have to stay if it's going to bother you."

I thought perhaps he was a little lightheaded and after giving him the prescribed capsules at eleven o'clock I went out

50   for a while. It was a bright, cold day, the ground covered with a sleet that had frozen so that it seemed as if all the bare trees, the bushes, the cut brush and all the grass and the bare ground had been varnished with ice. I took the young Irish setter for a little walk up the road and along a frozen creek, but it was difficult

55   to stand or walk on the glassy surface and the red dog slipped and slithered and I fell twice, hard, once dropping my gun and having it slide away over the ice.

We flushed[2] a covey of quail under a high clay bank with overhanging brush and I killed two as they went out of sight

60   over the top of the bank. Some of the covey lit[3] in trees but most of them scattered into brush piles and it was necessary to jump on the ice-coated mounds of brush several times before they would flush. Coming out while you were poised unsteadily on the icy, springy brush they made difficult shooting, and I

65   killed two, missed five and started back pleased to have found a covey close to the house and happy there were so many left to find on another day.

At the house they said the boy had refused to let anyone come into the room.

70   "You can't come in," he said. "You mustn't get what I have."

I went up to him and found him in exactly the position I had left him, white-faced, but with the tops of his cheeks **flushed** by the fever, staring still as he had stared at the foot of the bed.

---

2. **flushed.** Frightened a game bird from cover
3. **covey lit.** Flock of birds came to rest

75 I took his temperature.

"What is it?"

"Something like a hundred," I said. It was one hundred and two and four tenths.

"It was a hundred and two," he said.

80 "Who said so?"

"The doctor."

"Your temperature is all right," I said. "It's nothing to worry about."

I don't worry," he said. "but I can't keep from thinking."

85 "Don't think," I said. "Just take it easy."

"I'm taking it easy," he said and looked straight ahead. He was evidently holding tight on to himself about something.

"Take this with water."

"Do you think it will do any good?"

90 "Of course it will."

I sat down and opened the Pirate book and commenced[4] to read, but I could see he was not following, so I stopped.

"About what time do you think I'm going to die?" he asked.

"What?"

95 "About how long will it be before I die?"

"You aren't going to die. What's the matter with you?"

"Oh, yes, I am. I heard him say a hundred and two."

"People don't die with a fever of one hundred and two. That's a silly way to talk."

100 "I know they do. At school in France the boys told me you can't live with forty-four degrees. I've got a hundred and two."

He had been waiting to die all day, ever since nine o'clock in the morning.

"You poor Schatz," I said. "Poor old Schatz. It's like miles
105 and kilometers. You aren't going to die. That's a different ther-mometer. On that thermometer thirty-seven is normal. On this kind it's ninety-eight."

"Are you sure?"

"Absolutely," I said. "It's like miles and kilometers. You
110 know, like how many kilometers we make when we drive seventy miles in the car?"

"Oh," he said.

But his gaze at the foot of the bed relaxed slowly. The hold over himself relaxed too, finally, and the next day it was very
115 slack and he cried very easily at little things that were of no importance. ✤

---

4. **commenced.** Began

Analyze Literature

Conflict What kind of conflict is Schatz facing today?

_____

_____

Read Aloud

Read the conversation between Schatz and his father in lines 82–103. Why is Schatz so upset?

_____

_____

Culture Note

Schatz was confused about the different temperatures in Celsius and Fahrenheit. His father explains that it is like the difference between miles and kilometers. The United States uses systems of measurement that are different from most other countries. Has this ever caused any confusion for you?

_____

_____

 Has a miscommunication or misunderstanding ever caused you to feel scared about something?

_____

_____

READING CHECK

Circle the letter of the correct answer.

1. What is wrong with Schatz today?
   A. He has a fever.
   B. He has pneumonia.
   C. He wants to stay in bed instead of going to school.

2. How does Schatz's father know that his son had a fever?
   A. He would not come downstairs.
   B. He felt his forehead.
   C. The young boy was sweating.

3. What does the father do to try to comfort his son while he is sick?
   A. They listen to some music together.
   B. He takes him for a walk outside in the fresh air.
   C. He reads him a story in bed.

4. What is Schatz's temperature?
   A. 102°
   B. 44°
   C. 104°

5. Why does Schatz think that he is going to die?
   A. Boys from school told him that influenza is deadly.
   B. Boys from school told him that you can't live with a temperature above 44°.
   C. Boys from school told him that he shouldn't take the medicine.

VOCABULARY CHECK

Circle the letter of the correct answer.

1. The doctor gives Schatz three different *capsules*. What are they?
   A. small, round pieces of medicine
   B. boxes to open during the day
   C. tests to see why he has a fever

2. Does the doctor think that *influenza* is a serious problem for Schatz?
   A. It is nothing to worry about if he avoids pneumonia.
   B. It is a serious problem; he is very concerned.
   C. Schatz is not sick at all.

3. This is a light *epidemic* of the flu. Why is it only a light epidemic?
   A. Many people are sick all over the country.
   B. This is a contagious disease, but only some people are sick with it now.
   C. Many people are dying of pneumonia.

4. The father thinks that Schatz is a little *lightheaded*. Why would he think that?
   A. The father thinks the comments about staying and bothering him are strange.
   B. Schatz was dizzy when he was walking around.
   C. It is very hot in the bedroom.

5. The tops of Schatz's cheeks are *flushed* with fever. What color are they?
   A. white
   B. red
   C. yellow

ANALYZE LITERATURE: Conflict

Write a paragraph about the conflict that Schatz has in the story. Explain the difference between what he thinks is going to happen to him and what is the reality of the conflict.

_____

_____

_____

_____

USE READING SKILLS: Draw Conclusions

1. Look at your chart from page 11. Why do you think that the author chose to repeat and stress those specific words?

_____

_____

2. What do you think is the main idea, or theme, of the story? How did the repetition help you recognize the main idea?

_____

_____

BUILD LANGUAGE SKILLS: Contractions

Contractions are shortened forms of words in which the missing letters are replaced with an apostrophe. They are often used in everyday, spoken English. Look at these contractions used in the story and rewrite the phrase without the contraction. The first one is done for you.

With a Contraction	Without a Contraction
1. What's the matter?	What is the matter?
2. I've got a headache.	
3. I'm all right.	
4. You're sick.	
5. I'll wake you up for the medicine.	
6. It doesn't bother me.	
7. You can't come in.	
8. Don't think.	
9. That's a silly way to talk.	
10. It's like miles and kilometers.	

SPEAKING & LISTENING

Work with a partner to research the 1918 influenza pandemic. Where did this take place? What happened and what were the effects? Prepare a short oral report with your partner about one interesting aspect of this problem. Use new vocabulary learned in the story as you present your information to the class.

Differentiated Instruction: Literacy & Reading Skills

page 59

The War of the Wall

A Short Story by Toni Cade Bambara

ABOUT THE STORY

"The War of the Wall" is a story about two neighborhood children who are angry because a stranger started to paint a mural on "their" wall. The two children make plans to stop the stranger's work. Before they can stop the mural, they discover that the mural is not what the neighborhood expected.

MAKE CONNECTIONS

Where do you gather to have fun and relax with friends and family? Why is this place special to you?

_____

_____

_____

_____

ANALYZE LITERATURE: Dialect

Dialect is a version of a language spoken by people from a particular group, location, or time. For example, you can often tell what part of the country a person is from by the words that he or she chooses to use. As you read, pay attention to the examples of dialect in the story.

USE READING SKILLS: Evaluate Cause and Effect

When you evaluate **cause and effect**, you are looking for a logical relationship between a cause or causes and one or more effects. In a story, sometimes one event explains why another one happens. The event that explains why is the cause. The event that explains the result is the effect. Keep track of the causes and effects in "The War of the Wall" in the chart below.

Causes	Effects

Differentiated Instruction: Literacy & Reading Skills

PREVIEW VOCABULARY

Key Words and Phrases Read each key word and rate it using this scale: ① I don't know this word or phrase at all. ② I've seen this word or phrase before. ③ I know this word or phrase and use it.	Words and Phrases in Context Read to see how the key word or phrase can be used in a sentence.	Definition Write down what you think the word or phrase means. Then use a dictionary to check your definition.	Practice Practice using the key words and phrases by completing the following sentences.
masterpiece mas · ter · piece (mas´ tər pēs) *noun* ①　②　③	The song is very beautiful. It is the composer's **masterpiece**.		Another example of a **masterpiece** is…
trance trance (tran[t]s) *noun* ①　②　③	I was so tired after the long walk; I felt as if I was in a **trance**.		Something that can put you in a **trance** is…
strict strict (strikt) *adjective* ①　②　③	That teacher is very **strict**. He doesn't accept late homework.		A **strict** parent would not let you…
beckoned beck · oned (bek und) *verb* ①　②　③	She **beckoned** the children inside the house.		A supervisor might **beckon** the employees to…
liberation lib · er · a · tion (li' bə rā´ shən) *noun* ①　②　③	Many national anthems are songs of **liberation**.		The opposite of **liberation** is…
cracking up crack · ing up (krak iŋ əp) *verb* ①　②　③	The comedian was so funny that my sister and I were **cracking up**.		Something that has made me **crack up** before was…

The War of the Wall

A Short Story by Toni Cade Bambara

Me and Lou had no time for courtesies. We were late for school. So we just flat out told the painter lady to quit messing with the wall. It was our wall, and she had no right coming into our neighborhood painting on it. Stirring in the paint bucket and
5 not even looking at us, she mumbled something about Mr. Eubanks, the barber, giving her permission. That had nothing to do with it as far as we were concerned. We've been pitching pennies against that wall since we were little kids. Old folks have been dragging their chairs out to sit in the shade of the
10 wall for years. Big kids have been playing handball against the wall since so-called integration[1] when the crazies 'cross town poured cement in our pool so we couldn't use it. I'd sprained my neck one time boosting my cousin Lou up to chisel Jimmy Lyons's name into the wall when we found out he was never
15 coming home from the war in Vietnam to take us fishing.

Think and Reflect

How would you react if a stranger started making changes to a place or an object that you thought of as yours?

_____

"If you lean close," Lou said, leaning hipshot against her beat-up car, "you'll get a whiff of bubble gum and kids' sweat. And that'll tell you something—that this wall belongs to the kids of Taliaferro Street." I thought Lou sounded very convincing.
20 But the painter lady paid us no mind. She just snapped the brim of her straw hat down and hauled her bucket up the ladder.

"You're not even from around here," I hollered up after her. The license plates on her old piece of car said "New York." Lou dragged me away because I was about to grab hold of that
25 ladder and shake it. And then we'd really be late for school.

When we came from school, the wall was slick with white. The painter lady was running string across the wall and taping it here and there. Me and Lou leaned against the gumball

---

1. **integration.** Referring to legislation in the 1960s that outlawed segregation, the separation of the races in public places

machine outside the pool hall and watched. She had strings up
30 and down and back and forth. Then she began chalking them
with a hunk of blue chalk.

The Morris twins crossed the street, hanging back at the
curb next to the beat-up car. The twin with the red ribbons was
hugging a jug of cloudy lemonade. The one with yellow ribbons
35 was holding a plate of dinner away from her dress. The painter
lady began snapping the strings. The blue chalk dust measured
off halves and quarters up and down and sideways too. Lou was
about to say how hip it all was, but I dropped my book **satchel**
on his toes to remind him we were at war.

40   Some good aromas were drifting our way from the plate
leaking pot likker² onto the Morris girl's white socks. I could
tell from where I stood that under the tinfoil was baked ham,
collard greens, and candied yams. And knowing Mrs. Morris,
who sometimes bakes for my mama's restaurant, a slab of
45 buttered cornbread was probably up under there too, sopping
up some of the pot likker. Me and Lou rolled our eyes, wishing
somebody would send us some dinner. But the painter lady
didn't even turn around. She was pulling the strings down and
prying bits of tape loose.

50   Side Pocket came strolling out of the pool hall to see what
Lou and me were studying so hard. He gave the painter lady the
once-over, checking out her paint-spattered jeans, her chalky
T-shirt, her floppy-brimmed straw hat. He hitched up his pants
and glided over toward the painter lady, who kept right on with
55 what she was doing.

"Watcha got there, sweetheart?" he asked the twin with
the plate.

"Suppah," she said all soft and countrylike.

"For her," the one with the jug added, jerking her chin
60 toward the painter lady's back.

Still she didn't turn around. She was rearing back on her
heels, her hands jammed into her back pockets, her face
squinched up like the **masterpiece** she had in mind was taking
shape on the wall by magic. We could have been gophers
65 crawled up into a rotten hollow for all she cared. She didn't even
say hello to anybody. Lou was muttering something about how

satch•el (sa chəl) *noun,* small bag for carrying belongings, especially clothes or books

Note the Facts

Whose supper is one of the Morris twins holding?

_____

_____

mas • ter • piece (mas´ tər pēs)
n, artist's greatest work

---

2. **pot likker.** Liquid left in a pot after cooking something

great her concentration was. I butt him with my hip, and his elbow slid off the gum machine.

70   "Good evening," Side Pocket said in his best ain't-I-fine voice. But the painter lady was moving from the milk crate to the step stool to the ladder, moving up and down fast, scribbling all over the wall like a crazy person. We looked at Side Pocket. He looked at the twins. The twins looked at us. The painter lady was giving a show. It was like those old-timey

75 music movies where the dancer taps on the tabletop and then starts jumping all over the furniture, kicking chairs over and not skipping a beat. She didn't even look where she was stepping. And for a minute there, hanging on the ladder to reach a far spot, she looked like she was going to tip right over.

80   "Ahh," Side Pocket cleared his throat and moved fast to catch the ladder. "These young ladies here have brought you some supper."

    "Ma'am?" The twins stepped forward. Finally the painter turned around, her eyes "full of sky," as my grandmama would

85 say. Then she stepped down like she was in a **trance**. She wiped her hands on her jeans as the Morris twins offered up the plate and the jug. She rolled back the tinfoil, then wagged her head as though something terrible was on the plate.

    "Thank your mother very much," she said, sounding like

90 her mouth was full of sky too. "I've brought my own dinner along." And then, without even excusing herself, she went back up the ladder, drawing on the wall in a wild way. Side Pocket whistled one of those oh-brother breathy whistles and went back into the pool hall. The Morris twins shifted their weight

95 from one foot to the other, then crossed the street and went home. Lou had to drag me away, I was so mad. We couldn't wait to get to the firehouse to tell my daddy all about this rude woman who'd stolen our wall.

    All the way back to the block to help my mama out at the

100 restaurant, me and Lou kept asking my daddy for ways to run the painter lady out of town. But my daddy was busy talking about the trip to the country and telling Lou he could come too because Grandmama can always use an extra pair of hands on the farm.

    Later that night, while me and Lou were in the back doing

105 our chores, we found out that the painter lady was a liar. She came into the restaurant and leaned against the glass of the steam table, talking about how starved she was. I was scrubbing pots and Lou was chopping onions, but we could hear her through the service window. She was asking Mama was that a

trance (tran[t]s) *n,* state of detachment from one's physical surroundings

110 ham hock in the greens, and was that a neck bone in the pole
beans, and were there any vegetables cooked without meat,
especially pork.

"I don't care who your spiritual leader is," Mama said in
that way of hers. "If you eat in the community, sistuh, you
115 gonna eat pig by-and-by, one way or t'other."

Me and Lou were cracking up in the kitchen, and several
customers at the counter were clearing their throats, waiting
for Mama to really fix her wagon for not speaking to the elders
when she came in. The painter lady took a stool at the counter
120 and went right on with her questions. Was there cheese in
the baked macaroni, she wanted to know? Were there eggs in
the salad? Was it honey or sugar in the iced tea? Mama was
fixing Pop Johnson's plate. And every time the painter lady
asked a fool question, Mama would dump another spoonful of
125 rice on the pile. She was tapping her foot and heating up in a
dangerous way. But Pop Johnson was happy as he could be. Me
and Lou peeked through the service window, wondering what
planet the painter lady came from. Who ever heard of baked
macaroni without cheese, or potato salad without eggs?

130 "Do you have any bread made with unbleached flour?" the
painter lady asked Mama. There was a long pause, as though
everybody in the restaurant was holding their breath, wondering
if Mama would dump the next spoonful on the painter lady's
head. She didn't. But when she set Pop Johnson's plate down, it
135 came down with a bang. When Mama finally took her order, the
starving lady all of a sudden couldn't make up her mind whether
she wanted a vegetable plate or fish and a salad. She finally settled
on the broiled trout and a tossed salad. But just when Mama
reached for a plate to serve her, the painter lady leaned over the
140 counter with her finger all up in the air.

"Excuse me," she said. "One more thing." Mama was
holding the plate like a Frisbee, tapping that foot, one hand on
her hip. "Can I get raw beets in that tossed salad?"

"You will get," Mama said, leaning her face close to the painter
145 lady's, "whatever Lou back there tossed. Now sit down." And the
painter lady sat back down on her stool and shut right up.

All the way to the country, me and Lou tried to get Mama to
open fire on the painter lady. But Mama said that seeing as how
she was from the North, you couldn't expect her to have any
150 manners. Then Mama said she was sorry she'd been so impatient
with the woman because she seemed like a decent person and
was simply trying to stick to a very **strict** diet. Me and Lou didn't

Analyze Literature

Dialect Many of the characters in this story speak in a **dialect**, or a different form of English. For example, look at what Mama says to the painter lady in the restaurant. What does *sistuh* mean?

_____

_____

_____

Build Vocabulary

Idioms *Cracking up* means laughing really hard. What do Lou and the narrator think is so funny?

_____

_____

Use Reading Skills

Evaluate Cause and Effect
Describe the causes and effects of Mama's conversation with the painter lady.

_____

_____

_____

strict (strikt) *adjective,* close, careful observance of rules and requirements

Think and Reflect

How does the narrator's mother feel about the artist?

drawl (drо̄ l) *verb*, speak in a slow way, drawing out the syllables

want to hear that. Who did that lady think she was, coming into our neighborhood and taking over our wall?

155 "Wellllll," Mama **drawled,** pulling into the filling station so Daddy could take the wheel, "it's hard on an artist, ya know. They can't always get people to look at their work. So she's just doing her work in the open, that's all."

Me and Lou definitely did not want to hear that. Why
160 couldn't she set up an easel downtown or draw on the sidewalk in her own neighborhood? Mama told us to quit fussing so much; she was tired and wanted to rest. She climbed into the back seat and dropped down into the warm hollow Daddy had made in the pillow.

scheme (skēm) *verb*, plan in a deceitful way, plot

165 All weekend long, me and Lou tried to **scheme** up ways to recapture our wall. Daddy and Mama said they were sick of hearing about it. Grandmama turned up the TV to drown us out. On the late news was a story about the New York subways. When a train came roaring into the station all covered from top
170 to bottom, windows too, with writings and drawings done with spray paint, me and Lou slapped five. Mama said it was too bad kids in New York had nothing better to do than spray paint all over the trains. Daddy said that in the cities, even grown-ups wrote all over the trains and buildings too. Daddy called it
175 "graffiti." Grandmama called it a shame.

Note the Facts

What do Lou and the narrator plan to do to the mural?

_____

_____

We couldn't wait to get out of school on Monday. We couldn't find any black spray paint anywhere. But in a junky hardware store downtown we found a can of white epoxy[3] paint, the kind you touch up old refrigerators with when
180 they get splotchy and peely. We spent our whole allowance on it. And because it was too late to use our bus passes, we had to walk all the way home lugging our book satchels and gym shoes, and the bag with the epoxy. When we reached the corner of Taliaferro and Fifth, it looked like a block party
185 or something. Half the neighborhood was gathered on the sidewalk in front of the wall. I looked at Lou, he looked at me. We both looked at the bag with the epoxy and wondered

---

3. **epoxy.** Substance used to make glue or tough lacquer

how we were going to work our scheme. The painter lady's car was nowhere in sight. But there were too many people
190 standing around to do anything. Side Pocket and his buddies were leaning on their cue sticks, hunching each other. Daddy was there with a lineman[4] he catches a ride with on Mondays. Mrs. Morris had her arms flung around the shoulders of the twins on either side of her. Mama was talking with some of
195 her customers, many of them with napkins still at the throat. Mr. Eubanks came out of the barbershop, followed by a man in a striped poncho, half his face shaved, the other half full of foam.

"She really did it, didn't she?" Mr. Eubanks huffed out his
200 chest. Lots of folks answered right quick that she surely did when they saw the straight razor in his hand.

Mama **beckoned** us over. And then we saw it. The wall. Reds, greens, figures outlined in black. Swirls of purple and orange. Storms of blues and yellows. It was something. I
205 recognized some of the faces right off. There was Martin Luther King, Jr. And there was a man with glasses on and his mouth open like he was laying down a heavy rap. Daddy came up alongside and reminded us that was Minister Malcolm X. The serious woman with a rifle I knew was Harriet Tubman[5]
210 because my grandmama has pictures of her all over the house. And I knew Mrs. Fannie Lou Hamer[6] 'cause a signed photograph of her hangs in the restaurant next to the calendar.

beck·oned (bek´nd) *verb,* signaled or directed with the head or the hand

---

4. **lineman.** Person who works on telephone or electric power lines
5. **Harriet Tubman.** American abolitionist
6. **Mrs. Fannie Lou Hamer.** Civil Rights activist

Then I let my eyes follow what looked like a vine. It trailed past a man with a horn[7], a woman with a big white flower in
215 her hair[8], a handsome dude in a tuxedo seated at a piano[9], and a man with a goatee holding a book[10]. When I looked more closely, I realized that what had looked like flowers were really faces. One face with yellow petals looked just like Frieda Morris. One with red petals looked just like Hattie Morris. I could
220 hardly believe my eyes.

"Notice," Side Pocket said, stepping close to the wall with his cue stick like a classroom pointer. "These are the flags of **liberation**," he said in a voice I'd never heard him use before. We all stepped closer while he pointed and spoke. "Red, black and
225 green," he said, his pointer falling on the leaflike flags of the vine. "Our liberation flag. And here, Ghana, there Tanzania. Guinea-Bissau, Angola, Mozambique."[11] Side Pocket sounded very tall, as though he'd been waiting all his life to give this lesson.

lib · er · a · tion (li' bə rā´ shən)
n, state of being free or of achieving civil rights

Culture Note

A mural is a piece of art that is painted on a wall. In the United States, there have been several decades during which murals have been popular forms of expression. Murals were very popular on public buildings in the 1960s and 1970s. Describe a mural you have seen in a city in which you have lived or visited.

_____

_____

Think and Reflect

How does Lou feel about the artist before school? What does he think now?

_____

---

7. **man with a horn.** Most likely refers to musician Louis Armstrong
8. **woman with a big white flower in her hair.** Refers to jazz vocalist Billie Holiday
9. **handsome dude in a tuxedo seated at a piano.** Refers to composer, band leader, and pianist Duke Ellington
10. **man with a goatee holding a book.** Refers to author W. E. B. Du Bois
11. **Ghana, Tanzania, Guinea-Bissau, Angola, Mozambique.** Nations in Africa

Mama tapped us on the shoulder and pointed to a high
230 section of the wall. There was a fierce-looking man with his
arms crossed against his chest guarding a bunch of children.
His muscles bulged, and he looked a lot like my daddy. One
kid was looking at a row of books. Lou hunched me 'cause the
kid looked like me. The one that looked like Lou was spinning
235 a globe on the tip of his finger like a basketball. There were
other kids there with microscopes and compasses. And the
more I looked, the more it looked like the fierce man was not
so much guarding the kids as defending their right to do what
they were doing.

240 Then Lou gasped and dropped the paint bag and ran
forward, running his hands over a rainbow. He had to tiptoe
and stretch to do it, it was so high. I couldn't breathe either.
The painter lady had found the chisel marks and had painted
Jimmy Lyons's name in a rainbow.

245 "Read the inscription, honey," Mrs. Morris said, urging little
Frieda forward. She didn't have to urge much. Frieda marched
right up, bent down, and in a loud voice that made everybody
quit oohing and ahhing and listen, she read,
   To the People of Taliaferro Street
250   *I Dedicate This Wall of Respect*
   Painted in Memory of My Cousin
   Jimmy Lyons ✤

> ## MIRRORS & WINDOWS
>
> If you were going to make a mural of people who are important to you, who would you include?
>
> _____
>
> _____
>
> _____

READING CHECK

Circle the letter of the correct answer.

1. What does the painter lady do to the wall first?
   A. She paints the wall completely white.
   B. She uses strings and chalk to mark the wall.
   C. She chisels something into the wall.

2. Which of the following does *not* describe the narrator's feelings about the wall being painted?
   A. angry
   B. possessive
   C. welcoming

3. How does the painter lady interact with the community?
   A. She is very friendly and makes new friends.
   B. She is aggressive and hostile toward the people in the neighborhood.
   C. She is quiet and spends most of her time concentrating on the wall.

4. How does Mama feel about the artist?
   A. They have become good friends.
   B. She loses her patience with her.
   C. She wants her out of the town right away.

5. Why are there so many people out on the sidewalk in front of the wall?
   A. The artist is finished and people are admiring the mural.
   B. The artist did a poor job and the people want to fix it.
   C. Lou and the narrator ruined the mural with spray paint.

VOCABULARY CHECK

Circle the letter of the correct answer.

1. What does the line "her face squinched up like the *masterpiece* she had in her mind was taking shape on the wall" mean?
   A. The artist is concentrating really hard on what she is going to paint.
   B. The artist is angry about the resistance she is getting in the neighborhood.
   C. She can't see where she is supposed to start the mural.

2. What does it mean that the artist is on a very *strict* diet?
   A. The artist cooks all her own food.
   B. The artist will not eat anything from the restaurant.
   C. The artist avoids certain foods and chooses more healthful items.

3. What does it mean to speak with a *drawl*?
   A. to speak a different language
   B. to speak in a slow and relaxed way
   C. to be nervous when speaking

4. What plan is the narrator and Lou trying to *scheme* all weekend?
   A. They are scheming to recapture the wall.
   B. They want the painter lady to eat pork.
   C. They want to skip their chores in the restaurant.

5. Why does Mama *beckon* the children over to the wall?
   A. The children are in trouble for trying to ruin the mural.
   B. She wants the children to come and see the finished mural.
   C. She wants them to finish painting part of the wall.

ANALYZE LITERATURE: Dialect

The artist and Mama have a different way of speaking. This shows us that the artist is not from the same community. Write a paragraph about the way Mama uses her regional dialect when speaking to the painter lady.

_____

_____

USE READING SKILLS: Evaluate Cause and Effect

1. What are the painter's motivations (causes) for painting the mural?

   _____

   _____

2. What are some positive outcomes (effects) the mural has on the community?

   _____

   _____

BUILD LANGUAGE SKILLS: Punctuation

When a story includes dialogue, quotation marks are used before and after the words that people say. A comma is used to separate the quotation from the rest of the sentence. The sentences below are taken from "The War of the Wall." Rewrite each sentence using the correct punctuation. Remember that other punctuation always goes inside the quotation marks. The first one has been done for you.

1. If you lean close Lou said you'll get a whiff of bubble gum and kids' sweat

   <u>"If you lean close," Lou said, "you'll get a whiff of bubble gum and kids' sweat."</u>

2. You're not even from around here I hollered up after her

   _____

3. Suppah she said all soft and country like

   _____

4. I don't care who your spiritual leader is Mama said in that way of hers

   _____

5. Do you have any bread made with unbleached flour the painter lady asked Mama

   _____

6. You will get whatever Lou back there tossed. Now sit down

   _____

7. These are the flags of the liberation he said in a voice I'd never heard him use before

   _____

WORK TOGETHER: Reader's Theater

Work in small groups to perform a reader's theater of a section of this story. Decide as a group which section of the story you would like to present. Make sure that there are enough people speaking in the section you choose so that everyone in the group can participate. Mark each line with the name or initials of the person who will read that part.

Name: _____ Date:_____

 page E5

Rikki-Tikki-Tavi

A Short Story by Rudyard Kipling

ABOUT THE STORY

"Rikki-Tikki-Tavi" is the story of a young mongoose that is taken by an English family. Read this story to find out how this little mongoose becomes so much more than just a pet.

MAKE CONNECTIONS

Who is the most courageous person you have ever met? What do you think made that person brave?

_____

_____

_____

_____

ANALYZE LITERATURE: Suspense

Suspense is the feeling of being nervous or curious about what will happen next. The author writes the story in a way that raises questions in your mind about what will happen to the character or what the outcome will be. As you read, note which sections of the story create a feeling of suspense.

USE READING SKILLS: Understand Literary Elements

Personification

Personification is a figure of speech that gives human characteristics to something that is not human, such as an animal, object, or idea. For example, "The stars winked at us from the dark sky." Stars don't really wink, but you understand from this sentence that the stars must have been sparkling that night. When authors use personification, they assign a human characteristic to an object. Make a list of the animals in the story and note examples in which the author uses personification to develop their characters.

PERSONIFICATION CHART	
Animal	**Examples of Personification**
Rikki-tikki-tavi	The author describes his "war cry." This makes it seem like animals have an understanding of war.

USE READING SKILLS: Understand Literary Elements

PREVIEW VOCABULARY

Key Words and Phrases Read each key word and rate it using this scale: ①I don't know this word or phrase at all. ②I've seen this word or phrase before. ③I know this word or phrase and use it.	Words and Phrases in Context Read to see how the key word or phrase can be used in a sentence.	Definition Write down what you think the word or phrase means. Then use a dictionary to check your definition.	Practice Practice using the key words and phrases by completing the following sentences.
cultivated cul · ti · vat · ed (kʉl´ tə vāt' əd) *verb* ①　②　③	The farmer **cultivated** the land to prepare it for growing corn.		It is important to **cultivate** land because…
cower co · wer (kaủ´ [ə]r) *verb* ①　②　③	The dog **cowers** in the corner every time the door slams.		Something that might make a person **cower** is…
peculiar pe · cu · liar (pe kü lēär) *adjective* ①　②　③	I heard a **peculiar** sound coming from the basement.		The opposite of **peculiar** is…
providence prov · i · dence (präv ´ əd əns) *noun* ①　②　③	It was an instance of **providence** that the supplies came before the soldiers went hungry.		An example of **providence** is…
singed (si ŋd) *verb* ①　②　③	The curling iron was very hot and **singed** the ends of my hair.		An example of something that could be easily **singed** is…

　　Differentiated Instruction: Literacy & Reading Skills

Rikki-Tikki-Tavi

A Short Story by Rudyard Kipling

This is the story of the great war that Rikki-tikki-tavi fought single-handed, through the bathrooms of the big **bungalow** in Segowlee cantonment.[1] Darzee, the tailorbird, helped him, and Chuchundra, the muskrat, who never comes out into the
5 middle of the floor but always creeps round by the wall, gave him advice; but Rikki-tikki did the real fighting.

He was a mongoose, rather like a little cat in his fur and his tail but quite like a weasel in his head and his habits. His eyes and the end of his restless nose were pink; he could scratch
10 himself anywhere he pleased with any leg, front or back, that he chose to use; he could fluff up his tail till it looked like a bottlebrush, and his war cry as he **scuttled** through the long grass was *Rikk-tikk-tikki-tikki-tchk*!

One day, a high summer flood washed him out of the
15 burrow where he lived with his father and mother and carried him, kicking and clucking, down a roadside ditch. He found a little wisp of grass floating there and clung to it till he lost his senses. When he revived, he was lying in the hot sun in the middle of a garden path, very draggled indeed, and a small boy
20 was saying: "Here's a dead mongoose. Let's have a funeral."

"No," said his mother; "let's take him in and dry him. Perhaps he isn't really dead."

They took him into the house, and a big man picked him up between his finger and thumb and said he was not dead but half
25 choked; so they wrapped him in cotton wool and warmed him over a little fire, and he opened his eyes and sneezed.

"Now," said the big man (he was an Englishman who had just moved into the bungalow), "don't frighten him, and we'll see what he'll do."

30 It is the hardest thing in the world to frighten a mongoose, because he is eaten up from nose to tail with curiosity. The **motto** of all the mongoose family is "Run and find out," and Rikki-tikki was a true mongoose. He looked at the cotton wool, decided that it was not good to eat, ran all round the table, sat
35 up and put his fur in order, scratched himself, and jumped on the small boy's shoulder.

"Don't be frightened, Teddy," said his father. "That's his way of making friends."

---

1. **Segowlee cantonment.** Living quarters for British troops in the town of Segowlee in India

"Ouch! He's tickling under my chin," said Teddy.

40 Rikki-tikki looked down between the boy's collar and neck, snuffed at his ear, and climbed down to the floor, where he sat rubbing his nose.

"Good gracious," said Teddy's mother, "and that's a wild creature! I suppose he's so tame because we've been kind to him."

45 "All mongooses are like that," said her husband. "If Teddy doesn't pick him up by the tail or try to put him in a cage, he'll run in and out of the house all day long. Let's give him something to eat."

They gave him a little piece of raw meat. Rikki-tikki liked
50 it immensely, and when it was finished, he went out into the veranda and sat in the sunshine and fluffed up his fur to make it dry to the roots. Then he felt better.

"There are more things to find out about in this house," he said to himself, "than all my family could find out in all their
55 lives. I shall certainly stay and find out."

He spent all that day roaming over the house. He nearly drowned himself in the bathtubs, put his nose into the ink on a writing table, and burnt it on the end of the big man's cigar, for he climbed up in the big man's lap to see how writing was done.
60 At nightfall he ran into Teddy's nursery to watch how kerosene lamps were lighted, and when Teddy went to bed, Rikki-tikki climbed up too; but he was a restless companion, because he had to get up and attend to every noise all through the night and find out what made it. Teddy's mother and father came in,
65 the last thing, to look at their boy, and Rikki-tikki was awake on the pillow. "I don't like that," said Teddy's mother; "he may bite the child." "He'll do no such thing," said the father. "Teddy's safer with that little beast than if he had a bloodhound to watch him. If a snake came into the nursery now—"
70 But Teddy's mother wouldn't think of anything so awful.

Early in the morning, Rikki-tikki came to early breakfast in the veranda riding on Teddy's shoulder, and they gave him banana and some boiled egg; and he sat on all their laps one after the other, because every well-brought-up mongoose
75 always hopes to be a house mongoose someday and have rooms to run about in; and Rikki-tikki's mother (she used to live in the General's house at Segowlee) had carefully told Rikki what to do if ever he came across white men.

Then Rikki-tikki went out into the garden to see what was
80 to be seen. It was a large garden, only half **cultivated**, with bushes, as big as summer houses, of Marshal Niel roses; lime

Note the Facts

Where does Rikki-tikki sleep? How does Teddy's mother feel about Rikki-tikki sleeping there?

_____

_____

cul · ti · vat · ed (kʉlʹ tə vātʹ əd) _adj.,_ prepared for growing plants

and orange trees; clumps of bamboos; and thickets of high grass. Rikki-tikki licked his lips. "This is a splendid hunting ground," he said, and his tail grew bottlebrushy at the thought
85 of it, and he scuttled up and down the garden, snuffing here and there till he heard very sorrowful voices in a thorn bush.

It was Darzee, the tailorbird, and his wife. They had made a beautiful nest by pulling two big leaves together and stitching them up the edges with fibers and had filled the hollow with
90 cotton and downy fluff. The nest swayed to and fro as they sat on the rim and cried.

"What is the matter?" asked Rikki-tikki.

"We are very miserable," said Darzee. "One of our babies fell out of the nest yesterday and Nag ate him."

95 "H'm!" said Rikki-tikki, "that is very sad—but I am a stranger here. Who is Nag?"

Darzee and his wife only **cowered** down in the nest without answering, for from the thick grass at the foot of the bush there came a low hiss—a horrid, cold sound that made Rikki-
100 tikki jump back two clear feet. Then inch by inch out of the grass rose up the head and spread hood of Nag, the big black cobra, and he was five feet long from tongue to tail. When he had lifted one third of himself clear of the ground, he stayed balancing to and fro exactly as a dandelion tuft balances in the
105 wind, and he looked at Rikki-tikki with the wicked snake's eyes that never change their expression, whatever the snake may be thinking of.

"Who is Nag?" said he. "*I* am Nag. The great God Brahm[2] put his mark upon all our people, when the first cobra spread
110 his hood to keep the sun off Brahm as he slept. Look, and be afraid!"

He spread out his hood more than ever, and Rikki-tikki saw the spectacle mark on the back of it that looks exactly like the eye part of a hook-and-eye fastening. He was afraid for the
115 minute; but it is impossible for a mongoose to stay frightened for any length of time, and though Rikki-tikki had never met a live cobra before, his mother had fed him on dead ones, and he knew that all a grown mongoose's business in life was to fight and eat snakes. Nag knew that too, and at the bottom of his
120 cold heart, he was afraid.

"Well," said Rikki-tikki, and his tail began to fluff up again, "marks or no marks, do you think it is right for you to eat **fledglings** out of a nest?"

2. **Brahm.** Short for *Brahma*, the creator of the universe according to Hindu religion

Note the Facts

Who is Nag?

_____

_____

Read Aloud

Read aloud lines 108–111 What do you predict about the relationship between Nag and Rikki-tikki?

_____

_____

fledg·ling (flej lin) *noun*, a young bird

Nag was thinking to himself and watching the least little
125 movement in the grass behind Rikki-tikki. He knew that
mongooses in the garden meant death sooner or later for him
and his family, but he wanted to get Rikki-tikki off his guard. So
he dropped his head a little and put it on one side.

"Let us talk," he said. "You eat eggs. Why should not I eat
130 birds?"

"Behind you! Look behind you!" sang Darzee.

Rikki-tikki knew better than to waste time in staring. He
jumped up in the air as high as he could go, and just under
him whizzed by the head of Nagaina, Nag's wicked wife. She
135 had crept up behind him as he was talking, to make an end
of him; and he heard her savage hiss as the stroke missed. He
came down almost across her back, and if he had been an old
mongoose, he would have known that then was the time to
break her back with one bite; but he was afraid of the terrible
140 lashing return stroke of the cobra. He bit, indeed, but did not
bite long enough, and he jumped clear of the whisking tail,
leaving Nagaina torn and angry.

"Wicked, wicked Darzee!" said Nag, lashing up as high as he
could reach toward the nest in the thorn bush; but Darzee had
145 built it out of reach of snakes, and it only swayed to and fro.

Rikki-tikki felt his eyes growing red and hot (when a mongoose's eyes grow red, he is angry), and he sat back on his tail and hind legs like a little kangaroo, and looked all round him, and chattered with rage. But Nag and Nagaina

150 had disappeared into the grass. When a snake misses its stroke, it never says anything or gives any sign of what it means to do next. Rikki-tikki did not care to follow them, for he did not feel sure that he could manage two snakes at once. So he trotted off to the gravel path near the house and

155 sat down to think. It was a serious matter for him. If you read the old books of natural history, you will find they say that when the mongoose fights the snake and happens to get bitten, he runs off and eats some herb that cures him. That is not true. The victory is only a matter of quickness of eye

160 and quickness of foot—snake's blow against the mongoose's jump—and as no eye can follow the motion of a snake's head when it strikes, this makes things much more wonderful than any magic herb. Rikki-tikki knew he was a young mongoose, and it made him all the more pleased to think

165 that he had managed to escape a blow from behind. It gave him confidence in himself, and when Teddy came running down the path, Rikki-tikki was ready to be petted. But just as Teddy was stooping, something wriggled a little in the dust and a tiny voice said: "Be careful. I am Death!" It was Karait,

170 the dusty brown snakeling that lies for choice on the dusty earth; and his bite is as dangerous as the cobra's. But he is so small that nobody thinks of him, and so he does the more harm to people.

Rikki-tikki's eyes grew red again, and he danced up to

175 Karait with the **peculiar** rocking, swaying motion that he had inherited from his family. It looks very funny, but it is so perfectly balanced a gait that you can fly off from it at any angle you please; and in dealing with snakes this is an advantage. If Rikki-tikki had only known, he was doing a much more

180 dangerous thing than fighting Nag, for Karait is so small and can turn so quickly that unless Rikki bit him close to the back of the head, he would get the return stroke in his eye or his lip. But Rikki did not know; his eyes were all red, and he rocked back and forth, looking for a good place to hold. Karait struck

185 out, Rikki jumped sideways and tried to run in, but the wicked little dusty gray head lashed within a fraction of his shoulder, and he had to jump over the body, and the head followed his heels close.

Note the Facts

Does Rikki-tikki hurt Nagaina when she strikes at him from the grass?

_____

_____

Note the Facts

Why is Karait more dangerous than Nag?

_____

_____

pe·cu·liar (pi lyül yər) *adjective,* strange, odd, unusual

Teddy shouted to the house: "Oh, look here! Our mongoose
190 is killing a snake," and Rikki-tikki heard a scream from Teddy's
mother. His father ran out with a stick, but by the time he
came up, Karait had lunged out once too far, and Rikki-tikki
had sprung, jumped on the snake's back, dropped his head far
between his forelegs, bitten as high up the back as he could get
195 hold, and rolled away. That bite paralyzed Karait, and Rikki-
tikki was just going to eat him up from the tail, after the custom
of his family at dinner, when he remembered that a full meal
makes a slow mongoose, and if he wanted all his strength and
quickness ready, he must keep himself thin. He went away for
200 a dust bath under the castor-oil bushes, while Teddy's father
beat the dead Karait. "What is the use of that?" thought Rikki-
tikki; "I have settled it all"; and then Teddy's mother picked
him up from the dust and hugged him, crying that he had
saved Teddy from death, and Teddy's father said that he was a
205 **providence**, and Teddy looked on with big, scared eyes. Rikki-
tikki was rather amused at all the fuss, which, of course, he did
not understand. Teddy's mother might just as well have petted
Teddy for playing in the dust. Rikki was thoroughly enjoying
himself.
210   That night at dinner, walking to and fro among the wine-
glasses on the table, he might have stuffed himself three times
over with nice things; but he remembered Nag and Nagaina,
and though it was very pleasant to be patted and petted by
Teddy's mother and to sit on Teddy's shoulder, his eyes would
215 get red from time to time, and he would go off into his long war
cry of *Rikk-tikk-tikki-tikki-tchk*!
    Teddy carried him off to bed and insisted on Rikki-tikki's
sleeping under his chin. Rikki-tikki was too well bred to bite
or scratch, but as soon as Teddy was asleep, he went off for
220 his nightly walk round the house, and in the dark he ran up
against Chuchundra, the muskrat, creeping round by the wall.
Chuchundra is a brokenhearted little beast. He whimpers and
cheeps all night, trying to make up his mind to run into the
middle of the room; but he never gets there.
225   "Don't kill me," said Chuchundra, almost weeping. "Rikki-
tikki, don't kill me!"
    "Do you think a snake killer kills muskrats?" said Rikki-
tikki scornfully.
    "Those who kill snakes get killed by snakes," said
230 Chuchundra, more sorrowfully than ever. "And how am I to be
sure that Nag won't mistake me for you some dark night?"

prov-i-dence (präv´ əd əns) *n*, a
valuable gift, godsend

Read Aloud

Read lines 225–233 of the
story. Change your voice to
match Chuchundra's words
and Rikki's responses. Why is
Chuchundra so upset when he
meets Rikki?

_____

_____

"There's not the least danger," said Rikki-tikki, "but Nag is in the garden, and I know you don't go there."

235 "My cousin Chua, the rat, told me—" said Chuchundra, and then he stopped.

"Told you what?"

"H'sh! Nag is everywhere, Rikki-tikki. You should have talked to Chua in the garden."

"I didn't—so you must tell me. Quick, Chuchundra, or I'll
240 bite you!"

Chuchundra sat down and cried till the tears rolled off his whiskers. "I am a very poor man," he sobbed. "I never had spirit enough to run out into the middle of the room. H'sh! I mustn't tell you anything. Can't you *hear*, Rikki-tikki?"

245 Rikki-tikki listened. The house was as still as still, but he thought he could just catch the faintest *scratch-scratch* in the world—a noise as faint as that of a wasp walking on a windowpane—the dry scratch of a snake's scales on brickwork.

250 "That's Nag or Nagaina," he said to himself, "and he is crawling into the bathroom sluice.[3] You're right, Chuchundra; I should have talked to Chua."

He stole off to Teddy's bathroom, but there was nothing there, and then to Teddy's mother's bathroom. At the
255 bottom of the smooth plaster wall there was a brick pulled out to make a sluice for the bathwater, and as Rikki-tikki stole in by the masonry curb where the bath is put, he heard Nag and Nagaina whispering together outside in the moonlight.

260 "When the house is emptied of people," said Nagaina to her husband, "*he* will have to go away, and then the garden will be our own again. Go in quietly, and remember that the big man who killed Karait is the first one to bite. Then come out and tell me, and we will hunt for Rikki-tikki together."

265 "But are you sure that there is anything to be gained by killing the people?" said Nag.

"Everything. When there were no people in the bungalow, did we have any mongoose in the garden? So long as the bungalow is empty, we are king and queen of the garden; and
270 remember that as soon as our eggs in the melon bed hatch (as they may tomorrow), our children will need room and quiet."

Use Reading Skills

Sensory Details How does Rikki-tikki know the snakes are coming inside the house?

_____

_____

Note the Facts

Why do Nagaina and Nag want the humans gone from the bungalow?

_____

_____

---

3. **sluice.** Valve through which water is run

"I had not thought of that," said Nag. "I will go, but there is no need that we should hunt for Rikki-tikki afterward. I will kill the big man and his wife, and the child if I can, and come 275 away quietly. Then the bungalow will be empty, and Rikki-tikki will go."

Rikki-tikki tingled all over with rage and hatred at this, and then Nag's head came through the sluice, and his five feet of cold body followed it. Angry as he was, Rikki-tikki was 280 very frightened as he saw the size of the big cobra. Nag coiled himself up, raised his head, and looked into the bathroom in the dark, and Rikki could see his eyes glitter.

"Now, if I kill him here, Nagaina will know; and if I fight him on the open floor, the odds are in his favor. What am I to 285 do?" said Rikki-tikki-tavi.

Nag waved to and fro, and then Rikki-tikki heard him drinking from the biggest water jar that was used to fill the bath. "That is good," said the snake. "Now, when Karait was killed, the big man had a stick. He may have that stick still, but 290 when he comes in to bathe in the morning, he will not have a stick. I shall wait here till he comes. Nagaina—do you hear me?—I shall wait here in the cool till daytime."

There was no answer from outside, so Rikki-tikki knew Nagaina had gone away. Nag coiled himself down, coil by coil, 295 round the bulge at the bottom of the water jar, and Rikki-tikki stayed still as death. After an hour he began to move, muscle by muscle, toward the jar. Nag was asleep, and Rikki-tikki looked at his big back, wondering which would be the best place for a good hold. "If I don't break his back at the 300 first jump," said Rikki, "he can still fight; and if he fights—O Rikki!" He looked at the thickness of the neck below the hood, but that was too much for him; and a bite near the tail would only make Nag savage.

Differentiated Instruction: Literacy & Reading Skills   © Carnegie Learning, Inc.

"It must be the head," he said at last, "the head above the
305 hood; and when I am once there, I must not let go."

Then he jumped. The head was lying a little clear of the
water jar, under the curve of it; and as his teeth met, Rikki
braced his back against the bulge of the red earthenware to hold
down the head. This gave him just one second's purchase,[4] and
310 he made the most of it. Then he was battered to and fro as a rat
is shaken by a dog—to and fro on the floor, up and down, and
round in great circles, but his eyes were red and he held on as
the body cartwhipped over the floor, upsetting the tin dipper
and the soap dish and the flesh brush, and banged against the
315 tin side of the bath. As he held, he closed his jaws tighter and
tighter, for he made sure he would be banged to death, and for
the honor of his family, he preferred to be found with his teeth
locked. He was dizzy, aching, and felt shaken to pieces, when
something went off like a thunderclap just behind him; a hot
320 wind knocked him senseless and red fire **singed** his fur. The big
man had been wakened by the noise and had fired both barrels
of a shotgun into Nag just behind the hood.

Rikki-tikki held on with his eyes shut, for now he was quite
sure he was dead; but the head did not move, and the big man
325 picked him up and said: "It's the mongoose again, Alice; the
little chap has saved *our* lives now." Then Teddy's mother
came in with a very white face and saw what was left of Nag,
and Rikki-tikki dragged himself to Teddy's bedroom and spent
half the rest of the night shaking himself tenderly to find out
330 whether he really was broken into forty pieces, as he fancied.

When morning came, he was very stiff but well pleased with
his doings. "Now I have Nagaina to settle with, and she will be
worse than five Nags, and there's no knowing when the eggs
she spoke of will hatch. Goodness! I must go and see Darzee,"
335 he said.

Without waiting for breakfast, Rikki-tikki ran to the thorn
bush, where Darzee was singing a song of triumph at the top of
his voice. The news of Nag's death was all over the garden, for
the sweeper had thrown the body on the rubbish heap.
340 "Oh, you stupid tuft of feathers!" said Rikki-tikki angrily. "Is
this the time to sing?"

"Nag is dead—is dead—is dead!" sang Darzee. "The valiant
Rikki-tikki caught him by the head and held fast. The big man
brought the bang-stick, and Nag fell in two pieces! He will
345 never eat my babies again."

---

4. **purchase.** Firm hold

singed (sinjd) *verb*, slightly burned or burned the ends of something like hair or cloth

Think and Reflect

How would you react if you found a snake in your bathroom?

_____

_____

Build Vocabulary

Darzee says that the man "brought the *bang-stick*, and Nag fell in two pieces." What is a *bang-stick*?

_____

_____

"All that's true enough, but where's Nagaina?" said Rikki-tikki, looking carefully round him.

"Nagaina came to the bathroom sluice and called for Nag," Darzee went on; "and Nag came out on the end of a stick—the 350 sweeper picked him up on the end of a stick and threw him upon the rubbish heap. Let us sing about the great, the red-eyed Rikki-tikki!" and Darzee filled his throat and sang.

"If I could get up to your nest, I'd roll your babies out!" said Rikki-tikki. "You don't know when to do the right thing at the 355 right time. You're safe enough in your nest there, but it's war for me down here. Stop singing a minute, Darzee."

"For the great, beautiful Rikki-tikki's sake I will stop," said Darzee. "What is it, O Killer of the terrible Nag?"

"Where is Nagaina, for the third time?"

360 "On the rubbish heap by the stables, mourning for Nag. Great is Rikki-tikki with the white teeth."

"Bother my white teeth! Have you ever heard where she keeps her eggs?"

"In the melon bed, on the end nearest the wall, where the 365 sun strikes nearly all day. She hid them there weeks ago."

"And you never thought it worthwhile to tell me? The end nearest the wall, you said?"

"Rikki-tikki, you are not going to eat her eggs?"

"Not eat exactly; no. Darzee, if you have a grain of sense, 370 you will fly off to the stables and pretend that your wing is broken and let Nagaina chase you away to the bush. I must get to the melon bed, and if I went there now, she'd see me."

Darzee was a featherbrained little fellow who could never hold more than one idea at a time in his head, and just because 375 he knew that Nagaina's children were born in eggs like his own, he didn't think at first that it was fair to kill them. But his wife was a sensible bird, and she knew that cobra's eggs meant young cobras later on; so she flew off from the nest and left Darzee to keep the babies warm and continue his song about 380 the death of Nag. Darzee was very like a man in some ways.

She fluttered in front of Nagaina by the rubbish heap and cried out, "Oh, my wing is broken! The boy in the house threw a stone at me and broke it." Then she fluttered more desperately than ever.

385 Nagaina lifted up her head and hissed, "You warned Rikki-tikki when I would have killed him. Indeed and truly, you've chosen a bad place to be lame in." And she moved toward Darzee's wife, slipping along over the dust.

"The boy broke it with a stone!" shrieked Darzee's wife.

390   "Well! It may be some consolation to you when you're dead to know that I shall settle accounts with the boy. My husband lies on the rubbish heap this morning, but before night the boy in the house will lie very still. What is the use of running away? I am sure to catch you. Little fool, look at me!"

395   Darzee's wife knew better than to do that, for a bird who looks at a snake's eyes gets so frightened that she cannot move. Darzee's wife fluttered on, piping sorrowfully and never leaving the ground, and Nagaina quickened her pace.

    Rikki-tikki heard them going up the path from the stables, 400 and he raced for the end of the melon patch near the wall. There, in the warm litter above the melons, very cunningly hidden, he found twenty-five eggs about the size of a bantam's eggs but with whitish skins instead of shells.

    "I was not a day too soon," he said, for he could see the 405 baby cobras curled up inside the skin, and he knew that the minute they were hatched, they could each kill a man or a mongoose. He bit off the tops of the eggs as fast as he could, taking care to crush the young cobras, and turned over the litter from time to time to see whether he had missed any. At last 410 there were only three eggs left, and Rikki-tikki began to chuckle to himself, when he heard Darzee's wife screaming:

    "Rikki-tikki, I led Nagaina toward the house, and she has gone into the veranda, and—oh, come quickly—she means killing!"

    Rikki-tikki smashed two eggs, and tumbled backward down 415 the melon bed with the third egg in his mouth, and scuttled to the veranda as hard as he could put foot to the ground. Teddy and his mother and father were there at early breakfast, but Rikki-tikki saw that they were not eating anything. They sat stone still, and their faces were white. Nagaina was coiled up on 420 the matting by Teddy's chair, within easy striking distance of Teddy's bare leg, and she was swaying to and fro, singing a song of triumph.

    "Son of the big man that killed Nag," she hissed, "stay still. I am not ready yet. Wait a little. Keep very still, all you three! If 425 you move, I strike, and if you do not move, I strike. Oh, foolish people, who killed my Nag!"

    Teddy's eyes were fixed on his father, and all his father could do was to whisper, "Sit still, Teddy. You mustn't move. Teddy, keep still."

430   Then Rikki-tikki came up and cried: "Turn round, Nagaina; turn and fight!"

Analyze Literature

Setting The main setting of "Rikki-Tikki-Tavi" is around the bungalow. What are some other small settings in which part of the action of the story takes place?

_____

_____

Note the Facts

What happens when Nagaina tries to bite Rikki?

_____

_____

_____

_____

"All in good time," said she, without moving her eyes. "I will settle my account with you presently. Look at your friends, Rikki-tikki. They are still and white. They are afraid. They dare
435 not move, and if you come a step nearer, I strike."

"Look at your eggs," said Rikki-tikki, "in the melon bed near the wall. Go and look, Nagaina!"

The big snake turned half round and saw the egg on the veranda. "Ah-h! Give it to me," she said.
440 Rikki-tikki put his paws one on each side of the egg, and his eyes were blood-red. "What price for a snake's egg? For a young cobra? For a young king cobra? For the last—the very last of the brood? The ants are eating all the others down by the melon bed."

Nagaina spun clear round, forgetting everything for the sake
445 of the one egg; and Rikki-tikki saw Teddy's father shoot out a big hand, catch Teddy by the shoulder, and drag him across the little table with the teacups, safe and out of reach of Nagaina.

"Tricked! Tricked! Tricked! _Rikk-tck-tck_!" chuckled _Rikki-tikki_. "The boy is safe, and it was I—I—I that caught Nag by the hood
450 last night in the bathroom." Then he began to jump up and down, all four feet together, his head close to the floor. "He threw me to and fro, but he could not shake me off. He was dead before the big man blew him in two. I did it! Rikki-tikki-tck-tck! Come then, Nagaina. Come and fight with me. You shall not be a widow long."

455 Nagaina saw that she had lost her chance of killing Teddy, and the egg lay between Rikki-tikki's paws. "Give me the egg, Rikki-tikki. Give me the last of my eggs, and I will go away and never come back," she said, lowering her hood.

"Yes, you will go away, and you will never come back; for
460 you will go to the rubbish heap with Nag. Fight, widow! The big man has gone for his gun! Fight!"

Rikki-tikki was bounding all round Nagaina, keeping just out of reach of her stroke, his little eyes like hot coals. Nagaina gathered herself together and flung out at him. Rikki-tikki jumped up
465 and backwards. Again and again and again she struck, and each time her head came with a whack on the matting of the veranda and she gathered herself together like a watch spring. Then Rikki-tikki danced in a circle to get behind her, and Nagaina spun round to keep her head to his head, so that the rustle of her tail
470 on the matting sounded like dry leaves blown along by the wind.

He had forgotten the egg. It still lay on the veranda, and Nagaina came nearer and nearer to it, till at last, while Rikki-tikki was drawing breath, she caught it in her mouth, turned to the veranda steps, and flew like an arrow down the path, with

475 Rikki-tikki behind her. When the cobra runs for her life, she goes like a whiplash flicked across a horse's neck. Rikki-tikki knew that he must catch her or all the trouble would begin again. She headed straight for the long grass by the thorn bush, and as he was running, Rikki-tikki heard Darzee still singing

480 his foolish little song of triumph. But Darzee's wife was wiser. She flew off her nest as Nagaina came along and flapped her wings about Nagaina's head. If Darzee had helped, they might have turned her, but Nagaina only lowered her hood and went on. Still, the instant's delay brought Rikki-tikki up to her, and

485 as she plunged into the rat hole where she and Nag used to live, his little white teeth were clenched on her tail and he went down with her—and very few mongooses, however wise and old they may be, care to follow a cobra into its hole. It was dark in the hole, and Rikki-tikki never knew when it might open out

490 and give Nagaina room to turn and strike at him. He held on savagely and stuck out his feet to act as brakes on the dark slope of the hot, moist earth. Then the grass by the mouth of the hole stopped waving, and Darzee said: "It is all over with Rikki-tikki! We must sing his death song. Valiant Rikki-tikki is dead! For

495 Nagaina will surely kill him underground."

So he sang a very mournful song that he made up on the spur of the minute, and just as he got to the most touching part, the grass quivered again, and Rikki-tikki, covered with dirt, dragged himself out of the hole leg by leg, licking his whiskers.

500 Darzee stopped with a little shout. Rikki-tikki shook some of the dust out of his fur and sneezed. "It is all over," he said. "The widow will never come out again." And the red ants that live between the grass stems heard him and began to troop down one after another to see if he had spoken the truth.

Note the Facts

What does Darzee think will happen to Rikki-tikki?

_____

_____

505   Rikki-tikki curled himself up in the grass and slept where he was—slept and slept till it was late in the afternoon, for he had done a hard day's work.

     "Now," he said, when he awoke, "I will go back to the house. Tell the Coppersmith, Darzee, and he will tell the garden that
510 Nagaina is dead."

     The Coppersmith is a bird who makes a noise exactly like the beating of a little hammer on a copper pot, and the reason he is always making it is because he is the town crier to every Indian garden and tells all the news to everybody who
515 cares to listen. As Rikki-tikki went up the path, he heard his "attention" notes like a tiny dinner gong and then the steady "*Ding-dong-tock*! Nag is *dead—dong*! Nagaina is dead! Ding-dong-tock!" That set all the birds in the garden singing and the frogs croaking, for Nag and Nagaina used to eat frogs as
520 well as little birds.

     When Rikki got to the house, Teddy and Teddy's mother (she looked very white still, for she had been fainting) and Teddy's father came out and almost cried over him; and that night he ate all that was given him till he could eat no more and
525 went to bed on Teddy's shoulder, where Teddy's mother saw him when she came to look late at night.

     "He saved our lives and Teddy's life," she said to her husband. "Just think, he saved all our lives."

     Rikki-tikki woke up with a jump, for the mongooses are
530 light sleepers.

     "Oh, it's you," he said. "What are you bothering for? All the cobras are dead; and if they weren't, I'm here."

     Rikki-tikki had a right to be proud of himself, but he did not grow too proud, and he kept that garden as a mongoose
535 should keep it, with tooth and jump and spring and bite, till never a cobra dared show its head inside the walls. ❖

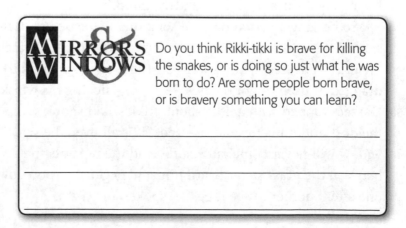

MIRRORS & WINDOWS Do you think Rikki-tikki is brave for killing the snakes, or is doing so just what he was born to do? Are some people born brave, or is bravery something you can learn?

_____

_____

_____

READING CHECK

Circle the letter of the correct answer.

1. In what condition does the family first find Rikki-tikki?
   A. He is fighting a snake.
   B. He is dead.
   C. He is wet and sick from being dragged by the flood waters.

2. Why are the tailorbirds sad?
   A. They are scared of Rikki-tikki.
   B. A snake ate one of their babies.
   C. They have a lot of work to do on their nest.

3. Who warns Rikki-tikki that Nagaina is coming up behind him?
   A. Darzee
   B. Darzee's wife
   C. Nag

4. Who kills Karait?
   A. Teddy
   B. Rikki-tikki
   C. the father

5. Where does Rikki-tikki catch and kill Nagaina?
   A. in the bathtub
   B. in a rat hole
   C. in the thorn bush

VOCABULARY CHECK

Circle the letter of the correct answer.

1. Rikki-tikki can see that half of the garden is *cultivated*. How would you describe the other half?
   A. ready for planting crops
   B. natural and wild with different plants and grasses
   C. not fit for animals or other living things

2. Why do Darzee and his wife *cower* in the nest?
   A. They are cold.
   B. They are afraid of Nag.
   C. They are sewing the two leaves together.

3. Why is the way that Rikki-tikki moves *peculiar*?
   A. He rocks and sways as he walks.
   B. He is a very small animal.
   C. He is an animal that walks on four legs.

4. Why does Teddy's father say that Rikki-tikki is a gift of *providence*?
   A. He is very brave.
   B. He saves Teddy's life.
   C. He will bring wealth to the family.

5. The blast of the gun *singes* Rikki-tikki's fur. Does this incident hurt him?
   A. No, but Nag bites him badly.
   B. Yes, it burns him badly.
   C. No, the heat just burns the ends of his fur.

ANALYZE LITERATURE: Suspense

Write a paragraph describing the part of the story you think is the most suspenseful. What questions does the author leave in your mind about what might happen next? Describe how you feel after reading this section.

_____

_____

_____

_____

_____

USE READING SKILLS: Understand Literary Elements
Personification

1. Rikki-tikki is a mongoose, but the story attributes many human qualities to him. Name some of these qualities.

   _____

2. What other examples of personification do you see in this story? List some examples.

   _____

BUILDING LANGUAGE SKILLS: Past Tense

The **past tense** describes actions that already occurred. Use the past tense to rewrite the following sentences so that they describe actions or events that already happened.

1. Rikki-tikki scratches himself anywhere he pleases with any leg, front or back, that he chooses to use.

   _____

2. He can fluff up his tail so that it looks like a bottle brush.

   _____

3. Nagaina creeps up in the grass and waits to strike at Rikki-tikki.

   _____

4. Chuchundra hears that a snake is crawling into the bathroom.

   _____

SPEAKING & LISTENING: Word Emphasis

An author may put certain words in italics to emphasize those words. If you see a word in italics, you should read the word with more stress or with a different intonation than the other words in the sentence. Work with a partner and practice reading aloud the sentences with italics from the story.

1. "Who is Nag," said he. "*I* am Nag."

2. "I never had spirit enough to run out into the middles of the room. H'sh! I mustn't tell you anything. Can't you *hear*, Rikki-tikki?"

3. "When the house is emptied of people," said Nagaina to her husband, "*he* will have to go away, and then the garden will be our own again."

Differentiated Instruction: Literacy & Reading Skills

◆ page E5

The Green Mamba

An Autobiography by Roald Dahl

ABOUT THE STORY

"The Green Mamba" is an autobiography about a surprising visit to a friend's house. The author arrives and sees a poisonous snake sliding into the front door. The family and the visitor are very nervous ab out what will happen next.

MAKE CONNECTIONS

Do you think people should live in the same area as dangerous animals? Why or why not?

_____

_____

_____

_____

ANALYZE LITERATURE: Autobiography

Autobiography is a form of nonfiction in which a person tells his or her own life story. In "The Green Mamba," the author tells a short, true story that happened to him in Africa. An autobiography has many of the same elements as works of fictions. These elements include setting, plot, and characters. As you read, think about how the author of this autobiography describes the characters and develops the plot.

USE READING SKILLS: Understand Literary Elements
Plot

The plot is what happens in a story. A **plot** is a series of events related to a *central conflict*, or struggle. A plot usually involves the introduction of a conflict, its development, and its eventual resolution. The elements of a plot include exposition, rising action, climax, falling action, and resolution. In the spaces provided, describe the exposition, rising action, climax, falling action, and resolution of "The Green Mamba."

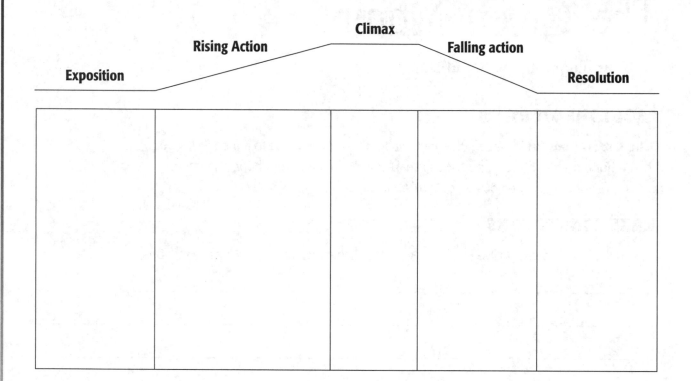

Differentiated Instruction: Literacy & Reading Skills   © Carnegie Learning, Inc.

PREVIEW VOCABULARY

Key Words and Phrases	Words and Phrases in Context	Definition	Practice
Read each key word and rate it using this scale: ①I don't know this word or phrase at all. ②I've seen this word or phrase before. ③I know this word or phrase and use it.	Read to see how the key word or phrase can be used in a sentence.	Write down what you think the word or phrase means. Then use a dictionary to check your definition.	Practice using the key words and phrases by completing the following sentences.
glide (glīd) *verb* ① ② ③	The Olympic skaters **glide** across the ice.		An animal, other than a snake, that **glides** as it moves is…
implement im • ple • ment (im ple ment) *noun* ① ② ③	The chef uses many different cooking **implements** for her creations.		An **implement** used for carpentry is…
trickle trick • le (trikl´) *noun* ① ② ③	The water faucet is broken. There is a constant **trickle** of water in the sink.		The river was reduced to only a **trickle** of water because…
forlorn for • lorn (fər lôrn´) *adjective* ① ② ③	The tuba and the trombone played a sad, **forlorn** duet.		The opposite of **forlorn** is…
manipulate man • ip • u • late (mə nip´ yə lāt) *verb* ① ② ③	The child **manipulated** the puzzle until every piece fit perfectly.		A mechanic often **manipulates**…

The Green Mamba

An Autobiography by Roald Dahl

Culture Note

This story takes place in the British colony of Tanganyika. Tanganyika achieved independence in 1961 and joined with Zanzibar in 1964 to form present-day Tanzania in East Africa.

Analyze Literature

Setting

Describe the setting of the story. Would you like to live in a place like that?

_____

_____

_____

_____

_____

> **glide** (glīd) *verb*, move smoothly without much effort

Read Aloud

Read aloud lines 17–22. Why is the narrator so scared?

_____

_____

_____

Note the Facts

How does Mr. Fuller get his family out of the house?

_____

_____

_____

Oh, those snakes! How I hated them! They were the only fearful thing about Tanganyika, and a newcomer very quickly learned to identify most of them and to know which were deadly and which were simply poisonous. The killers, apart from the
5 black mambas, were the green mambas, the cobras and the tiny little puff adders that looked very much like small sticks lying motionless in the middle of a dusty path, and so easy to step on.

One Sunday evening I was invited to go and have a sundowner[1] at the house of an Englishman called Fuller who
10 worked in the Customs office[2] in Dar es Salaam. He lived with his wife and two small children in a plain white wooden house that stood alone some way back from the road in a rough grassy piece of ground with coconut trees scattered about. I was walking across the grass toward the house and was about
15 twenty yards away when I saw a large green snake go **gliding** straight up the veranda[3] steps of Fuller's house and in through the open front door. The brilliant yellowy-green skin and its great size made me certain it was a green mamba, a creature almost as deadly as the black mamba, and for a few seconds I
20 was so startled and dumbfounded and horrified that I froze to the spot. Then I pulled myself together and ran round to the back of the house shouting, "Mr. Fuller! Mr. Fuller!"

Mrs. Fuller popped her head out of an upstairs window. "What on earth's the matter?" she said.
25 "You've got a large green mamba in your front room!" I shouted. "I saw it go up the veranda steps and right in through the door!"

"Fred!" Mrs. Fuller shouted, turning round. "Fred! Come here!"

Freddy Fuller's round red face appeared at the window
30 beside his wife. "What's up?" he asked.

"There's a green mamba in your living room!" I shouted.

Without hesitation and without wasting time with more questions, he said to me, "Stay there. I'm going to lower the children down to you one at a time." He was completely cool
35 and unruffled.[4] He didn't even raise his voice.

---

1. **sundowner.** Evening refreshment
2. **Customs office.** Government agency that controls taxes on imports and exports
3. **veranda.** Open-air porch, usually with a roof
4. **unruffled.** Poised; calm

A small girl was lowered down to me by her wrists and I was able to catch her easily by the legs. Then came a small boy. Then Freddy Fuller lowered his wife and I caught her by the waist and put her on the ground. Then came Fuller himself. He

40 hung by his hands from the windowsill and when he let go he landed neatly on his two feet.

We stood in a little group on the grass at the back of the house and I told Fuller exactly what I had seen.

The mother was holding the two children by the hand,

45 one on each side of her. They didn't seem to be particularly alarmed.

"What happens now?" I asked.

"Go down to the road, all of you," Fuller said. "I'm off to **fetch** the snake-man." He trotted away and got into his small

50 ancient black car and drove off. Mrs. Fuller and the two small children and I went down to the road and sat in the shade of a large mango tree.

"Who is this snake-man?" I asked Mrs. Fuller.

"He is an old Englishman who has been out here for years,"

55 Mrs. Fuller said. "He actually likes snakes. He understands them and never kills them. He catches them and sells them to zoos and laboratories all over the world. Every native for miles around knows about him and whenever one of them sees a snake, he marks its hiding place and runs, often for great

60 distances, to tell the snake-man. Then the snake-man comes along and captures it. The snake-man's strict rule is that he will never buy a captured snake from the natives."

"Why not?" I asked.

"To discourage them from trying to catch snakes them-

65 selves," Mrs. Fuller said. "In his early days he used to buy caught snakes, but so many natives got bitten trying to catch them, and so many died, that he decided to put a stop to it. Now any native who brings in a caught snake, no matter how rare, gets turned away."

70 "That's good," I said.

"What is the snake-man's name?" I asked.

"Donald Macfarlane," she said. "I believe he's Scottish."

"Is the snake in the house, Mummy?" the small girl asked.

"Yes, darling. But the snake-man is going to get it out."

75 "He'll bite Jack," the girl said.

"Oh, my God!" Mrs. Fuller cried, jumping to her feet. "I forgot about Jack!" She began calling out, "Jack! Come here, Jack! Jack!...Jack!...Jack!"

> **fetch** (fĕch) *verb*, go get something and bring it back

How do the children react when they realize the dog is still in the house?

_____

_____

Think and Reflect

Who do you think will be the victim in this story? Explain your choice.

_____

_____

clev·er (klev ər) adjective, smart, intelligent, or witty

imp·le·ment (im ple ment) noun, a piece of equipment or a tool

prong (prôŋ) noun, a pointed projecting part, like on a fork

The children jumped up as well and all of them started
80 calling to the dog. But no dog came out of the open front door.

"He's bitten Jack!" the small girl cried out. "He must have bitten him!" She began to cry and so did her brother, who was a year or so younger than she was. Mrs. Fuller looked grim.

"Jack's probably hiding upstairs," she said. "You know how
85 **clever** he is."

Mrs. Fuller and I seated ourselves again on the grass, but the children remained standing. In between their tears they went on calling to the dog.

"Would you like me to take you down to the Maddens'
90 house?" their mother asked.

"No!" they cried. "No, no, no! We want Jack!"

"Here's Daddy!" Mrs. Fuller cried, pointing at the tiny black car coming up the road in a swirl of dust. I noticed a long wooden pole sticking out through one of the car windows.

95 The children ran to meet the car. "Jack's inside the house and he's been bitten by the snake!" they wailed. "We know he's been bitten! He doesn't come when we call him!"

Mr. Fuller and the snake-man got out of the car. The snake-man was small and very old, probably over seventy. He
100 wore leather boots made of thick cowhide and he had long gauntlet-type gloves[5] on his hands made of the same stuff. The gloves reached above his elbows. In his right hand he carried an extraordinary **implement**, an eight-foot-long wooden pole with a forked end. The two **prongs** of the fork were made, so it
105 seemed, of black rubber, about an inch thick and quite flexible, and it was clear that if the fork was pressed against the ground the two prongs would bend outward, allowing the neck of the fork to go down as close to the ground as necessary. In his left hand he carried an ordinary brown sack.

110 Donald Macfarlane, the snake-man, may have been old and small but he was an impressive-looking character. His eyes were pale blue, deep-set in a face round and dark and wrinkled as a walnut. Above the blue eyes, the eyebrows were thick and startlingly white, but the hair on his head was almost black. In
115 spite of the thick leather boots, he moved like a leopard, with soft slow catlike strides, and he came straight up to me and said, "Who are you?"

"He's with Shell,"[6] Fuller said. "He hasn't been here long."

---

5. **gauntlet-type gloves.** Protective gloves
6. **Shell.** Shell Oil, the company Dahl flew for

"You want to watch?" the snake-man said to me.

120   "Watch?" I said, wavering. "Watch? How do you mean watch? I mean where from? Not in the house?"

"You can stand out on the veranda and look through the window," the snake-man said.

"Come on," Fuller said. "We'll both watch."

125   "Now don't do anything silly," Mrs. Fuller said.

The two children stood there **forlorn** and miserable, with tears all over their cheeks.

The snake-man and Fuller and I walked over the grass toward the house, and as we approached the veranda steps the

130 snake-man whispered, "Tread softly on the wooden boards or he'll pick up the vibration. Wait until I've gone in, then walk up quietly and stand by the window."

The snake-man went up the steps first and he made absolutely no sound at all with his feet. He moved soft and catlike

135 onto the veranda and straight through the front door and then he quickly but very quietly closed the door behind him.

I felt better with the door closed. What I mean is I felt better for myself. I certainly didn't feel better for the snake-man. I figured he was committing suicide. I followed

140 Fuller onto the veranda and we both crept over to the window. The window was open, but it had a fine mesh mosquito netting all over it. That made me feel better still. We peered through the netting.

The living room was simple and ordinary, coconut matting

145 on the floor, a red sofa, a coffee table and a couple of armchairs. The dog was sprawled on the matting under the coffee table, a large Airedale with curly brown and black hair. He was stone dead.

for·lorn (fər lôrn´) adjective, sad, lonely; hopeless

The snake-man was standing absolutely still just inside the
150 door of the living room. The brown sack was now slung over
his left shoulder and he was grasping the long pole with both
hands, holding it out in front of him, parallel to the ground. I
couldn't see the snake. I didn't think the snake-man had seen it
yet either.

155 A minute went by...two minutes...three...four...five. Nobody
moved. There was death in that room. The air was heavy with
death and the snake-man stood as motionless as a pillar of
stone, with the long rod held out in front of him.

And still he waited. Another minute...and another...and
160 another.

And now I saw the snake-man beginning to bend his knees.
Very slowly he bent his knees until he was almost **squatting** on
the floor, and from that position he tried to peer under the sofa
and the armchairs.

165 And still it didn't look as though he was seeing anything.

Slowly he straightened his legs again, and then his head began
to swivel around the room. Over to the right, in the far corner, a
staircase led up to the floor above. The snake-man looked at the
stairs, and I knew very well what was going through his head.
170 Quite abruptly, he took one step forward and stopped.

Nothing happened.

A moment later I caught sight of the snake. It was lying
full-length along the skirting[7] of the right-hand wall, but hidden
from the snake-man's view by the back of the sofa. It lay there
175 like a long, beautiful, deadly shaft of green glass, quite motionless, perhaps asleep. It was facing away from us who were at the
window, with its small triangular head resting on the matting
near the foot of the stairs.

I nudged Fuller and whispered, "It's over there against the
180 wall." I pointed and Fuller saw the snake. At once, he started
waving both hands, palms outward, back and forth across
the window, hoping to get the snake-man's attention. The
snake-man didn't see him. Very softly, Fuller said, "Pssst!"
and the snake-man looked up sharply. Fuller pointed. The
185 snake-man understood and gave a nod.

Now the snake-man began working his way very very slowly
to the back wall of the room so as to get a view of the snake
behind the sofa. He never walked on his toes as you or I would
have done. His feet remained flat on the ground all the time.

squat (skwät) *verb*, almost sit in a
low position with knees bent

Note the Facts

Who sees the snake first? What
does he do?

_____

_____

---

7. **skirting.** Baseboard

190 The cowhide boots were like moccasins, with neither soles nor heels. Gradually, he worked his way over to the back wall, and from there he was able to see at least the head and two or three feet of the snake itself.

But the snake also saw him. With a movement so fast it was 195 invisible, the snake's head came up about two feet off the floor and the front of the body arched backwards, ready to strike. Almost simultaneously, it bunched its whole body into a series of curves, ready to flash forward.

The snake-man was just a bit too far away from the snake to 200 reach it with the end of his pole. He waited, staring at the snake, and the snake stared back at him with two small malevolent[8] black eyes.

Then the snake-man started speaking to the snake. "Come along, my pretty," he whispered in a soft wheedling[9] voice. 205 "There's a good boy. Nobody's going to hurt you. Nobody's going to harm you, my pretty little thing. Just lie still and relax..." He took a step forward toward the snake, holding the pole out in front of him.

What the snake did next was so fast that the whole move- 210 ment couldn't have taken more than a hundredth of a second, like the flick of a camera shutter. There was a green flash as the snake darted forward at least ten feet and struck at the snake- man's leg. Nobody could have got out of the way of that one. I heard the snake's head strike against the thick cowhide boot with 215 a sharp little crack, and then at once the head was back in that same deadly backward-curving position, ready to strike again.

---

8. **malevolent.** Having or showing hatred
9. **wheedling.** Coaxing; flattering

Think and Reflect

How does the snake-man feel about snakes?

_____

_____

trick·le (trikl´) noun, flow slowly or fall by drops

Use Reading Skills

Make Predictions

How do you think the snake-man will get the snake out of the house?

_____

_____

Build Vocabulary

What are *prongs*? Draw a picture of the tool that the snake-man will use to capture the snake.

ma·nip·u·late (mə nip´ yə lāt) *verb*, treat or operate with the hands in a skillful manner

"There's a good boy," the snake-man said softly. "There's a clever boy. There's a lovely fellow. You mustn't get excited. Keep calm and everything's going to be all right." As he was

220 speaking, he was slowly lowering the end of the pole until the forked prongs were about twelve inches above the middle of the snake's body. "There's a lovely fellow," he whispered. "There's a good kind little chap. Keep still now, my beauty. Keep still, my pretty. Keep quite still. Daddy's not going to

225 hurt you."

I could see a thin dark **trickle** of venom running down the snake-man's right boot where the snake had struck.

The snake, head raised and arcing[10] backwards, was as tense as a tight-wound spring and ready to strike again. "Keep still,

230 my lovely," the snake-man whispered. "Don't move now. Keep still. No one's going to hurt you."

Then wham, the rubber prongs came down right across the snake's body, about midway along its length, and pinned it to the floor. All I could see was a green blur as the snake

235 thrashed around furiously in an effort to free itself. But the snake-man kept up the pressure on the prongs and the snake was trapped.

What happens next? I wondered. There was no way he could catch hold of that madly twisting flailing length of green

240 muscle with his hands, and even if he could have done so, the head would surely have flashed around and bitten him in the face.

Holding the very end of the eight-foot pole, the snake-man began to work his way round the room until he was at the

245 tail end of the snake. Then, in spite of the flailing and the thrashing, he started pushing the prongs forward along the snake's body toward the head. Very very slowly he did it, pushing the rubber prongs forward over the snake's flailing body, keeping the snake pinned down all the time and pushing,

250 pushing, pushing the long wooden rod forward millimeter by millimeter. It was a fascinating and frightening thing to watch, the little man with white eyebrows and black hair carefully **manipulating** his long implement and sliding the fork ever so slowly along the length of the twisting snake

255 toward the head. The snake's body was thumping against the coconut matting with such a noise that if you had been upstairs you might have thought two big men were wrestling on the floor.

---

10. **arcing.** Following a curved course

Then at last the prongs were right behind the head itself,
260 pinning it down, and at that point the snake-man reached
forward with one gloved hand and grasped the snake very
firmly by the neck. He threw away the pole. He took the sack
off his shoulder with his free hand. He lifted the great, still
twisting length of the deadly green snake and pushed the head
265 into the sack. Then he let go the head and bundled the rest of
the creature in and closed the sack. The sack started jumping
about as though there were fifty angry rats inside it, but the
snake-man was now totally relaxed and he held the sack
casually in one hand as if it contained no more than a few
270 pounds of potatoes. He stooped and picked up his pole from
the floor, then he turned and looked toward the window where
we were peering in.

"Pity about the dog," he said. "You'd better get it out of the
way before the children see it." ❖

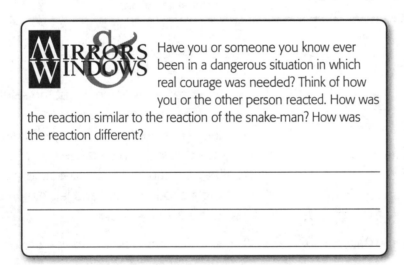

MIRRORS & WINDOWS
Have you or someone you know ever been in a dangerous situation in which real courage was needed? Think of how you or the other person reacted. How was the reaction similar to the reaction of the snake-man? How was the reaction different?

_____

_____

_____

READING CHECK

Circle the letter of the correct answer.

1. Who is the snake-man?
   A. He is a government official.
   B. He is an African neighbor who comes to kill the snake.
   C. He is an old Englishman who likes to capture snakes.

2. Why doesn't the snake-man buy snakes from the natives?
   A. The snake-man does not want to spend the money on captured snakes; he wants to make as much money as possible.
   B. The snake-man doesn't want to encourage the natives to deal with dangerous snakes and possibly get bitten.
   C. The snake-man has a strict rule that he never speaks to any of the natives.

3. Who is Jack?
   A. Jack is the family dog.
   B. Jack is Mr. Fuller's son.
   C. Jack is the real name of the snake-man.

4. Which words best describe the snake-man?
   A. scared and uncertain
   B. prepared and capable
   C. violent and aggressive

5. What happens when the snake strikes at the snake-man?
   A. The snake-man grabs the snake immediately and puts it in a bag.
   B. The snake-man falls stone dead onto the living room floor.
   C. The snake only strikes his boot, and a trickle of venom runs down the cowhide.

VOCABULARY CHECK

Circle the letter of the correct answer.

1. The author describes the snake's movement as *gliding* because…
   A. it moves very quickly and aggressively.
   B. it moves smoothly and effortlessly.
   C. it makes a lot of noise as it moves.

2. Which *implement* was most important for handling the situation with the snake?
   A. the long pole with prongs
   B. the venom of the green mamba
   C. the veranda in front of the house

3. There was a *trickle* of snake venom on the snake-man's boot. What does *trickle* mean?
   A. tear something to pieces
   B. some small drops
   C. roll it up into a ball

4. Why are the children *forlorn* when they are standing outside the house?
   A. They are very worried about the safety of their father on the veranda.
   B. They are scared of the old English snake-man dressed in his strange outfit.
   C. They are sad and crying because they forgot about the dog and left him in the house with the snake.

5. Is the snake-man able to *manipulate* his tools to capture the snake?
   A. No, he catches the snake in his hands and puts it in the bag.
   B. Yes, he slowly moves the fork toward the head of the snake.
   C. Yes, he uses a gun to shoot the snake behind the hood.

ANALYZE LITERATURE: Autobiography

Use this story as an example to write a short autobiography about a memorable event in your life. Make sure that all the details and characters are real.

_____

_____

USE READING SKILLS: Understand Literary Elements

Examine Plot Development

1. Look at the diagram that you completed on page 30. Explain how you determined which section of the story is the climax.

_____

_____

How did you feel when you read that part of the story?

_____

_____

2. Describe the resolution of the story.

_____

_____

How did you feel when you read that part of the story?

_____

_____

BUILDING LANGUAGE SKILLS: Hyphenated Words

A **hyphen** is a short line used to join words or parts of words. Writers often create adjectives by connecting two or more words with hyphens. Read each set of hyphenated words from the story and write what the words describe.

1. gauntlet-type   _____

2. eight-foot-long   _____

3. impressive-looking   _____

4. deep-set   _____

5. backward-curving   _____

SPEAKING & LISTENING SKILLS: Debate

Refer back to the Make Connections question on page 54. Pair up with another student who answered the question differently than you did. Prepare a short oral debate to express your ideas in front of the class. Note: If there are not an equal number of students who answered yes and no to the questions, some students may have to argue a different position for the sake of the debate.

BEFORE READING

 page E51

The Courage That My Mother Had

A Lyric Poem by Edna St. Vincent Millay

ABOUT THE POEM

"The Courage That My Mother Had" is a poem in which the speaker remembers her mother and one of her mother's special qualities. The mother gave the speaker a brooch, but the speaker would rather have inherited something else.

MAKE CONNECTIONS

What is one object you would like to inherit from your mother or father?

_____

_____

_____

_____

ANALYZE LITERATURE: Tone

Tone is the writer's attitude about the subject. The words and punctuation that writers use show how they feel about the topic. As you read, think about the writer's attitude toward her mother. What words in the poem create this tone?

USE READING SKILLS: Find the Main Idea

The **main idea** is a brief statement of what you think the author wants you to know, think, or feel after reading the text. You can find the main idea by identifying the important details. Read this poem several times and use the important details to identify the main idea. Write important details from the poem in the smaller circles of the graphic organizer below. Then write the main idea in the center circle of the graphic organizer.

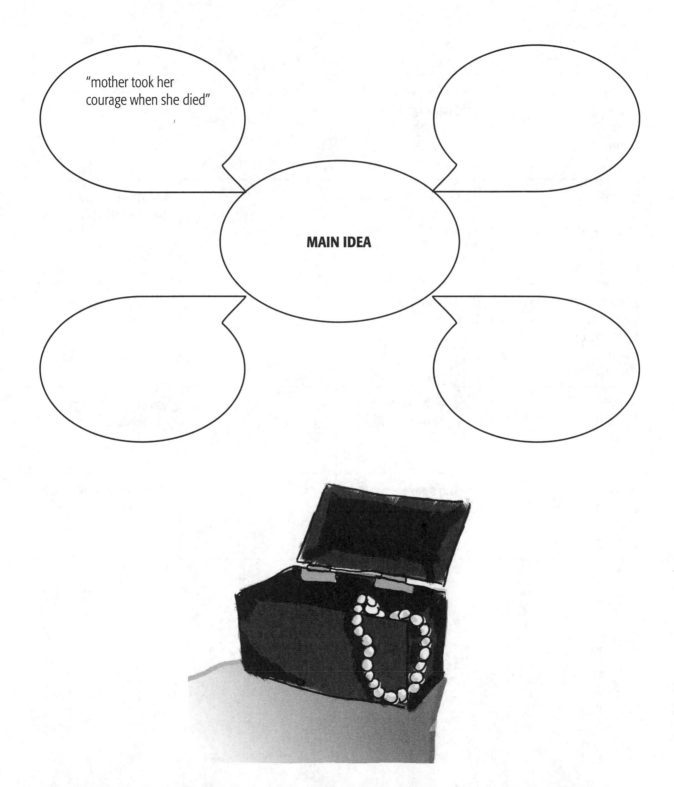

"mother took her courage when she died"

MAIN IDEA

PREVIEW VOCABULARY

Key Words and Phrases	Words and Phrases in Context	Definition	Practice
Read each key word and rate it using this scale: ① I don't know this word or phrase at all. ② I've seen this word or phrase before. ③ I know this word or phrase and use it.	Read to see how the key word or phrase can be used in a sentence.	Write down what you think the word or phrase means. Then use a dictionary to check your definition.	Practice using the key words and phrases by completing the following sentences.
courage cour · age (kər ij) *noun* ① ② ③	The firefighters showed great **courage** when they ran into the building.		Something that requires a lot of **courage** is…
quarry quar · ry (kwȯr e) *verb* ① ② ③	They wanted to **quarry** the beautiful stone from the side of the mountain.		Materials that you might **quarry** include…
granite gran · ite (gra nət) *noun* ① ② ③	The statue was made of **granite.**		**Granite** can be used for…
brooch (broch) *noun* ① ② ③	The silver **brooch** has a sharp pin on the back.		Someone that might wear a **brooch** is…
spare (sper) *verb* ① ② ③	Can you **spare** a cup of sugar?		I forgot my backpack. Can you **spare**…

Differentiated Instruction: Literacy & Reading Skills

The Courage That My Mother Had

A Lyric Poem by Edna St. Vincent Millay

> The courage that my mother had
> Went with her, and is with her still:
> Rock from New England quarried;[1]
> Now granite in a granite[2] hill.
>
> 5   The golden brooch[3] my mother wore
> She left behind for me to wear;
> I have no thing I treasure more:
> Yet, it is something I could spare.
>
>   Oh, if instead she'd left to me
> 10 The thing she took into the grave!—
> That courage like a rock, which she
> Has no more need of, and I have. ❧

1. **quarried.** Excavated; dug
2. **granite.** Very hard igneous rock
3. **brooch.** Piece of jewelry worn as a pin near the neck

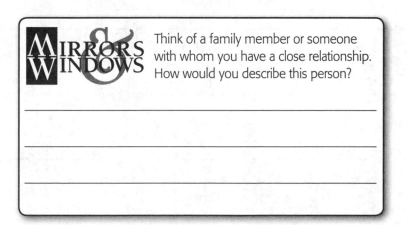

MIRRORS & WINDOWS

Think of a family member or someone with whom you have a close relationship. How would you describe this person?

_____

_____

_____

Analyze Literature

Tone How do the words *rock* and *granite* add to the tone of the poem?

Note the Facts

What did the speaker's mother leave her?

Build Vocabulary

Why does the speaker say that she can *spare* her mother's brooch?

_____

_____

Culture Note

The author's parents were divorced in the year 1900. It was much less common to be a single mother at that time. Do you think these facts could have contributed to the courage of the author's mother?

_____

_____

Think and Reflect

What quality do you admire about one of your relatives?

READING CHECK

Circle the letter of the correct answer.

1. What did the speaker's mother take to the grave?
   A. her money
   B. her jewelry
   C. her courage

2. What does the speaker say courage is like?
   A. a rock
   B. a brooch
   C. a grave

3. What object does the speaker treasure?
   A. granite
   B. a brooch
   C. a rock

4. What does the brooch look like?
   A. It is made of rock.
   B. It is made of gold.
   C. It is made of silver.

5. Is the speaker a courageous person?
   A. Yes, she has courage like a rock.
   B. No, she wishes she had more courage.
   C. She sometimes has courage.

VOCABULARY CHECK

Circle the letter of the correct answer.

1. What is the opposite of having *courage*?
   A. being fearful
   B. having strength
   C. being different than your mother

2. How is rock *quarried*?
   A. It is blasted, dug, or cut from the ground.
   B. It is only from New England.
   C. It is made in a factory.

3. What kind of material is *granite*?
   A. It is a hard rock.
   B. It is part of courage.
   C. It is a New England hill.

4. How do you usually use a *brooch*?
   A. You wear it as jewelry.
   B. You give it to your children.
   C. You use it for courage.

5. Why can the speaker *spare* the brooch?
   A. She needs a different brooch.
   B. It makes her sad to remember her mother.
   C. She doesn't really need it as much as she needs courage.

ANALYZE LITERATURE: Tone

Look at the sentences below and change the underlined words to add to the tone of the sentence. Rewrite your new sentence on the line.

1. I feel <u>fine</u> today.

   _____

2. The lunch in the school cafeteria is <u>OK</u>.

   _____

3. The weather yesterday was <u>normal</u>.

   _____

4. His grades at the end of the semester were <u>average</u>.

_____

5. The new students were dressed in <u>ordinary</u> clothes.

_____

USE READING SKILLS: Find the Main Idea

1. Why is the part of the poem about the mother written in the past tense?

_____

_____

2. What does the speaker want that she does not have?

_____

_____

BUILDING LANGUAGE SKILLS: Simile

A **simile** is a comparison of two items, ideas, characteristics, or traits that seem different. A simile uses the word *like* or *as* to make the comparison. For example the speaker says that *courage is like a rock* because courage is strong. Use your creativity to complete the similes below.

1. Friends and family are like _____

2. Snow is like _____

3. Fire is like _____

4. Travel is like _____

5. The English language is like _____

6. Music is like _____

SPEAKING & LISTENING: Presentation

Practice reading this poem in front of a mirror or take a video of yourself reading the poem. Think about ways to improve your presentation. Practice at least five times or until you feel comfortable reading the poem in front of a group. Your teacher will choose several students to present the poem to the class.

Name: _____ Date: _____

 page E59

Antaeus

A Short Story by Borden Deal

ABOUT THE STORY

"Antaeus" tells the story of a boy who moved from the rural South to a big city in the North with his family. He makes some new friends and tries to share some of his culture and country knowledge with the city boys in his apartment building.

MAKE CONNECTIONS

Think of a place to which you felt attached. Do you think that you could feel that same way about another place? Why or why not?

_____

_____

_____

_____

ANALYZE LITERATURE: Conflict

Conflict is the problem that is presented in the story. An external conflict is a conflict between two characters or between a character and another force. An internal conflict is a conflict within the character. As you read, think about the different kinds of conflict that are presented in the story.

USE READING SKILLS: Use Context Clues

Context clues are words and phrases near a difficult word that provide hints about its meaning. You can use usually use context clues to figure out the meaning of unfamiliar words. As you read, look for words that are unfamiliar to you. Then follow the steps below.

1. When you come across a sentence in the story with an unfamiliar word, copy the sentence into the first column of the chart below.
2. Underline the unfamiliar word and circle other parts of the sentence that might give you a clue about the unknown word's meaning.
3. In the second column, write your best guess for the definition of the unknown word.

An example has been done for you.

Unfamiliar Word	Definition
laborious	Something hard or difficult

PREVIEW VOCABULARY

Key Words and Phrases Read each key word and rate it using this scale: ①I don't know this word or phrase at all. ②I've seen this word or phrase before. ③I know this word or phrase and use it.	Words and Phrases in Context Read to see how the key word or phrase can be used in a sentence.	Definition Write down what you think the word or phrase means. Then use a dictionary to check your definition.	Practice Practice using the key words and phrases by completing the following sentences.
domain do · main (dō mān') *noun* ①　②　③	A tiger freely walks around the jungle because the jungle is its **domain.**		Your **domain** is a place where you…
laborious la · bo · ri · ous (lä bōr' ē äs) *adjective* ①　②　③	Growing a good garden and keeping the weeds out is **laborious.**		The most **laborious** part of my week is…
inert in · ert (i nʉrt') *adjective* ①　②　③	We knew the batteries were dead because the toy car was completely **inert.**		An example of something **inert** is…
desecrate des · e · crate (des' i krāt') *verb* ①　②　③	Burglars often **desecrate** the windows and doors of the stores they rob.		The opposite of **desecrate** is …
flourish flour · ish (flʉr' ish) *verb* ①　②　③	Those flowers **flourish** in the full sunlight.		Something that can **flourish** in water is…

Differentiated Instruction: Literacy & Reading Skills

Antaeus

A Short Story by Borden Deal

This was during the wartime, when lots of people were coming North for jobs in factories and war industries, when people moved around a lot more than they do now, and sometimes kids were thrown into new groups and new lives
5 that were completely different from anything they had ever known before. I remember this one kid, T. J. his name was, from somewhere down South, whose family moved into our building during that time. They'd come North with everything they owned piled into the back seat of an old-model sedan that
10 you wouldn't expect could make the trip, with T. J. and his three younger sisters riding shakily on top of the load of junk.

Our building was just like all the others there, with families crowded into a few rooms, and I guess there were twenty-five or thirty kids about my age in that one building. Of course,
15 there were a few of us who formed a gang and ran together all the time after school, and I was the one who brought T. J. in and started the whole thing.

The building right next door to us was a factory where they made walking dolls. It was a low building with a flat, tarred
20 roof that had a parapet¹ all around it about head-high, and we'd found out a long time before that no one, not even the watchman, paid any attention to the roof because it was higher than any of the other buildings around. So my gang used the roof as a headquarters. We could get up there by crossing over
25 to the fire escape from our own roof on a plank and then going on up. It was a secret place for us, where nobody else could go without our permission.

I remember the day I first took T. J. up there to meet the gang. He was a **stocky**, robust kid with a shock of white hair,
30 nothing sissy about him except his voice; he talked in this slow, gentle voice like you never heard before. He talked different from any of us and you noticed it right away. But I liked him anyway, so I told him to come on up.

We climbed up over the parapet and dropped down on the
35 roof. The rest of the gang were already there.

"Hi," I said. I jerked my thumb at T. J. "He just moved into the building yesterday."

---

1. **parapet.** Low wall around the edge of a roof or platform

Culture Note

The narrator mentions that T.J. speaks differently that the other boys. T.J. speaks in a southern *dialect*, which means that he says words differently than the other boys, and he may use words or phrases that the other boys do not use. Dialects can be a clue of where a person is from, because different regions often have different dialects. Authors use dialects to add dimension to a character and provide some insight as to where the characters are from.

---

stock•y ('stä kē) *adj.*, solid, thick, and short

Note the Facts

What do the other boys notice about T. J.'s voice?

_____

_____

He just stood there, not scared or anything, just looking, like the first time you see somebody you're not sure you're
40 going to like.

"Hi," Blackie said. "Where are you from?"

"Marion County," T. J. said.

We laughed. "Marion County?" I said. "Where's that?"

He looked at me for a moment like I was a stranger, too.
45 "It's in Alabama," he said, like I ought to know where it was.

"What's your name?" Charley said.

"T. J.," he said, looking back at him. He had pale blue eyes that looked washed-out[2] but he looked directly at Charley, waiting for his reaction. He'll be all right, I thought. No sissy in
50 him, except that voice. Who ever talked like that?

"T. J.," Blackie said. "That's just initials. What's your real name? Nobody in the world has just initials."

"I do," he said. "And they're T. J. That's all the name I got."

His voice was **resolute** with the knowledge of his rightness,
55 and for a moment no one had anything to say. T. J. looked around at the rooftop and down at the black tar under his feet. "Down yonder where I come from," he said, "we played out in the woods. Don't you-all have no woods around here?"

"Naw," Blackie said. "There's the park a few blocks over, but
60 it's full of kids and cops and old women. You can't do a thing."

T. J. kept looking at the tar under his feet. "You mean you ain't got no fields to raise nothing in?...no watermelons or nothing?"

"Naw," I said scornfully. "What do you want to grow
65 something for? The folks can buy everything they need at the store."

He looked at me again with that strange, unknowing look. "In Marion County," he said, "I had my own acre of cotton and my own acre of corn. It was mine to plant and make ever' year."
70 He sounded like it was something to be proud of, and in some obscure way it made the rest of us angry. Blackie said, "Who'd want to have their own acre of cotton and corn? That's just work. What can you do with an acre of cotton and corn?"

T. J. looked at him. "Well, you get part of the bale offen your
75 acre,"[3] he said seriously. "And I fed my acre of corn to my calf."

We didn't really know what he was talking about, so we were more puzzled than angry; otherwise, I guess, we'd have chased him off the roof and wouldn't let him be part of

res·o·lute (ˈre zə lüt) *adj.*, adjective, determined, set in purpose or opinion

---

2. **washed out.** With very little color
3. **you get part of the bale offen your acre.** When T. J. farmed someone else's land, he shared the crop with the owner and was able to keep part of it for himself.

Differentiated Instruction: Literacy & Reading Skills   © Carnegie Learning, Inc.

our gang. But he was strange and different, and we were all
80 attracted by his stolid[4] sense of rightness and belonging, maybe
by the strange softness of his voice contrasting our own tones of
speech into harshness.

He moved his foot against the black tar. "We could make
our own field right here," he said softly, thoughtfully. "Come
85 spring we could raise us what we want to—watermelons and
garden truck[5] and no telling what all."

"You'd have to be a good farmer to make these tar roofs
grow any watermelons," I said. We all laughed.

But T. J. looked serious. "We could haul us some dirt up
90 here," he said. "And spread it out even and water it, and before
you know it, we'd have us a crop in here." He looked at us
intently. "Wouldn't that be fun?"

"They wouldn't let us," Blackie said quickly.

"I thought you said this was you-all's roof," T. J. said to me.
95 "That you-all could do anything you wanted to up here."

"They've never bothered us," I said. I felt the idea beginning
to catch fire in me. It was a big idea, and it took a while for it
to sink in; but the more I thought about it, the better I liked
it. "Say," I said to the gang. "He might have something there.
100 Just make us a regular roof garden, with flowers and grass and
trees and everything. And all ours, too," I said. "We wouldn't let
anybody up here except the ones we wanted to."

"It'd take a while to grow trees," T. J. said quickly, but we
weren't paying any attention to him. They were all talking about
105 it suddenly, all excited with the idea after I'd put it in a way they
could catch hold of it. Only rich people had roof gardens, we
knew, and the idea of our own private **domain** excited them.

"We could bring it up in sacks and boxes," Blackie said.
"We'd have to do it while the folks weren't paying any attention
110 to us, for we'd have to come up to the roof of our building and
then cross over with it."

"Where could we get the dirt?" somebody said worriedly.

"Out of those **vacant** lots over close to school," Blackie said.
"Nobody'd notice if we scraped it up."
115 I slapped T. J. on the shoulder. "Man, you had a wonderful
idea," I said, and everybody grinned at him, remembering that
he had started it. "Our own private roof garden."

He grinned back. "It'll be ourn," he said. "All ourn." Then
he looked thoughtful again. "Maybe I can lay my hands on

Note the Facts

What is T. J.'s idea for the roof?

_____

_____

do·main (dō mān´) *n.*, land that a
person owns; rightful territory

va·cant (´va kənt) *adj.*, empty,
unoccupied

---

4. **stolid.** Unemotional
5. **garden truck.** Vegetables grown for market

120 some cotton seed, too. You think we could raise us some
cotton?" We'd started big projects before at one time or
another, like any gang of kids, but they'd always petered out[6]
for lack of organization and direction. But this one didn't;
somehow or other T. J. kept it going all through the winter
125 months. He kept talking about the watermelons and the cotton
we'd raise, come spring, and when even that wouldn't work,
he'd switch around to my idea of flowers and grass and trees,
though he was always honest enough to add that it'd take a
while to get any trees started. He always had it on his mind, and
130 he'd mention it in school, getting them lined up to carry dirt
that afternoon, saying in a casual way that he reckoned a few
more weeks ought to see the job through.

   Our little area of private earth grew slowly. T. J. was smart
enough to start in one corner of the building, heaping up
135 the carried earth two or three feet thick so that we had an
immediate result to look at, to contemplate with awe. Some of
the evenings T. J. alone was carrying earth up to the building,
the rest of the gang distracted by other enterprises or interests,
but T. J. kept plugging along on his own, and eventually we'd
140 all come back to him again, and then our own little acre would
grow more rapidly.

   He was careful about the kind of dirt he'd let us carry up
there, and more than once he dumped a sandy load over the
parapet into the areaway below because it wasn't good enough.
145 He found out the kinds of earth in all the vacant lots for blocks
around. He'd pick it up and feel it and smell it, frozen though it
was sometimes, and then he'd say it was good growing soil or it
wasn't worth anything, and we'd have to go on somewhere else.

   Thinking about it now, I don't see how he kept us at it. It
150 was hard work, lugging paper sacks and boxes of dirt all the

---

6. **petered out.** Quit or stopped

way up the stairs of our own building, keeping out of the way of the grown-ups so they wouldn't catch on to what we were doing. They probably wouldn't have cared, for they didn't pay much attention to us, but we wanted to keep it secret anyway.

155 Then we had to go through the trap door to our roof, teeter[7] over a plank to the fire escape, then climb two or three stories to the parapet, and drop them down onto the roof. All that for a small pile of earth that sometimes didn't seem worth the effort. But T. J. kept the vision bright within us, his words shrewd and

160 calculated toward the fulfillment of his dream; and he worked harder than any of us. He seemed driven toward a goal that we couldn't see, a particular point in time that would be definitely marked by signs and wonders that only he could see.

The **laborious** earth just lay there during the cold months,

165 **inert** and lifeless, the clods lumpy and cold under our feet when we walked over it. But one day it rained, and afterward there was a softness in the air, and the earth was live and giving again with moisture and warmth.

That evening T. J. smelled the air, his nostrils dilating with

170 the odor of the earth under his feet. "It's spring," he said, and there was a gladness rising in his voice that filled us all with the same feeling. "It's mighty late for it, but it's spring. I'd just about decided it wasn't never gonna get here at all."

We were all sniffing at the air, too, trying to smell it the way

175 that T. J. did, and I can still remember the sweet odor of the earth under our feet. It was the first time in my life that spring and spring earth had meant anything to me. I looked at T. J. then, knowing in a faint way the hunger within him through the toilsome winter months, knowing the dream that lay behind his

180 plan. He was a new Antaeus,[8] preparing his own bed of strength.

"Planting time," he said. "We'll have to find us some seed."

"What do we do?" Blackie said. "How do we do it?"

"First we'll have to break up the clods," T. J. said. "That won't be hard to do. Then we plant the seed, and after a while

185 they come up. Then you got you a crop." He frowned. "But you ain't got it raised yet. You got to tend it and hoe it and take care of it, and all the time it's growing and growing, while you're awake and while you're asleep. Then you lay it by when it's growed[9] and let it **ripen**, and then you got you a crop."

---

7. **teeter.** Wobble
8. **Antaeus.** Mythological giant who gained strength from touching Earth. Hercules defeated Antaeus by holding him off the ground until he weakened and died.
9. **Then you lay it by when it's growed.** To lay by a crop is to tend to it for the last time before harvesting. After laying by, a farmer leaves the crop to mature on its own.

---

la·bo·ri·ous (lə bōr´ ē əs) *adj.*, produced by hard work

in·ert (i nʉrt´) *adj.*, still; unmoving

Build Vocabulary

What is the most *laborious* part of making the rooftop garden?

_____

_____

Culture Note

T. J. is referred to as "a new Antaeus," and "Antaeus" is also the title of the story. Antaeus was a giant who wrestled Hercules in Greek myth. What does T. J. have in common with Antaeus?

rip·en (´rī pən) *v.*, become mature and ready to be eaten

190   "There's these wholesale seed houses over on Sixth," I said. "We could probably swipe some grass seed over there."

     T. J. looked at the earth. "You-all seem mighty set on raising some grass," he said. "I ain't never put no effort into that. I spent all my life trying not to raise grass."

195   "But it's pretty," Blackie said. "We could play on it and take sunbaths on it. Like having our own lawn. Lots of people got lawns."

     "Well," T. J. said. He looked at the rest of us, hesitant for the first time. He kept on looking at us for a moment. "I did have it

200 in mind to raise some corn and vegetables. But we'll plant grass."

     He was smart. He knew where to give in. And I don't suppose it made any difference to him, really. He just wanted to grow something, even if it was grass.

     "Of course," he said. "I do think we ought to plant a row

205 of watermelons. They'd be mighty nice to eat while we was a-laying on that grass."

     We all laughed. "All right," I said. "We'll plant us a row of watermelons."

     Things went very quickly then. Perhaps half the roof

210 was covered with the earth, the half that wasn't broken by ventilators,[10] and we swiped pocketfuls of grass seed from the open bins in the wholesale seed house, mingling among the buyers on Saturdays and during the school lunch hour. T. J. showed us how to prepare the earth, breaking up the clods and

215 smoothing it and sowing the grass seed. It looked rich and black now with moisture, receiving of the seed, and it seemed that the grass sprang up[11] overnight, pale green in the early spring.

---

10. **ventilators.** Mechanisms, such as ducts or fans, for getting rid of old air and bringing fresh air into a building
11. **sprang up.** Grew very quickly

We couldn't keep from looking at it, unable to believe that we had created this delicate growth. We looked at T. J. with
220 understanding now, knowing the fulfillment of the plan he had carried alone within his mind. We had worked without full understanding of the task, but he had known all the time.

We found that we couldn't walk or play on the delicate blades, as we had expected to, but we didn't mind. It was
225 enough just to look at it, to realize that it was the work of our own hands, and each evening, the whole gang was there, trying to measure the growth that had been achieved that day.

One time a foot was placed on the plot of ground, one time only, Blackie stepping onto it with sudden bravado. Then he
230 looked at the crushed blades and there was shame in his face. He did not do it again. This was his grass, too, and not to be **desecrated**. No one said anything, for it was not necessary.

T. J. had reserved a small section for watermelons, and he was still trying to find some seed for it. The wholesale house
235 didn't have any watermelon seed, and we didn't know where we could lay our hands on them. T. J. shaped the earth into mounds, ready to receive them, three mounds lying in a straight line along the edge of the grass plot.

We had just about decided that we'd have to buy the seed
240 if we were to get them. It was a violation of our principles, but we were anxious to get the watermelons started. Somewhere or other, T. J. got his hands on a seed catalog and brought it one evening to our roof garden.

"We can order them now," he said, showing us the catalog.
245 "Look!"

We all crowded around, looking at the fat, green watermelons pictured in full color on the pages. Some of them were split open, showing the red, tempting meat, making our mouths water.
250　"Now we got to scrape up some seed money," T. J. said, looking at us. "I got a quarter. How much you-all got?"

We made up a couple of dollars among us and T. J. nodded his head. "That'll be more than enough. Now we got to decide what kind to get. I think them Kleckley Sweets. What do you-all think?"
255　He was going into esoteric[12] matters beyond our reach. We hadn't even known there were different kinds of melons. So we just nodded our heads and agreed that yes, we thought the Kleckley Sweets too.

> **des·e·crate** (des´ i krāt') *v.*, treat with disrespect

---

12. **esoteric.** Understood by only a small group of people

flour·ish (flŭr´ ish) *v.*, grow luxuriously

Note the Facts

Who is the man in the suit? How does T. J. feel?

_____

_____

_____

Use Reading Skills

Cause and Effect

What do you think could have caused the owner to come up on the roof?

_____

_____

_____

Read Aloud

On pages 80 and 81, read aloud the dialogue between T. J. and the building owner. Why is T. J. so honest with the man in the suit?

_____

_____

_____

"I'll order them tonight," T. J. said. "We ought to have them
260 in a few days."

"What are you boys doing up here?" an adult voice said
behind us.

It startled us, for no one had ever come up here before,
in all the time we had been using the roof of the factory. We
265 jerked around and saw three men standing near the trap door
at the other end of the roof. They weren't policemen, or night
watchmen, but three men in plump business suits, looking at
us. They walked toward us.

"What are you boys doing up here?" the one in the middle
270 said again.

We stood still, guilt heavy among us, levied by the tone of
voice,[13] and looked at the three strangers.

The men stared at the grass **flourishing** behind us. "What's
this?" the man said. "How did this get up here?"
275 "Sure is growing good, ain't it?" T. J. said conversationally.
"We planted it."

The men kept looking at the grass as if they didn't believe
it. It was a thick carpet over the earth now, a patch of deep
greenness startling in the sterile industrial surroundings.
280 "Yes, sir," T. J. said proudly. "We toted that earth up here
and planted that grass." He fluttered the seed catalog. "And
we're just fixing to plant us some watermelon."

The man looked at him then, his eyes strange and faraway.
"What do you mean, putting this on the roof of my building?"
285 he said. "Do you want to go to jail?"

T. J. looked shaken. The rest of us were silent, frightened
by the authority of his voice. We had grown up aware of adult
authority, of policemen and night watchmen and teachers, and
this man sounded like all the others. But it was a new thing to T. J.
290 "Well, you wasn't using the roof," T. J. said. He paused a
moment and added shrewdly, "So we just thought to pretty it
up a little bit."

"And sag it so I'd have to rebuild it," the man said sharply.
He started turning away, saying to another man beside him,
295 "See that all that junk is shoveled off by tomorrow."

"Yes, sir," the man said.

T. J. started forward. "You can't do that," he said. "We toted
it up here, and it's our earth. We planted it and raised it and
toted it up here."

---

13. **levied by the tone of voice.** Judged by the attitude more than by words

300　　The man stared at him coldly. "But it's my building," he said. "It's to be shoveled off tomorrow."

　　"It's our earth," T. J. said desperately. "You ain't got no right!"

　　The men walked on without listening and descended clumsily
305　through the trap door. T. J. stood looking after them, his body tense with anger, until they had disappeared. They wouldn't even argue with him, wouldn't let him defend his earth rights.

　　He turned to us. "We won't let 'em do it," he said fiercely. "We'll stay up here all day tomorrow and the day after that, and
310　we won't let 'em do it."

　　We just looked at him. We knew that there was no stopping it.

　　He saw it in our faces, and his face wavered for a moment before he gripped it into determination. "They ain't got no right," he said. "It's our earth. It's our land. Can't nobody touch
315　a man's own land."

　　We kept looking at him, listening to the words but knowing that it was no use. The adult world had descended on us even in our richest dream, and we knew there was no calculating the adult world, no fighting it, no winning against it.

320　　We started moving slowly toward the parapet and the fire escape, avoiding a last look at the green beauty of the earth that T. J. had planted for us, had planted deeply in our minds as well as in our experience. We filed slowly over the edge and down the steps to the plank, T. J. coming last, and all of us could feel
325　the weight of his grief behind us.

　　"Wait a minute," he said suddenly, his voice harsh with the effort of calling.

　　We stopped and turned, held by the tone of his voice, and looked up at him standing above us on the fire escape.

330　　"We can't stop them?" he said, looking down at us, his face strange in the dusky light. "There ain't no way to stop 'em?"

　　"No," Blackie said with finality. "They own the building."

We stood still for a moment, looking up at T. J., caught into inaction by the decision working in his face. He stared back at
335　us, and his face was pale and mean in the poor light, with a bald nakedness in his skin like cripples have sometimes.

"They ain't gonna touch my earth," he said fiercely. "They ain't gonna lay a hand on it! Come on."

He turned around and started up the fire escape again,
340　almost running against the effort of climbing. We followed more slowly, not knowing what he intended to do. By the time we reached him, he had seized a board and **thrust** it into the soil, scooping it up and flinging it over the parapet into the areaway below. He straightened and looked at us.
345　"They can't touch it," he said. "I won't let 'em lay a dirty hand on it!"

We saw it then. He stooped to his labor again, and we followed, the gusts of his anger moving in frenzied labor among us as we scattered along the edge of the earth, scooping it and
350　throwing it over the parapet, destroying with anger the growth we had nurtured with such tender care. The soil carried so laboriously upward to the light and the sun cascaded swiftly into the dark areaway, the green blades of grass crumpled and twisted in the falling.

thrust ('thərst) v., push with force

Think and Reflect

Why does T. J. throw the earth and grass over the edge of the building if the owner is going to remove it the next day?

355　It took less time than you would think; the task of destruction is infinitely easier than that of creation. We stopped at the end, leaving only a scattering of loose soil, and when it was finally over, a stillness stood among the group and over the factory building. We looked down at the bare sterility of black
360　tar, felt the harsh texture of it under the soles of our shoes, and the anger had gone out of us, leaving only a sore aching in our minds, like overstretched muscles.

T. J. stood for a moment, his breathing slowing from anger and effort, caught into the same contemplation of destruction
365　as all of us. He stooped slowly, finally, and picked up a lonely blade of grass left trampled under our feet and put it between his teeth, tasting it, sucking the greenness out of it into his mouth. Then he started walking toward the fire escape,

Analyze Literature

Narrator Do you think the narrator of this story is an adult or a child? Explain your choice.

_____

_____

370 moving before any of us were ready to move, and disappeared over the edge.

We followed him, but he was already halfway down to the ground, going on past the board where we crossed over, climbing down into the areaway. We saw the last section swing down with his weight, and then he stood on the concrete below

375 us, looking at the small pile of anonymous earth scattered by our throwing. Then he walked across the place where we could see him and disappeared toward the street without glancing back, without looking up to see us watching him.

They did not find him for two weeks.

380 Then the Nashville police caught him just outside the Nashville freight yards. He was walking along the railroad track, still heading South, still heading home.

As for us, who had no remembered home to call us, none of us ever again climbed the escapeway to the roof. ❖

MIRRORS & WINDOWS Have you ever created an artistic piece such as a decorative garden, a poem, or a piece of music? How does it feel to create something beautiful?

_____

_____

_____

READING CHECK

Circle the letter of the correct answer.

1. Where is T. J. from?
   A. New York, New York
   B. Marion County, Alabama
   C. Marion County, Mississippi

2. What does T. J. look like?
   A. short and strong
   B. tall and skinny
   C. medium height with black hair

3. What crop does T. J. want to plant the most?
   A. grass
   B. watermelon
   C. corn

4. What crop do the other boys want to plant the most?
   A. grass
   B. watermelon
   C. corn

5. Where is T. J. going when the police finally find him?
   A. up to the roof
   B. North
   C. South

VOCABULARY CHECK

Circle the letter of the correct answer.

1. Why are the boys excited to have their own *domain*?
   A. It would be a lot of work.
   B. It would be a private place, only for them.
   C. They could share the space with everyone.

2. Why is farming *laborious*?
   A. It is difficult to work in the hot sun.
   B. Farmers usually work seven days a week.
   C. All of the above

3. The narrator says that the dirt was *inert* during the winter. Why was the dirt *inert*?
   A. Winter is too cold for the dirt to grow anything.
   B. They had to throw the dirt off the roof.
   C. The dirt was very heavy.

4. The new grass is not to be *desecrated*. Why do the boys feel that way?
   A. Only certain people can walk on the grass.
   B. The boys do not want to ruin the grass or do anything disrespectful to it.
   C. The grass belongs to the building owner.

5. The building owner stares at the *flourishing* grass. What does he see?
   A. yellow, dying grass
   B. healthy, green growing grass
   C. new grass seeds being planted

ANALYZE LITERATURE: Conflict

One conflict in this story is over what to plant on the roof. T. J. wants to plant one crop, but the other boys want to plant something else. Write a short paragraph about what they decide to do.

_____

_____

_____

_____

USE READING SKILLS: Use Context Clues

1. When the narrator talks about starting the rooftop garden, he says, "I felt the idea beginning to *catch fire* in me." What does *catch fire* mean in this sentence?

   _____

2. Blackie steps onto the grass with *bravado*. After he sees that he crushed the blades of grass, he feels bad and there is shame in his face. What does *bravado* mean?

   _____

BUILDING LANGUAGE SKILLS: Dialect

Many words that T. J. uses are part of a Southern dialect that is a little different from the way the other boys speak. Match T. J.'s words on the left with their standard English meaning on the right. Use the footnotes from the story to help you.

_____ 1. down yonder   a. in the South

_____ 2. ourn   b. your

_____ 3. ain't   c. isn't

_____ 4. ever' year   d. ours

_____ 5. you-all's   e. every year

SPEAKING & LISTENING: Narrative

After reading the story, think about what tone of voice you think the narrator would use. Together with a partner, take turns reading the first two paragraphs of the story. Pay attention to the punctuation and practice pausing at appropriate places. Choose words or phrases to emphasize. On the lines below, write down words or phrases that your partner chose to emphasize.

_____

_____

BEFORE READING

page 193

Names/Nombres

A Personal Essay by Julia Alvarez

ABOUT THE STORY

"Names/Nombres" tells the story of Julia Alvarez. She talks about the many names by which she was known from the time that she arrived in the United States to the time that she began college. At first, she was upset by the way so many people mispronounced her name and the names of her family members. Read her story and see how her opinions changed.

MAKE CONNECTIONS

How would you feel if everyone suddenly started referring to you with a new name?

_____

_____

_____

_____

ANALYZE LITERATURE: Personal Essay

A **personal essay** is a short, true story that tells the author's opinion about a subject. Personal essays are written in the first person. That means they use pronouns such as *I* and *we* to tell the story. As you read, think about the opinions that the author shares in this personal essay.

Differentiated Instruction: Literacy & Reading Skills   © Carnegie Learning, Inc.

USE READING SKILLS: Identify Author's Purpose

A writer's **purpose** is his or her aim or goal. An important reading skill is to try to figure out what the author's purpose is. Look at the title, skim the story, and read the footnotes. Then write your observations in the Before Reading section of the chart below. Next, read the essay and list some of the author's ideas in the During Reading section. Then in the After Reading section, explain why you think the author wrote this essay.

AUTHOR'S PURPOSE CHART
Before Reading: (Predict the author's purpose.)
During Reading: (Record details that show the author's purpose.)
After Reading: (What is the author's purpose?)

PREVIEW VOCABULARY

Key Words and Phrases Read each key word and rate it using this scale: ① I don't know this word or phrase at all. ② I've seen this word or phrase before. ③ I know this word or phrase and use it.	Words and Phrases in Context Read to see how the key word or phrase can be used in a sentence.	Definition Write down what you think the word or phrase means. Then use a dictionary to check your definition.	Practice Practice using the key words and phrases by completing the following sentences.
ethnicity eth · ni · ci · ty (eth niˊ sə tē) *noun* ① ② ③	New York City has a population with a wide variety of **ethnicities**.		Some **ethnicities** represented in this city are…
specify spec · i · fy (speˊ sə fīˊ) *verb* ① ② ③	My mom asked me to **specify** the time I would be home.		I asked the teacher to **specify**…
chaotic cha · o ·tic (kā ätˊ ik) *adjective* ① ② ③	The amusement park was crowded and **chaotic**.		An example of something **chaotic** is…
commencement com · mence · ment (kəm men[t]sˊ mə nt) *noun* ① ② ③	She bought a new dress for her high school **commencement** speech.		High school **commencement** can be celebrated with…
portable port · a · ble (port a bleˊ) *adjective* ① ② ③	My grandfather often took walks with his **portable** radio.		The opposite of **portable** is…

Differentiated Instruction: Literacy & Reading Skills

Names/Nombres

A Personal Essay by Julia Alvarez

When we arrived in New York City, our names changed almost immediately. At Immigration, the officer asked my father, *Mister Elbures*, if he had anything to declare. My father shook his head no, and we were waved through.

5   I was too afraid we wouldn't be let in if I corrected the man's pronunciation, but I said our name to myself, opening my mouth wide for the organ blast of the a, trilling my tongue for the drumroll of the *r*, *All-vah-rrr-es*! How could anyone get *Elbures* out of that orchestra of sound?

10   At the hotel my mother was *Missus Alburest*, and I was little girl, as in, "Hey, little girl, stop riding the elevator up and down. It's *not* a toy."

When we moved into our apartment building, the super called my father *Mister Alberase*, and the neighbors who
15 became mother's friends pronounced her name *Jew-lee-ah* instead of *Hoo-lee-ah*. I, her namesake, was known as Hoo-lee-tah at home. But at school I was Judy or Judith, and once an English teacher mistook me for *Juliet*.

It took a while to get used to my new names. I wondered
20 if I shouldn't correct my teachers and new friends. But my mother argued that it didn't matter. "You know what your friend Shakespeare said, '*A rose by any other name would smell as sweet*.'" My family had gotten into the habit of calling any famous author "my friend" because I had begun to write poems
25 and stories in English class.

By the time I was in high school, I was a popular kid, and it showed in my name. Friends called me *Jules* or *Hey Jude*, and once a group of troublemaking friends my mother forbade me to hang out with called me *Alcatraz*.[1] I was *Hoo-lee-tah* only
30 to Mami and Papi and uncles and aunts who came over to eat *sancocho*[2] on Sunday afternoons—old world folk whom I would just as soon go back to where they came from and leave me to pursue whatever mischief I wanted to in America. *JUDY ALCATRAZ*, the name on the "Wanted" poster would read.
35 Who would ever trace her to me?

Note the Facts

Why didn't Julia correct the immigration officer's pronunciation of her last name?

_____

_____

Culture Note

"Hey Jude" was a popular song by the Beatles when Julia was in high school. Do any of your friends have nicknames that come from music or from another part of popular culture?

_____

---

1. **Alcatraz.** From the mid-1930s to the mid-1960s, a maximum-security prison for America's toughest criminals
2. *sancocho* (san kô´ chō). Caribbean meat stew (Spanish)

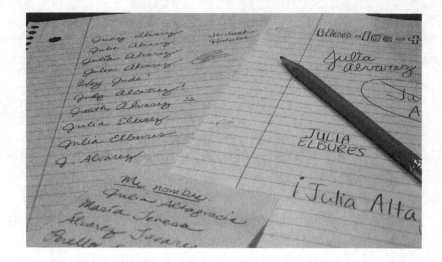

My older sister had the hardest time getting an American name for herself because *Mauricia* did not translate into English. Ironically, although she had the most foreign-sounding name, she and I were the Americans in the family. We had been born in New
40 York City when our parents had first tried immigration and then gone back "home," too homesick to stay. My mother often told the story of how she almost changed my sister's name in the hospital.

After the delivery, Mami and some other new mothers were cooing over their newborn sons and daughters and exchanging
45 names, weights and delivery stories. My mother was embarrassed among the Sallys and Janes, Georges and Johns to reveal the rich, noisy name of *Mauricia*, so when her turn came to brag, she gave her baby's name as Maureen.

"Why'd ya give her an Irish name with so many pretty
50 Spanish names to choose from?" one of the women asked.

My mother blushed and admitted her baby's real name to the group. Her mother-in-law had recently died, she apologized, and her husband had insisted that the first daughter be named after his mother, *Mauran*. My mother thought it the
55 ugliest name she had ever heard, and talked my father into what she believed was an improvement, a combination of *Mauran* and her own mother's name, *Felicia*.

"Her name is Mao-ree-shee-ah," my mother said to the group of women.
60 "Why, that's a beautiful name," the other mothers cried. "*Moor-ee-sha, Moor-ee-sha,*" she cooed into the pink blanket. *Moor-ee-sha* it was when we returned to the States eleven years later. Sometimes, American tongues found that mispronunciation tough to say and called her *Maria* or *Marsha*
65 or *Maudy* from her nickname *Maury*. I pitied her. What an awful name to have to transport across borders!

My little sister, Ana, had the easiest time of all. She was plain
Anne—that is, only her name was plain, for she turned out to be
the pale, blond "American beauty" in the family. The only Hispanic
70   thing about her was the affectionate nicknames her boyfriends
sometimes gave her. *Anita*, or, as one goofy guy used to sing to her
to the tune of the banana advertisement, *Anita Banana*.

Later, during her college years in the late sixties, there was a
push to pronounce Third World[3] names correctly. I remember
75   calling her long distance at her group house and a roommate
answering.

"Can I speak to Ana?" I asked, pronouncing her name the
American way.

"Ana?" The man's voice hesitated. "Oh! You must mean
80   *Ah-nah!*"

Our first few years in the States, though, **ethnicity** was not
yet "in." Those were the blond, blue-eyed, bobby-sock years
of junior high and high school before the sixties ushered in
peasant blouses, hoop earrings, *sarapes*.[4] My initial desire to be
85   known by my correct Dominican name faded. I just wanted to
be Judy and merge with the Sallys and Janes in my class. But,
inevitably, my accent and coloring gave me away. "So where are
you from, Judy?"

"New York," I told my classmates. After all, I had been born
90   blocks away at Columbia-Presbyterian Hospital.

"I mean, *originally*."

"From the Caribbean," I answered vaguely, for if I
specified, no one was quite sure on what continent our island
was located.

95   "Really? I've been to Bermuda. We went last April for spring
vacation. I got the worst sunburn! So, are you from Portoriko?"[5]

"No," I sighed. "From the Dominican Republic."

"Where's that?"

"South of Bermuda."

100   They were just being curious, I knew, but I burned with
shame whenever they singled me out as a "foreigner," a rare,
exotic friend.

"Say your name in Spanish, oh, please say it!" I had made
mouths drop one day by rattling off my full name, which,
105   according to Dominican custom, included my middle names,
Mother's and Father's surnames for four generations back.

---

3. **Third World.** Developing countries of Latin America, Africa, and Asia
4. *sarapes* (sə rä´ pēs). Woolen shawls or ponchos (Spanish)
5. **Portoriko.** Puerto Rico

Build Vocabulary

What does it mean for *ethnicity*
to be "in" as Julia said?

_____

_____

eth·ni·ci·ty (eth ni´ sə tē) *n.*,
belonging to a racial, cultural, or
national group

spec·i·fy (spe´ sə fī´) *verb.*, state
explicitly

Read Aloud

Read aloud the paragraph with Julia's full name in lines 107–110. Can anyone in your class pronounce her full name really well?

_____

_____

cha·ot·ic (kā ät´ ik) *adj.*, in a state of disorder or confusion

Note the Facts

Who attended Julia's graduation? How were her guests different from the guests of other students?

_____

_____

Think and Reflect

Do you or any of your friends have names that are difficult for some people to pronounce? Is it important to you to have your name pronounced correctly?

com·mence·ment (kəm men[t]s´ mənt) *adj.*, graduation

port·a·ble (port a ble´) *adj.*, something that can be carried

"Julia Altagracia María Teresa Álvarez Tavares Perello Espaillat Julia Pérez Rochet González." I pronounced it slowly, a name as **chaotic** with sounds as a Middle Eastern bazaar or
110 market day in a South American village.

My Dominican heritage was never more apparent than when my extended family attended school occasions. For my graduation, they all came, the whole lot of aunts and uncles and the many little cousins who snuck in without tickets. They sat
115 in the first row in order to better understand the Americans' fast-spoken English. But how could they listen when they were constantly speaking among themselves in florid-sounding phrases, rococo[6] consonants, rich, rhyming vowels?

Introducing them to my friends was a further trial to me.
120 These relatives had such complicated names and there were so many of them, and their relationships to myself were so convoluted. There was my Tía[7] Josefina, who was not really an aunt but a much older cousin. And her daughter, Aida Margarita, who was adopted, *una hija de crianza*.[8] My uncle of affection,
125 Tío José, brought my *madrina*[9] Tía Amelia and her *comadre*[10] Tía Pilar. My friends rarely had more than a "Mom and Dad" to introduce.

After the **commencement** ceremony, my family waited outside in the parking lot while my friends and I signed
130 yearbooks with nicknames which recalled our high school good times: "Beans" and "Pepperoni" and "Alcatraz." We hugged and cried and promised to keep in touch.

Our goodbyes went on too long. I heard my father's voice calling out across the parking lot, "*Hoo-lee-tah! Vámonos!*"[11]
135 Back home, my *tíos* and *tías* and *primas*,[12] Mami and Papi, and *mis hermanas*[13] had a party for me with sancocho and a store-bought *pudín*,[14] inscribed with *Happy Graduation, Julie*. There were many gifts—that was a plus to a large family! I got several wallets and a suitcase with my initials and a graduation
140 charm from my godmother and money from my uncles. The biggest gift was a **portable** typewriter from my parents for writing my stories and poems.

---

6. **rococo.** Fancy, flamboyant
7. **Tía** (tē´ ä). Aunt (Spanish); Tío (tē´ ō) is uncle.
8. **una hija de crianza** (ù´ nä ē´ hä de krē än´ sä). An adopted daughter (Spanish)
9. **madrina** (mä drē nä). Godmother (Spanish)
10. **comadre** (kō mä´ drä). Close friend (Spanish)
11. **Vámonos** (vä´ mä nōs'). Let's go (Spanish)
12. **primas** (prē´ mäs'). Cousins (Spanish)
13. **mis hermanas** (mēs är mä´ näs). My sisters (Spanish)
14. **pudín** (pù dēn´). Pudding (Spanish)

Someday, the family predicted, my name would be well-known throughout the United States. I laughed to myself, wondering which one I would go by. ❖

MIRRORS & WINDOWS If your name were difficult for people in the United States to pronounce, would you change your name? Why or why not?

_____

_____

Analyze Literature

Dialogue Authors use *speaker tags* so that the reader knows who is talking in the story. These phrases tell who the speaker is and include a verb such as *said*. List a few speaker tags that the author uses to bring life to the dialogue.

_____

_____

READING CHECK

Circle the letter of the correct answer.

1. When Julia and her family came to the United States, they first stayed
   A. in a hotel.
   B. with family.
   C. in an apartment.

2. What is Julia's sister's real name?
   A. Maureen
   B. Mooresha
   C. Mauricia

3. Julia and her sisters were born in
   A. the United States.
   B. the Caribbean.
   C. the Dominican Republic.

4. Why did Julia's parents return to the Dominican Republic after they immigrated to the United States the first time?
   A. They were homesick.
   B. Their visas expired.
   C. Julia's sister was born.

5. What was the biggest gift Julia received for graduation?
   A. money
   B. a necklace
   C. a typewriter

VOCABULARY CHECK

Circle the letter of the correct answer.

1. Which of the following is a list of some *ethnicities*?
   A. Asian, Hispanic, African
   B. short, dark, beautiful
   C. verb, noun, adjective

2. Why didn't Julia want to *specify* exactly where she was from?
   A. No one knew where the Dominican Republic was located.
   B. It was her special secret.
   C. Her parents told her not to tell anyone.

3. Why does Julia describe her full name as *chaotic*?
   A. It is very long and is difficult for most people to say.
   B. She always argued with people about her name.
   C. She was very embarrassed to say it in front of people.

4. Julia's extended family all attended her *commencement* ceremony. What did they do at the ceremony?
   A. The met all of Julia's friends.
   B. They saw Julia graduate from high school.
   C. They saw the college where Julia would attend.

5. Why did Julia's parents give her a *portable* typewriter?
   A. She could take it to college with her.
   B. It was cheaper.
   C. It was the biggest gift.

ANALYZE LITERATURE: Personal Essay

Reread the first and last paragraphs of the story. How does the conclusion of the story connect back to the beginning?

_____

_____

_____

USE READING SKILLS: Identify Author's Purpose

1. List some of the author's memories that you enjoyed reading.

_____

_____

2. Why does the author use so many Spanish words in her essay?

_____

_____

BUILDING LANGUAGE SKILLS: Compound Sentences

A **compound sentence** is made of two ideas that are linked in one sentence with a comma and a conjunction such as *and* or *but*. Use a comma and a conjunction to combine each pair of sentences below into a compound sentence.

1. The immigration officer asked if my father had anything to declare. My father shook his head no.

_____

_____

2. At the hotel, my mother was *Missus Alburest*. I was *little girl*.

_____

_____

3. I was a popular kid. It showed in my name.

_____

_____

4. We were born in New York City. My parents decided to move back home.

_____

_____

WRITING SKILLS: Create an Outline

If you were going to write a personal essay, how would you start? What details would you include? Create an outline with a list of main ideas and some supporting details for each main idea.

_____

_____

Name: _____ Date: _____

page 227

FISH CHEEKS

A Personal Essay by Amy Tan

ABOUT THE STORY

"Fish Cheeks" tells the story of the narrator's Chinese family. The family invites the Caucasian minister's family to Christmas Eve dinner. The fourteen-year-old narrator is horrified. She has a crush on the minister's son and knows that he will not appreciate her family's traditions. Through this experience, the narrator learns something about who she really is.

MAKE CONNECTIONS

What are some traditional holiday foods in your family? Do you think these traditions are important to follow?

_____

_____

_____

_____

ANALYZE LITERATURE: Sensory Details

Sensory details are words that appeal to the five senses. As you read the story, notice the words used to describe sight, sound, touch, taste, and smell.

Differentiated Instruction: Literacy & Reading Skills   © Carnegie Learning, Inc.

USE READING SKILLS: Analyze Text Organization

Writing is organized in many different ways. To be a good reader, you need to be able to analyze how the text is organized. The author tells this story in **chronological order**, or in the same order that the events happened that evening. Use the Sequence Chart below to list the events in the order that they happened.

Sequence Chart

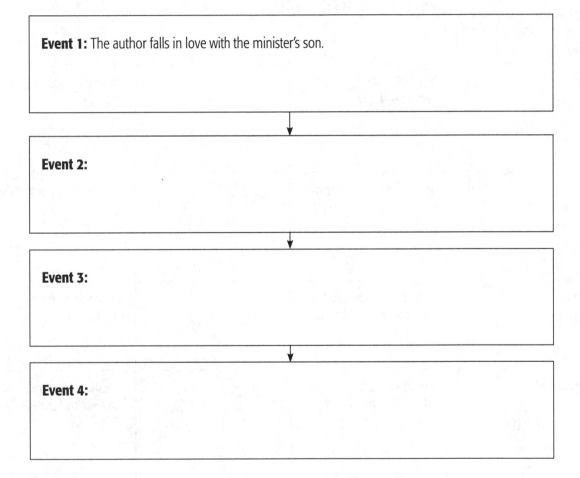

Event 1: The author falls in love with the minister's son.

Event 2:

Event 3:

Event 4:

PREVIEW VOCABULARY

Key Words and Phrases Read each key word and rate it using this scale: ①I don't know this word or phrase at all. ②I've seen this word or phrase before. ③I know this word or phrase and use it.	Words and Phrases in Context Read to see how the key word or phrase can be used in a sentence.	Definition Write down what you think the word or phrase means. Then use a dictionary to check your definition.	Practice Practice using the key words and phrases by completing the following sentences.
appalling ap • pall •ing (ə pôl´ iŋ) *adjective* ①　②　③	The smell of rotten eggs was **appalling**.		An **appalling** event in history was…
rumpled rum • pled (rʉm´ pəld) *adjective* ①　②　③	The T-shirt was **rumpled** when it was tossed on the floor.		The opposite of **rumpled** is…
pluck (plʉk) *verb* ①　②　③	The farmer **plucked** the feathers from the chicken.		Some things that can be **plucked** are…
astonished as • ton • ished (ə stä nishd) *adjective* ①　②　③	I was **astonished** to get a D on the test since I studied so hard.		The students were **astonished** because…
shame (shām) *noun* ①　②　③	The thief felt **shame** because he knew that stealing was wrong.		Some people feel **shame** when…

　　Differentiated Instruction: Literacy & Reading Skills

FISH CHEEKS

A Personal Essay by Amy Tan

I fell in love with the minister's son the winter I turned fourteen. He was not Chinese, but as white as Mary in the manger. For Christmas I prayed for this blond-haired boy, Robert, and a slim new American nose.

5   When I found out that my parents had invited the minister's family over for Christmas Eve dinner, I cried. What would Robert think of our shabby *Chinese* Christmas? What would he think of our noisy *Chinese* relatives who lacked proper American manners? What terrible disappointment would he

10 feel upon seeing not a roasted turkey and sweet potatoes but *Chinese* food?

On Christmas Eve I saw that my mother had outdone herself in creating a strange menu. She was pulling black veins out of the backs of fleshy prawns.[1] The kitchen was littered

15 with **appalling** mounds of raw food: A slimy rock cod[2] with bulging fish eyes that pleaded not to be thrown into a pan of hot oil. Tofu, which looked like stacked wedges of rubbery white sponges. A bowl soaking dried fungus back to life. A plate of squid, their backs crisscrossed with knife markings so they

20 resembled bicycle tires.

And then they arrived—the minister's family and all my relatives in a clamor of doorbells and **rumpled** Christmas packages. Robert grunted hello, and I pretended he was not worthy of existence.

25   Dinner threw me deeper into despair. My relatives licked the ends of their chopsticks and reached across the table, dipping them into the dozens or so plates of food. Robert and his family waited patiently for platters to be passed to them. My relatives murmured with pleasure when

30 my mother brought out the whole steamed fish. Robert grimaced.[3] Then my father poked his chopsticks just below the fish eye and **plucked** out the soft meat. "Amy, your favorite," he said, offering me the tender fish cheek. I wanted to disappear.

35   At the end of the meal my father leaned back and belched loudly, thanking my mother for her fine cooking. "It's a polite

---

1. **prawns.** Small shellfish that resemble shrimp
2. **rock cod.** Large, soft-finned fish that lives among rocks
3. **grimaced.** Twisted one's face to show disapproval or disgust

Note the Facts

What did the narrator pray for at Christmastime?

_____

_____

Culture Note

A traditional Chinese holiday meal may include fish, tofu, pickled vegetables, and rice.

Read Aloud

What are your impressions of the meal described in lines 12–20? Read the paragraph aloud in an appropriate tone.

_____

_____

Analyze Literature

Sensory Details
What word does the narrator use to describe the rock cod?

_____

What would that feel like?

_____

_____

ap · pall ·ing (ə pôl´ iŋ) *adjective*, inspiring disgust

rum · pled (rʊm´ pəld) *adjective*, wrinkled

pluck (plʊk) *verb*, pull off or out

Chinese custom to show you are satisfied," explained my father to our **astonished** guests. Robert was looking down at his plate with a reddened face. The minister managed to muster up a
40 quiet burp. I was stunned into silence for the rest of the night.

Think and Reflect

Amy was embarrassed during dinner. Would you feel the same way?

_____

After everyone had gone, my mother said to me, "You want to be the same as American girls on the outside." She handed me an early gift. It was a miniskirt in beige tweed. "But inside you must always be Chinese. You must be proud you are
45 different. Your only **shame** is to have shame."

And even though I didn't agree with her then, I knew that she understood how much I had suffered during the evening's dinner. It wasn't until many years later—long after I had gotten over my crush on Robert—that I was able to
50 fully appreciate her lesson and the true purpose behind our particular menu. For Christmas Eve that year, she had chosen all my favorite foods. ❖

MIRRORS & WINDOWS

What is it like to feel different from others? How are people who are different treated in our society?

_____

_____

_____

READING CHECK

Circle the letter of the correct answer.

1. How did the narrator react when she found out that the minister's family was coming to dinner?
   A. She cried.
   B. She was happy to see her crush.
   C. She was excited to wear her new outfit.

2. What did Amy's mother prepare for dinner?
   A. roasted turkey and sweet potatoes
   B. many different kinds of seafood
   C. fish cheeks

3. Who waited patiently for food to be passed around the table?
   A. Amy
   B. Robert and his family
   C. Amy's relatives

4. What does Amy's mother do to make her feel better?
   A. She burped after the meal.
   B. She washed all of the dishes.
   C. She gave her a new skirt so that she would look like other American girls.

5. What does Amy realize at the end of the story?
   A. She still has a crush on Robert.
   B. Her mother prepared all of her favorite foods.
   C. She doesn't like traditional Chinese food.

VOCABULARY CHECK

Circle the letter of the correct answer.

1. Why were the mounds of raw food *appalling* to Amy?
   A. She knew the guests would think the food was disgusting.
   B. She was very hungry and wanted to eat.
   C. It was a lot of work for her mother to prepare all of that food.

2. The Christmas packages were probably *rumpled* because
   A. they were very expensive.
   B. they were from China.
   C. many relatives were carrying packages and the house was crowded.

3. How did Amy's father *pluck* out the fish cheek for her?
   A. Amy plucked out the fish cheek, not her father.
   B. He used chopsticks and pushed below the fish eye.
   C. It was prepared in the kitchen.

4. What did Amy's father do that made the guests feel *astonished*?
   A. He belched after the meal.
   B. He turned red in the face.
   C. He yelled at his daughter.

5. According to Amy's mother, why shouldn't she feel *shame*?
   A. She should be proud to be different.
   B. Chinese people always eat seafood.
   C. She is wearing a new American skirt.

ANALYZE LITERATURE: Sensory Details

The author writes about the Christmas Eve dinner with words that describe the tastes, touches, smells, sounds, and sights of the evening. Use sensory details to write a description of a typical holiday meal from your culture.

_____

_____

_____

USE READING SKILLS: Analyze Text Organization

1. When did the narrator fall in love with the minister's son?

   _____

2. When did this dinner take place?

   _____

3. When did Amy's father belch?

   _____

4. What did Amy's mother do after all the guests went home?

   _____

BUILD LANGUAGE SKILLS: Sentence Improvement

A **sentence fragment** is a phrase that does not express a complete thought. Sentence fragments are often missing a verb. Identify whether each line below is a sentence or a fragment. Rewrite the fragments to make complete sentences.

1. The table with dishes, fish, and other seafood.

   _____

2. I was happy when my mother gave me the miniskirt.

   _____

3. Please make this the happiest Christmas I can remember.

   _____

4. Across the living room and down the hall.

   _____

5. The fish and slabs of tofu on red and green plates.

   _____

WRITING SKILLS: Italics

Italics are used for many reasons in writing. Authors use italics for foreign words, words used as vocabulary words, or titles. In the second paragraph, the author uses italics to emphasize the word *Chinese*. Write a paragraph explaining why the author chose to italicize this word. What do the italics show us about how Amy feels about being Chinese?

Name: _____ Date: _____

◆ page E90

A Bittersweet Memoir

A Biography by Jerry Izenberg

ABOUT THE STORY

"A Bittersweet Memoir" tells the story of Roberto Clemente. He played baseball for the Pittsburg Pirates from 1955 to 1972. A tragic event happened when Clemente was taking some emergency supplies to Nicaragua after a devastating earthquake. This is the story of his life with details from the people who loved him.

MAKE CONNECTIONS

Who from the past or present do you most admire and why?

_____

_____

_____

_____

ANALYZE LITERATURE: Setting

The **setting** is where the story happens. An author often describes the setting to set the mood of the story. A dark alley could create a scary feeling or a field of flowers could set a happy mood, for example. Watch for how the author describes the setting at the beginning of the story.

© Carnegie Learning, Inc.   *Differentiated Instruction: Literacy & Reading Skills*   UNIT 3   **103**

USE READING SKILLS: Understand Literary Elements

Characterization

The literary techniques writers use to create characters and make them come alive are called **characterization**. Authors create characterization in three major ways:

- showing what characters say, do, and think
- showing what other characters say about them
- and showing their physical features.

Look for the ways the author describes Roberto Clemente throughout the memoir. Then add details in the chart below.

CHARACTERIZATION CHART	
Characterization Type	Details from the Text
What Clemente says, does, and thinks	
What others say about Clemente	
How Clemente looks and acts	"…the <u>grace of his movements</u> and the <u>artistry of his reflexes</u>…"

What do you think of the character, based on the chart?

_____

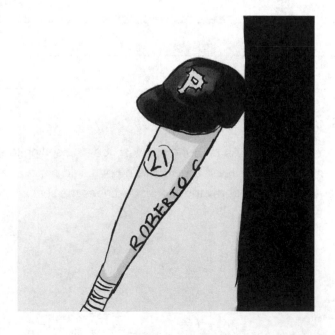

Differentiated Instruction: Literacy & Reading Skills   © Carnegie Learning, Inc.

PREVIEW VOCABULARY

Key Words and Phrases Read each key word and rate it using this scale: ①I don't know this word or phrase at all. ②I've seen this word or phrase before. ③I know this word or phrase and use it.	Words and Phrases in Context Read to see how the key word or phrase can be used in a sentence.	Definition Write down what you think the word or phrase means. Then use a dictionary to check your definition.	Practice Practice using the key words and phrases by completing the following sentences.
bittersweet bit • ter • sweet (bi tər swēt) *adjective* ①　②　③	Even though we won the last game of the season, it was **bittersweet**.		Moving can be **bittersweet** because…
harshly harsh • ly (härsh lē) *adverb* ①　②　③	The mean man spoke **harshly** with all the children.		I would treat someone **harshly** if…
rumble rum • ble (rəm bəl) *verb* ①　②　③	We heard the thunder **rumble** all night long.		Another sound that **rumbles** is…
prominent prom • i • nent (prom i nənt) *adjective* ①　②　③	The major is a **prominent** member of the community.		A **prominent** sports figure today is …
phony pho • ny (fō nē) *adjective* ①　②　③	She is **phony** and pretends she is someone that she is not.		Some people buy **phony**…

A Bittersweet Memoir

A Biography by Jerry Izenberg

> bit·ter·sweet (bi tər swēt) *adjective*,
> both pleasant and painful

I saw him play so often. I watched the grace of his move-
ments and the artistry of his reflexes from who knows how many
press boxes. None of us really appreciated how pure an athlete
he was until he was gone. What follows is a personal retracing of
5 *the steps that took Roberto Clemente from the narrow, crowded*
streets of his native Carolina to the local ball parks in San Juan
and on to the major leagues. But it is more. It is a remembrance
formed as I stood at the water's edge in Puerto Rico and stared at
daybreak into the waves that killed him. It is all the people I met
10 *in Puerto Rico who knew him and loved him. It is the way an*
entire island in the sun and a Pennsylvania city in the smog took
his death....

The record book will tell you that Roberto Clemente
collected 3,000 hits during his major-league career. It will say
15 that he came to bat 9,454 times, that he drove in 1,305 runs, and
played 2,433 games over an eighteen-year span.

But it won't tell you about Carolina, Puerto Rico; and the
old square; and the narrow, twisting streets; and the roots
that produced him. It won't tell you about the Julio Coronado
20 School and a remarkable woman named María Isabella Casares,
whom he called "Teacher" until the day he died and who helped
to shape his life in times of despair and depression. It won't
tell you about a man named Pedron Zarrilla who found him
on a country softball team and put him in the uniform of the
25 Santurce club and who nursed him from promising young
athlete to major-league superstar.

And most of all, those cold numbers won't begin to delineate
the man Roberto Clemente was. To even begin to understand
what this magnificent athlete was all about, you have to work
30 backward. The search begins at the site of its ending.

The car moves easily through the predawn streets of San
Juan. A heavy all-night rain has now begun to drive, and there
is that post-rain sweetness in the air that holds the promise of
a new, fresh, clear dawn. This is a journey to the site of one of
35 Puerto Rico's deepest tragedies. This last says a lot. Tragedy is
no stranger to the sensitive emotional people who make this
island the human place it is.

Read Aloud

Read aloud lines 17–26. What
won't the record books tell
you?

_____

_____

Shortly before the first rays of sunlight, the car turns down a bumpy secondary road and moves past small shantytowns,
40 where the sounds of the children stirring for the long walk toward school begin to drift out on the morning air. Then there is another turn, between a brace of trees and onto the hardpacked dirt and sand, and although the light has not yet quite begun to break, you can sense the nearness of the ocean.
45 You can hear its waves pounding **harshly** against the jagged rocks. You can smell its saltiness. The car noses to a stop, and the driver says, "From here you must walk. There is no other way." The place is called Puente Maldonado and the dawn does not slip into this angry place. It explodes in a million lights and
50 colors as the large fireball of the sun begins to nose above the horizon.

harsh·ly (härsh lē) *adverb*, in an ungentle, unpleasant way

"This is the nearest place," the driver tells me. "This is where they came by the thousands on that New Year's Eve and New Year's Day. Out there," he says, gesturing with his right
55 hand, "out there, perhaps a mile and a half from where we stand. That's where we think the plane went down."
The final hours of Roberto Clemente were like this. Just a month or so before, he had agreed to take a junior-league baseball team to Nicaragua and manage it in an all-star game
60 in Managua. He had met people and made friends there. He was not a man who made friends casually. He had always said that the people you wanted to give your friendship to were the people for whom you had to be willing to give something in return—no matter what the price.
65 Two weeks after he returned from that trip, Managua, Nicaragua exploded into flames. The earth trembled and people died. It was the worst earthquake anywhere in the Western Hemisphere in a long, long time.

Culture Note

The earthquake in Nicaragua on December 23, 1972, nearly destroyed the entire capital city. As many as 7,000 people died and 15,000 were injured. This was the most destructive earthquake ever recorded in Central America.

Back in Puerto Rico, a television personality named Luis
70　Vigereaux heard the news and was moved to try to help the
victims. He needed someone to whom the people would
listen, someone who could say what had to be said and get
the work done that had to be done and help the people who
had to be helped.

75　　"I knew," Luis Vigereaux said, "Roberto was such a person,
perhaps the only such person who would be willing to help."

And so the mercy project, which would eventually claim
Roberto's life, began. He appeared on television. But he needed a
staging area. The city agreed to give him Sixto Escobar Stadium.

80　　"Bring what you can," he told them. "Bring medicine...bring
clothes...bring food...bring shoes...bring yourself and help us
load. We need so much. Whatever you bring, we will use."

And the people of San Juan came. They walked through
the heat and they drove cars and battered little trucks, and the
85　mound of supplies grew and grew. Within two days, the first
mercy planes left for Nicaragua.

Meanwhile, a ship had been chartered and loaded. And as
it prepared to steam away, unhappy stories began to drift back
from Nicaragua. Not all the supplies that had been flown in, it was
90　rumored, were getting through. Puerto Ricans who had flown the
planes had no passports, and Nicaragua was in a state of panic.

"We have people there who must be protected. We have
black-market types that must not be allowed to get their hands
on these supplies," Clemente told Luis Vigereaux. "Someone
95　must make sure—particularly before the ship gets there. I'm
going on the next plane."

The plane they had rented was an old DC-7. It was sched-
uled to take off at 4:00 P.M. on December 31, 1972. Long before
take-off time, it was apparent that the plane needed more work.
100　It had even taxied onto the runway and then turned back. The
trouble, a mechanic who was at the airstrip that day conjec-
tured, had to do with both port [left side] engines. He worked
on them most of the afternoon.

The departure time was delayed an hour, and then two, and
105　then three. Across town, a man named Rudy Hernandez, who
had been a teammate of Roberto's when they were rookies[1]
in the Puerto Rican League and who had later pitched for
the Washington Senators, was trying to contact Roberto by
telephone. He had just received a five-hundred-dollar donation,

---

Use Reading Skills

Make Predictions

Can you guess what might
happen on Roberto's flight to
Nicaragua?

_____

_____

110 and he wanted to know where to send it. He called Roberto's
wife, Vera, who told him that Roberto was going on a trip and
that he might catch him at the airport. She had been there
herself only moments before to pick up some friends who were
coming in from the States, and she had left because she was
115 fairly sure that the trouble had cleared and Roberto had probably left already.

"I caught him at the airport and I was surprised," Rudy
Hernandez told me. "I said I had this money for Nicaraguan
relief and I wanted to know what to do with it. Then I asked him
120 where he was going."

"Nicaragua," Clemente told him.

"It's New Year's Eve, Roberto. Let it wait."

"Who else will go?" Roberto told him. "Someone has to do it."

At 9 p.m., even as the first stirrings of the annual New
125 Year's Eve celebration were beginning in downtown San Juan,
the DC-7 taxied onto the runway, received clearance, **rumbled**
down the narrow concrete strip, and pulled away from the
earth. It headed out over the Atlantic and banked toward
Nicaragua, and its tiny lights disappeared on the horizon.

130 Just ninety seconds later, the tower at San Juan
International Airport received this message from the pilot: "We
are coming back around."

Just that.

Nothing more.

135 And then there was a great silence.

"It was almost midnight," recalls Rudy Hernandez, a
former teammate of Roberto's. "We were having this party
in my restaurant, and somebody turned on the radio and the
announcer was saying that Roberto's plane was feared missing.
140 And then, because my place is on the beach, we saw these giant
floodlights crisscrossing the waves, and we heard the sound of
the helicopters and the little search planes."

Drawn by a common sadness, the people of San Juan began
to make their way toward the beach, toward Puente Maldonado.
145 A cold rain had begun to fall. It washed their faces and blended
with the tears.

They came by the thousands and they watched for three days.
Towering waves boiled up and made the search virtually impossible. The U.S. Navy sent a team of expert divers into the area, but
150 the battering of the waves defeated them too. Midway through the
week, the pilot's body was found in the swift-moving currents to
the north. On Saturday bits of the cockpit were sighted.

DURING READING

rum·ble (rəm bəl) *verb*, to make a deep heavy sound

Note the Facts

What happened out in the ocean?

_____

_____

And then—nothing else.

"I was born in the Dominican Republic," Rudy Hernandez
155 said, "but I've lived on this island for more than twenty years.
I have never seen a time or a sadness like that. The streets were
empty, the radios silent, except for the constant bulletins about
Roberto. Traffic? Forget it. All of us cried. All of us who knew
him and even those who didn't, wept that week.

160 "Manny Sanguillen, the Pittsburgh catcher, was down here
playing winter ball, and when Manny heard the news he ran to
the beach and he tried to jump into the ocean with skin-diving
gear. I told him, man, there's sharks there. You can't help. Leave
it to the experts. But he kept going back. All of us were a little
165 crazy that week.

"There will never be another like Roberto."

Who was he...I mean really?

Well, nobody can put together all the pieces of another
man's life. But there are so many who want the world to know
170 that it is not as impossible a search as you might think.

He was born in Carolina, Puerto Rico. Today the town has
about 125,000 people, but when Roberto was born there in
1934, it was roughly one-sixth its current size.

María Isabella Casares is a schoolteacher. She has taught the
175 children of Carolina for thirty years. Most of her teaching has
been done in tenth-grade history classes. Carolina is her home
and its children are her children. And among all of those whom
she calls her own (who are all the children she taught), Roberto
Clemente was something even more special to her.

180 "His father was an overseer on a sugar plantation. He did
not make much money," she explained in an empty classroom at
Julio Coronado School. "But then, there are no rich children here.
There never have been. Roberto was typical of them. I had known
him when he was a small boy because my father had run a grocery
185 store in Carolina, and Roberto's parents used to shop there."

There is this thing that you have to know about María
Isabella Casares before we hear more from her. What you have
to know is that she is the model of what a teacher should be.
Between her and her students even now, as back when Roberto
190 attended her school, there is this common bond of mutual
respect. Earlier in the day, I had watched her teach a class in
the history of the Abolition Movement in Puerto Rico. I don't
speak much Spanish, but even to me it was clear that this is how
a class should be, this is the kind of person who should teach,
195 and these are the kinds of students such a teacher will produce.

Note the Facts

What does the narrator say is
important to understand about
Roberto's teacher?

_____

_____

With this as a background, what she has to say about Roberto Clemente carries much more impact.

"Each year," she said, "I let my students choose the seats they want to sit in. I remember the first time I saw Roberto.
200 He was a very shy boy and he went straight to the back of the room and chose the very last seat. Most of the time he would sit with his eyes down. He was an average student. But there was something very special about him. We would talk after class for hours. He wanted to be an engineer, you know,
205 and perhaps he could have been. But then he began to play softball, and one day he came to me and said, 'Teacher, I have a problem.'

"He told me that Pedron Zarrilla, who was one of our most **prominent** baseball people, had seen him play, and that Pedron
210 wanted him to sign a professional contract with the Santurce Crabbers. He asked me what he should do.

"I have thought about that conversation many times. I believe Roberto could have been almost anything, but God gave him a gift that few have, and he chose to use that gift. I
215 remember that on that day I told him, 'This is your chance, Roberto. We are poor people in this town. This is your chance to do something. But if in your heart you prefer not to try, then Roberto, that will be your problem—and your decision.'"

220 There was and there always remained a closeness between this boy-soon-to-be-a-man and his favorite teacher.

"Once, a few years ago, I was sick with a very bad back. Roberto, not knowing this, had driven over from Rio Piedras, where his house was, to see me."

225 "Where is the teacher?" Roberto asked Mrs. Casares' step-daughter that afternoon.

"Teacher is sick, Roberto. She is in bed."

"Teacher," Roberto said, pounding on the bedroom door, "get up and put on your clothes. We are going to the doctor
230 whether you want to or not."

"I got dressed," Mrs. Casares told me, "and he picked me up like a baby and carried me in his arms to the car. He came every day for fifteen days, and most days he had to carry me, but I went to the doctor and he treated me. Afterward, I said to the
235 doctor that I wanted to pay the bill.

"'Mrs. Casares,' he told me, 'please don't start with that Clemente, or he will kill me. He has paid all your bills, and don't you dare tell him I have told you.'

prom·i·nent (prom i nənt) *adjective*, standing out, noticeable

Analyze Literature

Flashback A **flashback** is an interruption of the sequence of the story to describe an event that happened earlier. What advice did Roberto's teacher give him about playing baseball?

_____

_____

"Well, Roberto was like that. We had been so close. You
240 know, I think I was there the day he met Vera, the girl he later
married. She was one of my students, too. I was working part-
time in the pharmacy and he was already a baseball player by
then, and one day Vera came into the store.

"'Teacher,' Roberto asked me, 'who is that girl?'

245 "'That's one of my students,' I told him. 'Now don't you
dare bother her. Go out and get someone to introduce you.
Behave yourself.'

"He was so proper, you know. That's just what he did, and
that's how he met her, and they were married here in Carolina
250 in the big church on the square."

On the night Roberto Clemente's plane disappeared, Mrs.
Casares was at home, and a delivery boy from the pharmacy
stopped by and told her to turn on the radio and sit down. "I
think something has happened to someone who is very close
255 with you, Teacher, and I want to be here in case you need help."

María Isabella Casares heard the news. She is a brave
woman, and months later, standing in front of the empty crypt[2]
in the cemetery at Carolina where Roberto Clemente was to
have been buried, she said, "He was like a son to me. This is
260 why I want to tell you about him. This is why you must make
people—particularly our people, our Puerto Rican children—
understand what he was. He was like my son, and he is all
our sons in a way. We must make sure that the children never
forget how beautiful a man he was."

265 The next person to touch Roberto Clemente was Pedron
Zarrilla, who owned the Santurce club. He was the man who
discovered Clemente on the country softball team, and he was
the man who signed him for a four-hundred-dollar bonus.

"He was a skinny kid," Pedron Zarrilla recalls, "but even
270 then he had those large powerful hands, which we all noticed
right away. He joined us, and he was nervous. But I watched
him, and I said to myself, 'this kid can throw and this kid can
run, and this kid can hit. We will be patient with him.' The
season had been through several games before I finally sent him
275 in to play."

Luis Olmo remembers that game. Luis Olmo had been a
major-league outfielder with the Brooklyn Dodgers. He had
been a **splendid** ballplayer. Today he is in the insurance business in San Juan. He sat in his office and recalled very well that
280 first moment when Roberto Clemente stepped up to bat.

---

2. **crypt.** An underground burial place

Differentiated Instruction: Literacy & Reading Skills   © Carnegie Learning, Inc.

Build Vocabulary

The reading says that
Luis Olmo was a *splendid*
ballplayer. What does *splendid*
mean?

_____

_____

splen·did (splen dəd) *adjective,*
excellent, very good

"I was managing the other team. They had a man on base and this skinny kid comes out. Well, we had never seen him, so we didn't really know how to pitch to him. I decided to throw him a few bad balls and see if he'd bite.

"He hit the first pitch. It was an outside fast ball, and he never should have been able to reach it. But he hit it down the line for a double. He was the best bad-ball hitter I have ever seen, and if you ask major-league pitchers who are pitching today, they will tell you the same thing. After a while it got so that I just told my pitchers to throw the ball down the middle because he was going to hit it no matter where they put it, and at least if he decided not to swing we'd have a strike on him.

"I played in the big leagues. I know what I am saying. He was the greatest we ever had...maybe one of the greatest anyone ever had. Why did he have to die?"

Once Pedron Zarrilla turned him loose, there was no stopping Roberto Clemente. As Clemente's confidence grew, he began to get better and better. He was the one the crowd came to see out at Sixto Escobar Stadium.

"You know, when Clemente was in the lineup[3]," Pedron Zarrilla says, "there was always this undercurrent of excitement in the ball park. You knew that if he was coming to bat, he would do something spectacular. You knew that if he was on first base, he was going to try to get to second base. You knew that if he was playing right field and there was a man on third base, then that man on third base already knew what a lot of men on third base in the majors were going to find out—you don't try to get home against Roberto Clemente's arm.

"I remember the year that Willie Mays came down here to play in the same outfield with him for the winter season. I remember the wonderful things they did and I remember that Roberto still had the best of it.

"Sure I knew we were going to lose him. I knew it was just a matter of time. But I was only grateful that we could have him if only for that little time."

The major-league scouts[4] began to make their moves. Olmo was then scouting, and he tried to sign him for the Giants. But

Note the Facts

What did Olmo tell his pitchers to do when Roberto was up at bat?

_____

_____

---

3. **lineup.** A list with the order that the baseball players will hit
4. **major-league scouts.** People who attend baseball games and look for new players for their teams

it was the Dodgers who won the bidding war. The Dodgers had Clemente, but in having him, they had a major problem. He had to be hidden.

325   This part takes a little explaining. Under the complicated draft rules that baseball used at that time, if the Dodgers were not prepared to bring Clemente up to their major-league team within a year (and because they were winning with proven players, they couldn't), then Clemente could be claimed by another team.

330   They sent him to Montreal with instructions to the manager to use him as little as possible, to hide him as much as possible, and to tell everyone he had a sore back, a sore arm, or any other excuse the manager could give. But how do you hide a diamond when he's in the middle of a field of broken soda bottles?

335   In the playoffs that year against Syracuse, they had to use Clemente. He hit two doubles and a home run and threw a man out at home the very first try.

The Pittsburgh Pirates had a man who saw it all. They drafted him at the season's end.

340   And so Roberto Clemente came to Pittsburgh. He was the finest prospect the club had had in a long, long time. But the Pirates of those days were spectacular losers and even Roberto Clemente couldn't turn them around overnight.

"We were bad, all right," recalls Bob Friend, who later
345 became a great Pirate pitcher. "We lost over a hundred games, and it certainly wasn't fun to go to the ball park under those conditions. You couldn't blame the fans for being noisy and impatient. Branch Rickey, our general manager, had promised a winner. He called it his five-year plan. Actually, it took ten."

350   When Clemente joined the club, it was Friend who made it his business to try to make him feel at home. Roberto was, in truth, a moody man, and the previous season hadn't helped him any.

Differentiated Instruction: Literacy & Reading Skills   © Carnegie Learning, Inc.

"I will never forget how fast he became a superstar in this town," says Bob Friend. "Later he would have troubles because
355 he was either hurt or thought he was hurt, and some people would say that he was loafing. But I know he gave it his best shot and he helped make us winners."

The first winning year was 1960, when the Pirates won the pennant and went on to beat the Yankees in the seventh game
360 of the World Series. Whitey Ford, who pitched against him twice in that Series, recalls that Roberto actually made himself look bad on an outside pitch to encourage Whitey to come back with it. "I did," Ford recalls, "and he unloaded. Another thing I remember is the way he ran out a routine ground ball in the last
365 game and when we were a little slow covering, he beat it out. It was something most people forget but it made the Pirates' victory possible."

The season was over. Roberto Clemente had hit safely in every World Series game. He had batted over .300. He had been
370 a superstar. But when they announced the Most Valuable Player Award voting, Roberto had finished a distant third.

Think and Reflect

How did it make Clemente feel to get so few votes?

_____

_____

"I really don't think he resented the fact that he didn't win it," Bob Friend says. "What hurt—and in this he was right—was how few votes he got. He felt that he simply wasn't being accepted. He
375 brooded about that a lot. I think his attitude became one of 'Well, I'm going to show them from now on so that they will never forget.'

"And you know, he sure did."

Roberto Clemente went home and married Vera. He felt less alone. Now he could go on and prove what it was he had to
380 prove. And he was determined to prove it.

"I know he was driven by thoughts like that," explains Buck Canel, a newspaper writer who covers all sports for most of the hemisphere's Spanish language papers.

"He would talk with me often about his feelings. You know,
385 Clemente felt strongly about the fact that he was a Puerto Rican and that he was a black man. In each of these things he had pride.

"On the other hand, because of the early language barriers, I am sure that there were times when he *thought* people were laughing at him when they were not. It is difficult for

390 a Latin-American ballplayer to understand everything said
around him when it is said at high speed, if he doesn't speak
English that well. But, in any event, he wanted very much to
prove to the world that he was a superstar and that he could do
things that in his heart he felt he had already proven."

395   In later years, there would be people who would say that
Roberto was a hypochondriac (someone who *imagined* he was
sick or hurt when he was not). They could have been right, but
if they were, it made the things he did even more remarkable.
Because I can testify that I saw him throw his body into outfield

400 fences, teeth first, to make remarkable plays. If he thought he
was hurt at the time, then the act was even more courageous.

    His moment finally came. It took eleven years for the
Pirates to win a World Series berth again, and when they did
in 1971, it was Roberto Clemente who led the way. I will never

405 forget him as he was during that 1971 series with the Orioles, a
Series that the Pirates figured to lose, and in which they, in fact,
dropped the first two games down in Baltimore.

    When they got back to Pittsburgh for the middle slice of the
tournament, Roberto Clemente went to work and led this team.

410   He was a superhero during the five games that followed. He
was the big man in the Series. He was the MVP.⁵ He was everything he had ever dreamed of being on a ball field.

    Most important of all, the entire country saw him do it on
network television, and never again—even though nobody knew it

415 would end so tragically soon—was anyone ever to doubt his ability.

    The following year, Clemente ended the season by collecting
his three-thousandth hit. Only ten other men had ever done
that in the entire history of baseball.

    "It was a funny thing about that hit," Willie Stargell, his

420 closest friend on the Pirates, explains. "He had thought of
taking himself out of the lineup and resting for the playoffs, but
a couple of us convinced him that there had to be a time when a
man had to do something for himself, so he went on and played
and got it. I'm thankful that we convinced him, because, you

425 know, as things turned out, that number three thousand was his
last hit.

    "When I think of Roberto now, I think of the kind of man
he was. There was nothing **phony** about him. He had his own
ideas about how life should be lived, and if you didn't see it that

430 way, then he let you know in so many ways, without words, that
it was best you each go your separate ways.

pho·ny (fō nē) *adjective*, fake, not genuine

5. **MVP.** Most Valuable Player

"He was a man who chose his friends carefully. His was a friendship worth having. I don't think many people took the time and the trouble to try to understand him, and I'll admit it 435 wasn't easy. But he was worth it.

"The way he died, you know, I mean on that plane carrying supplies to Nicaraguans who'd been dying in that earthquake, well, I wasn't surprised he'd go out and do something like that. I wasn't surprised he'd go. I just never thought what happened 440 could happen to him.

"But I know this. He lived a full life. And if he knew at that moment what the Lord had decided, well, I really believe he would have said, 'I'm ready.'"

He was thirty-eight years old when he died. He touched the 445 hearts of Puerto Rico in a way that few people ever could.

He touched a lot of other hearts, too. He touched hearts that beat inside people of all colors of skin.

He was one of the proudest of The Proud People. ✤

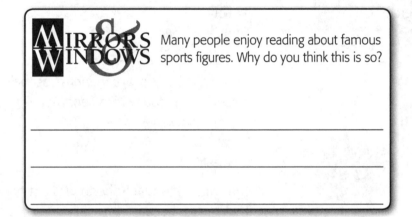

MIRRORS & WINDOWS Many people enjoy reading about famous sports figures. Why do you think this is so?

_____

_____

_____

READING CHECK

Circle the letter of the correct answer.

1. Why did Clemente believe he had to go to Nicaragua on New Year's Eve?
   A. A Central American had to go.
   B. He is a famous baseball player.
   C. He didn't know who else would go, and someone had to do it.

2. What did the people do when they heard the news about Roberto?
   A. They starting walking to the beach.
   B. They became interested in baseball.
   C. They moved to Puerto Rico.

3. Were the Pittsburg Pirates a good baseball team when Clemente first joined them?
   A. Yes, they won the championship.
   B. No, they were losers.
   C. They turned around overnight.

4. What award did Clemente win in his second World Series?
   A. The Gold Bat
   B. MVP
   C. VPM

5. How many hits did Roberto Clemente have in his baseball career?
   A. 30
   B. 300
   C. 3,000

VOCABULARY CHECK

Circle the letter of the correct answer.

1. Why is the story of Roberto Clemente *bittersweet*?
   A. He was a wonderful baseball player and person, but he died tragically.
   B. He was born in Puerto Rico, but he moved to the United States.
   C. He had a good teacher as a child, and he was married.

2. The waves pounded *harshly* against the rocks. Would this be a safe place to swim?
   A. no
   B. yes
   C. only for children

3. The airplane *rumbled* down the runway. How would you describe the sound of the plane?
   A. very quiet
   B. high-pitched screaming
   C. low and noisy

4. Pedron Zarilla was a *prominent* baseball person. What does *prominent* mean?
   A. well-known
   B. talented
   C. wealthy

5. The writer says that Roberto was not *phony*. That means he was
   A. a liar.
   B. genuine.
   C. a good pitcher.

ANALYZE LITERATURE: Setting

The author says that many Puerto Ricans came out to the beach when Roberto Clemente was declared missing. Write a few sentences describing what you think that scene looked like. You can use the description from the story and add details from your imagination.

_____

_____

_____

_____

USE READING SKILLS: Understand Literary Elements
Characterization

1. What was Roberto Clemente's last action before he died?

_____

_____

2. What does this say about him as a person?

_____

_____

BUILDING LANGUAGE SKILLS: Syntax

The way words are arranged in a sentence is called syntax. Put these sentences about Roberto Clemente in the correct order. Use every word given and add the correct punctuation.

1. was Roberto student an average Clemente

_____

2. Roberto was Puerto from Clemente Carolina Rico

_____

3. almost earthquake devastated 1972 Nicaragua An in

_____

4. The Series won Pittsburg the World Pirates

_____

5. New airplane Eve in the ocean Year's crashed The on

_____

6. Pedron to a wanted professional Roberto sign Zarrilla contract

_____

SPEAKING AND LISTENING: Persuasion

Willie Stargell and some of the other players on the Pirate's team persuaded Roberto to play in the playoffs to get his three-thousandth hit. What do you think they might have said to convince him? Write a few persuasive sentences and share them with your classmates.

_____

_____

Name: _____   Date: _____

BEFORE READING

◀◇ page E108

Madam C. J. Walker

A Biography by Jim Haskins

ABOUT THE STORY

"Madam C. J. Walker" is a biography of a woman who had many difficulties in her life, but worked hard and turned her life around. She had a mind for business, and one night, she dreamed of a wonderful business idea. She became the first American woman to earn a million dollars. Read the story to find out how she did it.

MAKE CONNECTIONS

What goals do you have for your life? Do you think you might run into any problems in achieving those goals?

_____

_____

_____

_____

ANALYZE LITERATURE: Introduction and Conclusion

An **introduction** should grab a reader's attention and present the main idea of the selection. A **conclusion** should bring a close to the details presented in the selection. As you read, pay close attention to the introduction and conclusion of this story.

Differentiated Instruction: Literacy & Reading Skills   © Carnegie Learning, Inc.

USE READING SKILLS: Use Context Clues

Dictionaries are a helpful tool, but you don't always have to look up every unknown word. **Context clues** are words and phrases near a difficult word that provide hints about its meaning. As you read, look for words that you don't know. Then follow the steps below.

1. Copy the sentence with the unknown word in the first column of the chart below.
2. Underline the word and circle other parts of the sentence that might give you a clue about the unknown word's meaning.
3. In the second column, give your best guess for the definition of the unknown word. An example has been done for you.

Sentence with Unknown Word or Phrase	My Definition
Madam Walker was the first woman to earn her fortune by setting up her own business and proving that women could be <u>financially independent of</u> men.	able to make money without

PREVIEW VOCABULARY

Key Words and Phrases Read each key word and rate it using this scale: ①I don't know this word or phrase at all. ②I've seen this word or phrase before. ③I know this word or phrase and use it.	Words and Phrases in Context Read to see how the key word or phrase can be used in a sentence.	Definition Write down what you think the word or phrase means. Then use a dictionary to check your definition.	Practice Practice using the key words and phrases by completing the following sentences.
segregate seg · re · gate (seg´ ri gāt') *verb* ① ② ③	The criminals were **segregated** from the rest of society.		I believe it is wrong to **segregate**...
recruit re · cruit (ri krüt´) *verb* ① ② ③	The Marines **recruit** new soldiers to train.		Companies **recruit** employees that are...
ambition am · bi · tion (am bi´ shən) *noun* ① ② ③	His **ambition** helped him get into his first-choice college.		**Ambition** helps you become...
lavish lav · ish (la´ vish) *adjective* ① ② ③	All of the chefs worked hard to prepare the **lavish** dinner.		If I had a million dollars, I would buy a **lavish**...
astute as · tute (ə stüt´) *adjective* ① ② ③	She always makes good life choices. She is very **astute.**		An **astute** person might know about...
fruits of their success *idiom* ① ② ③	Two friends enjoyed the **fruits of their success** by buying movie tickets with the money they'd earned.		People might enjoy the **fruits of their success** by...

Differentiated Instruction: Literacy & Reading Skills   © Carnegie Learning, Inc.

Madam C. J. Walker

A Biography by Jim Haskins

Madam C. J. Walker was the first American woman to earn a million dollars. There were American women millionaires before her time, but they had inherited their wealth, either from their husbands or from their families. Madam Walker was the

5 first woman to earn her fortune by setting up her own business and proving that women could be financially independent of men. The company she started in the early years of this century is still in operation today.

Madam C. J. Walker was born Sarah Breedlove on

10 December 23, 1867. She grew up in the South under very racist conditions. Her parents, Owen and Minerva Breedlove, had been slaves until President Abraham Lincoln's Emancipation Proclamation and the Union victory in the Civil War had freed the slaves.

15 After the war, few **provisions** were made to help former slaves become independent. They did not receive money to help them get started in their new lives. They were uneducated, they had few skills except the ability to grow crops, and many were unaware of what freedom meant. Like the majority of

20 former slaves, the Breedloves remained on the Burney family plantation in Delta, Louisiana. They had little choice but to stay on the same land where they had been slaves, only now they were sharecroppers.

Sharecroppers farm land for a landowner. In return, they

25 receive a place to live and part of the crop. But since they must buy what they cannot grow from the landowner, when they harvest the crop they find themselves owing whatever is their share to the landowner anyway.

The Breedloves sharecropped cotton. Like her brothers and

30 sisters, Sarah was working in the cotton fields by the time she was six. By the time she was seven, both her parents were dead, and she moved in with her older sister, Louvenia. A few years later, they moved across the river to Vicksburg, Mississippi.

Sarah had little schooling. Like other sharecroppers'

35 children, she had a chance to go to school only when there were no crops to be planted or harvested, which totaled about four months out of the year. She also had little happiness in her childhood. Not only was she an orphan, but she also suffered at the hands of her sister's cruel husband. Sarah was just fourteen

Build Vocabulary

Provisions are preparations to help meet people's needs. What are some *provisions* that could have helped the former slaves become more independent?

_____

_____

pro·vi·sion (prə vi′ zhən) *n.,* arrangement made beforehand to deal with a certain need

Note the Facts

What does a sharecropper do?

_____

_____

seg·re·gate (seg´ ri gāt') v., separate a race, class, or ethnic group from the rest of the population; set apart

Culture Note

The Ku Klux Klan (KKK) is an organization with a record of hate, terrorism, violence, and oppression of many minority groups including African Americans. They are known for committing acts of violence while hiding behind white hats, masks, and robes.

_____

_____

_____

Note the Facts

Why was Sarah's hair falling out?

_____

_____

40 when she married a man named McWilliams to get away from her sister's household.

By the time Sarah got married, conditions in the South for blacks were actually worse than they had been during slavery. This was the time when Jim Crow laws were passed,
45 **segregating** southern blacks from whites in nearly every area of life. It was the time when white supremacy groups like the Ku Klux Klan achieved their greatest power, and lynchings of blacks were common.

Sarah and her husband lived with the terror of being black
50 as best they could. In 1885 their daughter, Lelia, was born, and her parents dreamed of making a better life for their little girl. Then, when Lelia was two, McWilliams was killed by a lynch mob.[1]

Sarah was a widow at the age of twenty, and the sole
55 support of a two-year-old daughter. She took in laundry to earn a living and was determined to leave the South. With Lelia, she made her way up the Mississippi River and settled in St. Louis, where she worked fourteen hours a day doing other people's laundry. She enrolled Lelia in the St. Louis public schools and
60 was pleased that her daughter would get the education that had been denied to her. But she wanted more for her daughter and for herself.

Not long after they moved to St. Louis, Sarah McWilliams realized that her hair was falling out. She did not know why,
65 but it is likely that the practice of braiding her hair too tightly was part of the cause. At the time, few hair-care products were available for black women. The ideal was straight, "white," hair, and to achieve this effect black women divided their hair into sections, wrapped string tightly around each section, and
70 then twisted them. When the hair was later combed out, it was straighter. But this procedure pulled on the scalp and caused the hair to fall out.

Sarah was not the only black woman to suffer from hair loss. But she was one who refused to accept the idea that there
75 was nothing she could do about it. For years she tried every hair-care product available. But nothing worked.

Then one night she had a dream. As she told the story many years later, in her dream "a black man appeared to me and told me what to mix up for my hair. Some of the remedy was grown
80 in Africa, but I sent for it, mixed it, put it on my scalp, and in a

---

1. **McWilliams…mob.** No documentation actually proves that he died this way.

few weeks my hair was coming in faster than it had ever fallen out." Sarah never publicly revealed[2] the formula of her mixture.

Sarah's friends remarked on what a full and healthy head of hair she had, and she gave some of her mixture to them.

85 It worked on them, too, so she decided to sell it. She later said that she started her "Hair Grower" business with an investment of $1.50.

She had not been in business long when she received word that a brother who lived in Denver, Colorado, had died, leaving

90 a wife and daughters. Her own daughter, Lelia, was attending Knoxville College, a private black college in Tennessee, and did not need her around all the time. Sarah decided to go to Denver to live with her sister-in-law and nieces.

In Denver, Sarah began to sell her special haircare product

95 and did well. But she realized she needed to advertise to get more customers. Six months after arriving in Denver, she married C. J. Walker, a newspaperman who knew a lot about selling by mail order. With his help, she began to advertise her product, first in black newspapers across the state and later in

100 black newspapers nationwide, and to make more money.

But soon her marriage was in trouble. As Sarah Walker later said of her husband, "I had business disagreements with him, for when we began to make ten dollars a day, he thought that amount was enough and that I should be satisfied. But I

105 was convinced that my hair preparations would fill a longfelt want, and when we found it impossible to agree, due to his narrowness of vision, I embarked in business for myself."

In addition to helping her learn about advertising, her marriage gave Sarah Breedlove McWilliams Walker the name

110 she would use for the rest of her life—Madam C. J. Walker. The "Madam" part was an affectation,[3] but Sarah liked the way it sounded. She thought it would be good for her business. By 1906 her business was so well that she was able to stop doing laundry for a living and devote all her time to her hair-care

115 company. Her products by this time included "Wonderful Hair Grower," "Glossine" hair oil, "Temple Grower," and "Tetter Salve" for the scalp.

Madam Walker was very proud of being a woman, and she was convinced that she could make it in the business world

120 without the help of men. Almost from the start she determined that her business would be run by women. In 1906 she put her

Note the Facts

What are the two reasons she added *Madam* to the beginning of her name?

_____

_____

2. **revealed.** Showed; made known
3. **affectation.** Artificial behavior meant to impress others

twenty-one-year-old daughter, Lelia, in charge of her growing mail-order business. She herself started traveling throughout the South and East selling her preparations and teaching her
125 methods of hair care. She was so successful that two years later she and Lelia moved to Pittsburgh, Pennsylvania, and started Lelia College, which taught the Walker System of hair care.

Once again, Lelia ran the business while her mother traveled thousands of miles to spread the word. Madam Walker realized
130 that the normal outlets for her products—white department stores and pharmacies—were not open to her. These stores would not stock black products because they did not want black customers. In addition to advertising,
135 mostly in black newspapers, Madam Walker had to depend on the institutions in the black communities, the black churches, and the black women's clubs.

Madam Walker's lectures on hair
140 culture were widely attended. She was an excellent speaker and a commanding woman, nearly six feet tall, who was always beautifully dressed and coiffed.[4] She made a lasting impression wherever she went.

Her travels, and her personality, brought her into contact
145 with many important black people. She joined the National Association of Colored Women and through that organization met the educator Mary McLeod Bethune. She also met Ida B. Wells-Barnett, who worked for the right of women to vote, and against lynching in the South. She formed friendships with these
150 women, who helped her spread the word about her business.

Although she lacked the formal education that most of these women had, Madam Walker never felt ashamed of her shortcomings[5] in that area. She taught herself as much as she could and was not afraid to ask someone to define a word she
155 did not know or explain something she did not understand.

There were other black hair-care companies in business at this time. A couple of companies were owned by whites. But they stressed hair straightening. Madam Walker emphasized hair care. Most of the products she developed were aimed at
160 producing healthy hair, not straight hair. She did design a steel comb with teeth spaced far enough apart to go through thick hair, but its main purpose was not hair straightening.

---

4. **coiffed.** Styled, specifically hair
5. **shortcomings.** Less than what is expected or required

Analyze Literature

Characterization Describe Madam C. J. Walker. Include details about her appearance and personality.

_____

_____

_____

Differentiated Instruction: Literacy & Reading Skills   © Carnegie Learning, Inc.

Madam Walker also wanted black women to go into business. Why should they toil over hot laundry tubs and clean white
165　people's houses when they could be in business for themselves? Helping other black women also helped the Walker Company, and with this goal in mind Madam Walker **recruited** and trained scores of women to use and sell Walker products. Many of them set up salons in their own homes. Others traveled door-to-door
170　selling Walker products and demonstrating the Walker System. Madam Walker insisted that her agents sign contracts promising to abide by her strict standards of personal hygiene[6]—long before various states passed similar laws for workers in the cosmetics field. By 1910 the Walker Company had trained around 5,000
175　black female agents, not just in the United States but in England, France, Italy, and the West Indies. The company itself was taking in $1,000 a day, seven days a week.

That same year, Madam Walker's travels took her to Indianapolis, Indiana, a city that impressed her so much that
180　she decided to move her headquarters there. She put a man in charge of her operations, which was a departure from her usual philosophy, but Freeman B. Ransom was, in her opinion, an unusual man.

She had met him in her travels when he was working as
185　a train porter summers and during school vacations, while working his way through Columbia University Law School. He impressed her with his **ambition** and with his vision of progress for blacks. When he finished school, she put him in charge of her Indianapolis headquarters.

190　In 1913 Lelia moved from Pittsburgh to New York to expand the Walker Company's East Coast operations. Madam Walker built a **lavish** town house in Harlem at 108–110 West 136th Street and installed a completely equipped beauty parlor.

Lelia had become an **astute** businesswoman herself,
195　although she did not have the drive of her mother. Lelia, who changed her name to A'Lelia, liked to enjoy the fruits of their success. The Walker town house soon became the "in" place for parties in Harlem, attended by wealthy and artistic people, black and white.

200　Madam Walker also enjoyed spending the money she made. In 1917 she built a $250,000 mansion on the Hudson River in upstate New York. She hired the black architect Vertner Tandy to design it and named it Villa Lewaro. She drove around in an

---

6. **hygiene.** Cleanliness and sanitary practices

DURING READING

re·cruit (ri krüt´) *v.*, hire or engage the services

Note the Facts

Who did Madam C. J. Walker put in charge of her headquarters in Indianapolis? Why was that an unusual choice?

_____

_____

am·bi·tion (am bi´ shən) *n.*, drive to succeed

lav·ish (la´ vish) *adj.*, abundant; rich

as·tute (ə stüt´) *adj.*, possessing practical intelligence and the ability to make good decisions

Build Vocabulary

Idioms *Fruits of their success* are the nice items that Madam C. J. Walker and her daughter could buy with all the money that they earned. What are some of the ways Lelia enjoyed the *fruits of their success*?

_____

_____

electric car, dressed in the finest clothing, and was said to have
205 spent $7,000 on jewelry in a single afternoon.

> ## Think and Reflect
>
> How did Madam C. J. Walker spend her money? Would you have
> spent the money the same way?
>
> _____
>
> _____

Madam Walker also gave generously to charity. She had
a strong interest in education and took time out of her busy
schedule to be tutored by Booker T. Washington, founder of
Tuskegee Institute in Alabama. She became an avid reader of
210 literature and American history. She encouraged her friend
Mary McLeod Bethune and later gave money to Mrs. Bethune
to establish her Daytona Normal and Industrial Institute
for Negro Girls in Daytona, Florida. When the National
Association of Colored Women decided to pay off the mortgage
215 on the home of the late black abolitionist Frederick Douglass,
Madam Walker made the largest single contribution.

Madam Walker did not have much of a private life. She
spent her time thinking of new ways to increase her business.
The friends she had were people who could help her.
220 By 1917 the years of traveling and overwork began to take
their toll on her. She developed high blood pressure, and in
1918 her doctors warned her that she had to slow down. She
turned over her responsibilities in the business to her daughter,
to Freeman B. Ransom, and to other trusted associates, and
225 retired to her mansion, Villa Lewaro. There, she tried to relax,
but her mind was always on her business. She died quietly of
kidney failure resulting from hypertension in May 1919.

In her will, Madam Walker left the bulk of her estate and
the business to her daughter, A'Lelia. But she also provided
230 generously for a variety of educational institutions run by
black women, including $5,000 to Dr. Bethune's school. She
established a trust fund for an industrial and mission school in
West Africa and provided bequests[7] to Negro orphanages, old
people's homes, and Negro YWCA branches. In addition, she
235 made bequests to many friends and employees.

Also in her will, Madam Walker insisted that the Madam C.
J. Walker Company always be headed by a woman, and
her wishes were carried out. Her daughter, A'Lelia, became

Use Reading Skills

Context Clues What does
take their toll on her mean in
the sentence," By 1917 the
years of traveling and overwork
began to take their toll on her"?

_____

_____

_____

Note the Facts

How did Madam C. J. Walker
die?

_____

_____

---

7. **bequests.** Things handed down or passed on

president of the company after her death and presided at the
240 dedication of the new company headquarters in Indianapolis in
1927, fulfilling a long-held dream of her mother's.

Times have changed greatly since Madam C. J. Walker
made her millions. Drugstores and department stores owned by
both whites and blacks now stock hair- and skin-care products
245 for black women. Many more companies, white and black,
manufacture such products. In the midst of all that competition,
the Walker Company is not as active as it once was, although it
still sells some of the products Madam developed. The Walker
Building is being renovated[8] as part of the rejuvenation of
250 downtown Indianapolis. Now called the Madam Walker Urban
Life Center, it houses professional offices and a cultural center.

Madam C. J. Walker, the daughter of former slaves, with
little education, overcame the barriers of being black and a
woman and succeeded beyond everyone's expectations but
255 her own. ❖

---

8. **renovated.** Replaced worn and broken parts

MIRRORS & WINDOWS Madam C. J. Walker helped many African American women get out of poverty and become successful business women. What is one way you would choose to help others?

_____

_____

READING CHECK

Circle the letter of the correct answer.

1. Why didn't Sarah go to school very much?
   A. Slaves' children were not allowed to go to school.
   B. She could go to school only when she wasn't working on the farm.
   C. Her sister's husband would not let her go.

2. How did Sarah feel about her own daughter going to school?
   A. She was happy to see her daughter get an education.
   B. She was jealous that she did not have the same opportunity.
   C. She preferred her daughter to help her start a business.

3. How did Sarah know what to include in the first hair products?
   A. Her first husband made hair products.
   B. She learned about hair products in Africa.
   C. A man appeared to her in a dream and told her what to add in the mix.

4. Why did Madam C. J. Walker name her hair school Lelia College?
   A. She wanted to make more money.
   B. She loved her sister very much.
   C. She named the school after her daughter.

5. Why did Madam Walker separate from her second husband?
   A. They had business disagreements.
   B. She didn't want him to take her money.
   C. He did not love her anymore.

VOCABULARY CHECK

Circle the letter of the correct answer.

1. Who was *segregated* in the South?
   A. Blacks were segregated from whites
   B. Educated people were segregated from uneducated people.
   C. People from the North were segregated from people from the South.

2. Why did Madam C. J. Walker *recruit* many women?
   A. to sell Walker hair products
   B. to improve personal hygiene
   C. to provide food for the needy

3. Why did Madam C. J. Walker want someone with *ambition* to work in her company?
   A. She wanted only female workers.
   B. She wanted her workers to be hardworking and successful.
   C. She needed her workers to know about hair products.

4. What made the house in Harlem *lavish*?
   A. It had many expensive features including a beauty parlor.
   B. They built the house very quickly.
   C. Madam C. J. Walker lived there all her life.

5. Why did the author describe Lelia as an *astute* business person?
   A. She lost more money than she made
   B. She worked even harder than her mother.
   C. She was intelligent and made good business decisions.

ANALYZE LITERATURE: Introduction and Conclusion

Madam C. J. Walker grew up in poverty and worked long days doing laundry. By the end of her life, she "succeeded beyond everyone's expectations but her own." Write a paragraph to explain what this last phrase of the story means.

_____

_____

_____

USE READING SKILLS: Use Context Clues

1. Madam Walker's hair *lectures* were widely attended. She was an excellent speaker. What are hair *lectures*?

   _____

   _____

2. Madam Walker trained *scores* of women. Some of them set up salons in their homes and many others sold products door-to-door. How many women did she teach about the hair products?

   _____

   _____

BUILDING LANGUAGE SKILLS: Silent letters

Spelling some words can be difficult in the English language because of silent letters. **Silent letters** are letters that we write, but do not pronounce when we speak the word. Look at the underlined words below. Circle the silent letter or letters in each word. When you are finished, practice pronouncing those words as a class.

1. She worked fourteen <u>hours</u> a day doing other people's laundry.

2. Some black women <u>wrapped</u> string around sections of their hair.

3. She married a newspaperman who <u>knew</u> a lot about selling by mail order.

4. <u>Although</u> she lacked formal education, Madam Walker never felt ashamed.

5. She invented a steel <u>comb</u> for thick hair.

6. She hired Vertner Tandy to <u>design</u> her home in upstate New York.

WORK TOGETHER

Work in small groups to make a time line of Madam C. J. Walker's life. Start with her birth in 1867 and end with her death in 1919. Put each event in order in the appropriate place on the time line. Include details from the story like the names she used, the places she lived, events within her family, and incidents that happened in her business. Use a large sheet of paper so that you have room to write all the details from the story.

Name: _____ Date:_____

page 314

Father William

A Humorous Poem by Lewis Carroll

ABOUT THE POEM

"Father William" is a poem about a boy who asks why his father acts strangely in old age. The father stands on his head, eats whatever he likes, and has many other funny habits. The father explains all of his actions to the son, but starts to get a little impatient with the son at the end.

MAKE CONNECTIONS

How does it feel to receive bad advice?

_____

_____

_____

_____

ANALYZE LITERATURE: Rhyme

Sounds that are repeated at the ends of words are **rhymes**. For example, *car* and *star* rhyme because they both end with the same *-ar* sound. Look for more words that rhyme in "Father William."

Differentiated Instruction: Literacy & Reading Skills   © Carnegie Learning, Inc.

USE READING SKILLS: Analyze Text Organization

Writing can be organized in different ways. A good reader needs to know how to analyze text organization. When you **analyze** something, you break it down into parts and then think about how the parts are related to each other and to the whole. Analyzing the text organization can help you understand a poem.

This poem is like a conversation between a father and a son. Mark each section to the left of the poem below to show who is speaking. Write an *S* for "son" or an *F* for "father." After you mark the page, look for patterns in what each character says, and add these patterns to the chart below.

TEXT ORGANIZATION CHART	
In each pair of stanzas, the young man tells Father William…	That he is old…
In each pair of stanzas, the young man asks Father William…	
In each pair of stanzas, Father William answers…	

PREVIEW VOCABULARY

Key Words and Phrases Read each key word and rate it using this scale: ①I don't know this word or phrase at all. ②I've seen this word or phrase before. ③I know this word or phrase and use it.	Words and Phrases in Context Read to see how the key word or phrase can be used in a sentence.	Definition Write down what you think the word or phrase means. Then use a dictionary to check your definition.	Practice Practice using the key words and phrases by completing the following sentences.
incessantly in · ces · sant · ly (in' se´ s‿nt lē) *adverb* ① ② ③	The two best friends sent text messages **incessantly**.		A famous person who talks **incessantly** is...
uncommonly un · com · mon · ly (ən' kä´ mən lē) *adverb* ① ② ③	I've never had cookies like these; they're **uncommonly** good.		Something **uncommonly** difficult is...
sage (sāj) *noun* ① ② ③	My grandmother was a **sage**. She gave great advice.		A person is a **sage** if...
supple sup · ple (su´ pəl) *adjective* ① ② ③	The baby's skin was soft and **supple**.		The opposite of **supple** is...
clever clev · er (klev ʉr) *adjective* ① ② ③	He answered quickly with a **clever** joke.		A **clever** person can...

Differentiated Instruction: Literacy & Reading Skills

Father William

A Humorous Poem by Lewis Carroll

"You are old, Father William," the young man said,
    "And your hair has become very white;
And yet you **incessantly** stand on your head—
    Do you think, at your age, it is right?"

5 "In my youth," Father William replied to his son,
    "I feared it might injure the brain;
But, now that I'm perfectly sure I have none,
    Why, I do it again and again."

"You are old," said the youth, "as I mentioned before.
10   And have grown most **uncommonly** fat;
Yet you turned a back-somersault[1] in at the door—
    Pray, what is the reason of that?"

"In my youth," said the **sage**, as he shook his gray locks.
    "I kept all my limbs very **supple**
15 By the use of this ointment[2]—one shilling[3] the box—
    Allow me to sell you a couple?"

Think and Reflect

Do you think that this father and son have a good relationship?

"You are old," said the youth, "and your jaws are too weak
    For anything tougher than suet;[4]
Yet you finished the goose, with the bones and the beak—
20   Pray, how did you manage to do it?"

"In my youth," said his father, "I took to the law,
    And argued each case with my wife;
And the muscular strength, which it gave to my jaw
    Has lasted the rest of my life."

---

1. **back-somersault.** An acrobatic move in which the body rolls backward
2. **ointment.** A creamy medicine usually rubbed on the skin
3. **shilling.** British coin
4. **suet.** Fat used in cooking

DURING READING

Read Aloud

Read this poem aloud with a partner. One person should read the father's lines and the other should read the son's lines.

Build Vocabulary

The author says that Father William was *uncommonly* fat. What did he look like?

_____

_____

Note the Facts

What did Father William eat?

_____

_____

Culture Note

Pray is a very formal and old-fashioned way to say *please tell me*.

Analyze Literature

Rhyme Which word rhymes with *wife* in this poem?

_____

_____

in·ces·sant·ly (in' se´ s‚nt lē) *adv.,* constantly

un·com·mon·ly (ən' kä´ mən lē) *adv.,* amazingly

sage (sāj) *n.,* wise man

sup·ple (sʉ´ pəl) *adj.,* flexible

clev · er (klĕv ʉr) *adjective,*
intelligent or witty

Use Reading Skills

Analyze Text Organization
Each time the son begins to
speak, he uses the same words
to describe the father. What are
these words?

_____

_____

Note the Facts

What did Father William balance
on the end of his nose?

_____

_____

25 "You are old," said the youth, "one would hardly suppose
       That your eye was as steady as ever;
     Yet you balanced an eel on the end of your nose—
       What made you so awfully **clever**?"

     "I have answered three questions, and that is enough,"
30   Said his father. "Don't give yourself airs!
     Do you think I can listen all day to such stuff?
       Be off, or I'll kick you downstairs!" ❖

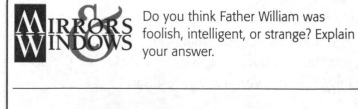

Do you think Father William was
foolish, intelligent, or strange? Explain
your answer.

_____

_____

_____

READING CHECK

Circle the letter of the correct answer.

1. What color is Father William's hair?
   A. white
   B. brown
   C. blond

2. What did Father William think about standing on his head in his youth?
   A. He did it again and again.
   B. He thought it might injure his brain.
   C. He never did it.

3. What did the father offer to sell his son?
   A. ointment
   B. suet
   C. an eel

4. How did Father William get a strong jaw?
   A. He always ate goose bones.
   B. He argued about law with his wife.
   C. He balanced objects on his nose.

5. What did Father William threaten to do to the son if the son did not stop asking questions?
   A. He threatened to listen to him all day.
   B. He threatened to make him clean the stairs.
   C. He threatened to kick him downstairs.

VOCABULARY CHECK

Circle the letter of the correct answer.

1. What did Father William do *incessantly*?
   A. stand on his head
   B. argue with his wife
   C. shake his gray hair

2. Was Father William always *uncommonly* fat?
   A. Yes, he has always been very fat.
   B. No, he has grown fat later in life.
   C. No, he is a thin man.

3. What makes Father William a *sage*?
   A. He is very slow to answer questions.
   B. He is very wise.
   C. He can do a somersault.

4. Why are Father William's arms and legs *supple*?
   A. He uses an ointment.
   B. He does a lot of exercise.
   C. He balances many objects.

5. What did the father do that made him so *clever*?
   A. He threatened to kick his son downstairs.
   B. He ate a whole goose.
   C. He balanced an eel on his nose.

ANALYZE LITERATURE: Rhyme

Choose the word from the list that does *not* rhyme with the numbered word.
Remember that rhymes are repeated sounds, and not always repeated letters.

_____ 1. right
   A. white
   B. light
   C. thought

_____ 2. son
   A. tone
   B. run
   C. none

_____ 3. fat
   A. cute
   B. that
   C. hat

_____ 4. law
   A. where
   B. jaw
   C. claw

_____ 5. enough
   A. through
   B. stuff
   C. rough

_____ 6. suppose
   A. roads
   B. nose
   C. close

_____ 7. head
   A. said
   B. red
   C. stand

_____ 8. before
   A. door
   B. ignore
   C. computer

USE READING SKILLS: Analyze Text Organization

1. How does the father start each of his answers?

   _____

   _____

2. List two of the questions the son asks his father.

   _____

   _____

BUILD LANGUAGE SKILLS: Thesaurus

A **thesaurus** is a book that gives synonyms of words. Look up a word to find a list of words with the same meaning. Use a thesaurus, or an online thesaurus, to find two synonyms for each of the following words.

1. young   _____   _____

2. old   _____   _____

3. injure   _____   _____

4. steady   _____   _____

5. clever   _____   _____

6. weak   _____   _____

WORK TOGETHER: Creative Writing

Work in a group to write a funny poem like "Father William." It does not have to be long, but try to include some words that rhyme in the same pattern as the poem you read today. When you are finished, share your poem with the class.

page 370

Annabel Lee

A Narrative Poem by Edgar Allan Poe

ABOUT THE POEM

"Annabel Lee" is a poem about the love the speaker has for a young woman. He loves her so much that he believes that the angels in heaven are jealous of his love. Read the poem to see if their love story continues to be so sweet.

MAKE CONNECTIONS

How would you react to a sudden change in your life?

_____

_____

_____

_____

ANALYZE LITERATURE: Narrative Poetry

A **narrative poem** has the same plot elements as a narrative story. Look for rising action, a conflict, and a resolution in this poem just as you would look for these elements in a story.

USE READING SKILLS: Understand Literary Elements

Mood

The mood of a piece of literature is the atmosphere or emotion that the author gives to the literary work. The author creates the mood in this poem by describing details of the setting, characters, and events. Complete the chart below with details from the poem that set the mood for each of the three categories.

Details	Mood
It was many years ago	The speaker is sad as he remembers

PREVIEW VOCABULARY

Key Words and Phrases Read each key word and rate it using this scale: ①I don't know this word or phrase at all. ②I've seen this word or phrase before. ③I know this word or phrase and use it.	Words and Phrases in Context Read to see how the key word or phrase can be used in a sentence.	Definition Write down what you think the word or phrase means. Then use a dictionary to check your definition.	Practice Practice using the key words and phrases by completing the following sentences.
maiden maid · en (mā-dᵊn) *noun* ① ② ③	The **maiden** wore a beautiful dress to the party.		The **maiden** wanted to marry…
chill chill (chil) *verb* ① ② ③	Mom always **chills** the pudding before serving it.		A beverage I like to **chill** is…
bore (bor) *verb* ① ② ③	The soldier **bore** a heavy bag.		Something heavy to **bear** is…
envy en · vy (en vē) *verb* ① ② ③	I **envy** people with shiny hair; my hair is so dull.		People often **envy** other people with…
soul (sōl) *noun* ① ② ③	The music touched my **soul.**		When someone dies, many people believe the **soul** goes…

Annabel Lee

A Narrative Poem by Edgar Allan Poe

Make Predictions

Why does the speaker use the past tense to talk about his love? What do you think will happen?

_____

_____

_____

bear (ber) v., carry; **bore** past tense

According to the speaker of the poem, how does Annabel Lee die?

_____

_____

_____

It was many and many a year ago,
    In a kingdom by the sea.
That a maiden there lived whom you may know
    By the name of Annabel Lee;
5 And this maiden she lived with no other thought
    Than to love and be loved by me.

I was a child and she was a child,
    In this kingdom by the sea;
But we loved with a love that was more than love—
10   I and my Annabel Lee—
With a love that the wingèd seraphs of heaven
    Coveted her and me.[1]

And this was the reason that, long ago,
    In this kingdom by the sea,
15 A wind blew out of a cloud, chilling
    My beautiful Annabel Lee;
So that her highborn kinsmen[2] came
    And **bore** her away from me,
To shut her up in a sepulcher[3]
20   In this kingdom by the sea.

The angels, not half so happy in heaven,
    Went envying her and me—
Yes!—that was the reason (as all men know,
    In this kingdom by the sea)
25 That the wind came out of a cloud, by night,
    Chilling and killing my Annabel Lee.

But our love it was stronger by far than the love
    Of those who were older than we—
    Of many far wiser than we—
30 And neither the angels in heaven above
    Nor the demons down under the sea,

---

1. **the wingèd seraphs...Coveted her and me.** The angels envied us.
2. **highborn kinsman.** Wealthy or noble relatives
3. **sepulcher.** Tomb or grave

Can ever dissever[4] my soul from the soul
    Of the beautiful Annabel Lee:

For the moon never beams, without bringing me dreams
35 Of the beautiful Annabel Lee;
And the stars never rise, but I feel the bright eyes
    Of the beautiful Annabel Lee;
And so, all the night-tide, I lie down by the side
Of my darling—my darling—my life and my bride,
40   In her sepulcher there by the sea—
    In her tomb by the sounding sea. ❖

---

4. **dissever.** Break; sever

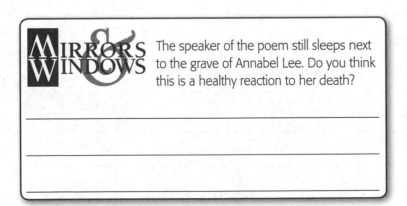

The speaker of the poem still sleeps next to the grave of Annabel Lee. Do you think this is a healthy reaction to her death?

_____

_____

_____

READING CHECK

Circle the letter of the correct answer.

1. How do these two young people feel about each other?
   A. They are in love.
   B. They are good friends.
   C. They are enemies.

2. How do the angels feel about the young couple's love?
   A. They are happy for the couple.
   B. They bring the couple together.
   C. They are jealous of the couple's love.

3. Who takes Annabel Lee away from the speaker?
   A. the sea
   B. her new husband
   C. her family

4. What parts of the two young people still remain together?
   A. their minds
   B. their children
   C. their souls

5. What reminds the speaker of Annabel Lee's eyes?
   A. the stars
   B. the waves
   C. the moon

VOCABULARY CHECK

Circle the letter of the correct answer.

1. Who is the *maiden* in the poem?
   A. an unknown person
   B. Edgar Allan Poe
   C. Annabel

2. What was the thing that *chilled* and killed Annabel Lee?
   A. her family
   B. the wind
   C. the water

3. What is another word for *bore*?
   A. carried
   B. pushed
   C. died

4. The speaker says that the angels *envy* the love the couple has. What does *envy* mean?
   A. to feel great love for someone
   B. to steal
   C. to desire something that belongs to someone else

5. Nothing can dissever the *souls* of the two young people in love. What is a *soul*?
   A. the spirit part of a human
   B. a wise person
   C. a young man

ANALYZE LITERATURE: Narrative Poetry

What is the conflict in this poem? How is the conflict resolved? Write a paragraph explaining your thoughts.

_____

_____

_____

_____

USE READING SKILLS: Understand Literary Elements
Mood

1. What does the line, "To shut her up in a sepulcher" mean?

   _____

   How does that line affect the mood of the poem?

   _____

2. What does, "For the moon never beams without bringing me dreams of the beautiful Annabel Lee" mean?

   _____

   How does that line affect the mood of the poem's ending?

   _____

BUILDING LANGUAGE SKILLS: Pronouns

Remember that a **pronoun** is a word that is used in the place of a noun. Circle the correct pronoun or pronouns in each of these sentences inspired by the poem.

1. (Me/I) was young when I fell in love with (her/she).

2. (We/Us) loved each other more than anything in the world.

3. The angels were jealous of (mine/my) beautiful Annabel Lee.

4. (Our/Us) love is stronger than the love of older couples.

5. (She/Her) loved (he/him) with all of her heart.

SPEAKING AND LISTENING SKILLS

Your teacher will read or play a recording of the first stanza of the poem. Fill in the missing words as you listen. Don't turn back to read the poem itself.

It was _____ and many a year _____,

In a _____ by the sea.

That a maiden there lived _____ you may know

_____ the name of Annabel Lee

And _____ maiden she _____ with no other _____

Than to love and _____ _____ by me.

Name: _____ Date: _____

BEFORE READING

 page E187

I'm Nobody

A Lyric Poem by Emily Dickinson

ABOUT THE STORY

In **"I'm Nobody,"** the speaker thinks about being "nobody." This poem can be read as a celebration of privacy and a quiet personal life.

MAKE CONNECTIONS

Are you a shy person? Have you ever felt it was better to not be noticed?

_____

_____

_____

_____

ANALYZE LITERATURE: Hyperbole

A **hyperbole** is an exaggeration for effect. The following statement is an example of a hyperbole: "Tom thinks of his girlfriend a million times a day." Tom probably doesn't actually think of her a million times a day, but this hyperbole tells that he thinks of his girlfriend a lot.

USE READING SKILLS: Compare and Contrast

As you read, look for how the speaker of the poem describes being Somebody and being Nobody. List the details of each type of person in the chart below.

SOMEBODY   NOBODY

PREVIEW VOCABULARY

Key Words and Phrases Read each key word and rate it using this scale: ①I don't know this word or phrase at all. ②I've seen this word or phrase before. ③I know this word or phrase and use it.	Words and Phrases in Context Read to see how the key word or phrase can be used in a sentence.	Definition Write down what you think the word or phrase means. Then use a dictionary to check your definition.	Practice Practice using the key words and phrases by completing the following sentences.
banish ban · ish (ban ish) *verb* ①　②　③	The king would **banish** every enemy from the country.		Something that is **banished** from school is…
dreary drear · y (dr ēr ē) *adjective* ①　②　③	What a **dreary** and cloudy day.		**Dreary** weather makes people feel…
livelong live · long (liv lôŋ) *adjective* ①　②　③	We picked apples the **livelong** day.		An activity I could do the **livelong** day is…
admiring ad · mir · ing (ad mīr iŋ) *adjective* ①　②　③	The movie star waved to her **admiring** fans.		The opposite of **admiring** is…
bog (bäg) *noun* ①　②　③	There were many mosquitoes around the **bog**.		The area around a **bog** sounds…

Differentiated Instruction: Literacy & Reading Skills

I'm Nobody

A Lyric Poem by Emily Dickinson

> I'm Nobody! Who are you?
> Are you—Nobody—too?
> Then there's a pair of us!
> Don't tell! they'd banish us—you know!
>
> 5   How dreary—to be—Somebody!
> How public—like a Frog—
> To tell your name—the livelong June—
> To an admiring Bog!¹ ❖

---

1. **bog.** Marsh or swamp

 If you were a famous person, would you welcome the attention or would you prefer to keep your life private?

_____

_____

_____

Read Aloud

Read this poem aloud with a partner. Take turns reading the whole poem.

_____

_____

Use Reading Skills

Summarize

Use your own words to write a few sentences about the main idea of this poem.

_____

_____

READING CHECK

Circle the letter of the correct answer.

1. How does the speaker describe herself?
   A. as Nobody
   B. as Somebody
   C. as a frog

2. What question does the speaker ask the reader?
   A. Who are you?
   B. Are you also Nobody?
   C. All of the above

3. Would the speaker like to be a more outgoing person?
   A. Yes, she would.
   B. No, she would not.
   C. She can't decide.

4. What does the speaker think about the life of more outgoing people?
   A. She thinks they must be very busy.
   B. She thinks that kind of life must be very sad and dreary.
   C. She wishes she could also be more outgoing.

5. According to the poem, what would you have to do all the time if you were Somebody?
   A. tell your name
   B. shake hands
   C. go to parties

VOCABULARY CHECK

Circle the letter of the correct answer.

1. Who would *banish* Nobody?
   A. Somebody
   B. another Nobody
   C. no one

2. What is the opposite of *dreary*?
   A. cheerful
   B. depressing
   C. a long time

3. What is another word for a *livelong* time?
   A. the whole time
   B. a short time
   C. in the past

4. The speaker does not want to tell her name to an admiring bog. What does *admiring* mean?
   A. in nature
   B. loud
   C. adoring

5. Which animal might live in a *bog*?
   A. an elephant
   B. a turtle
   C. a cat

ANALYZE LITERATURE: Hyperbole

Write a paragraph explaining how the speaker exaggerates in line 4 of the poem. What does this say about her attitude?

_____

_____

_____

_____

USE READING SKILLS: Compare and Contrast

1. Describe the main characteristics of Somebody.

   _____

   _____

2. Describe the main characteristics of Nobody.

   _____

   _____

3. If you could choose another name for this poem, what would you choose and why?

   _____

   _____

BUILDING LANGUAGE SKILLS: Connotation

Connotation is the feeling or emotion attached to a word. For example, the word *sunny* might make people think of bright, happy things. Describe the connotation of each of these words found in the poem.

1. nobody   _____

2. somebody   _____

3. dreary   _____

4. public   _____

5. banish   _____

6. bog   _____

WORK TOGETHER: Reader's Theater

Imagine that you are a journalist who would like to photograph and interview the author of this poem. You find her and get the chance to ask her for an interview. Perform a reader's theater of this meeting with a partner. One person will be the journalist and the other person will play the role of the author.

Name: _____ Date: _____

 page E214

The Monsters Are Due on Maple Street

A Screenplay by Rod Serling

ABOUT THE STORY

Maple Street is an ordinary street in the American suburbs. However, when something in the sky flashes overhead, machines and electronics stop working. As the residents try to figure out is happening, they begin to suspect one another. Read about what happens in **"The Monsters Are Due on Maple Street."**

MAKE CONNECTIONS

Think about a time you made a hasty decision. What happened when you jumped to conclusions?

_____

_____

_____

_____

_____

ANALYZE LITERATURE: Diction

The author's choice of words is known as **diction**. An author's diction may be formal or informal, simple or ornate, old-fashioned or modern. To help you determine the diction of this screenplay, write down words and phrases that suggest a specific type of diction.

USE READING SKILLS: Analyze Cause and Effect

As you read a dramatic script, identify cause-and-effect relationships created by stage directions, dialogue, and characters' actions. Determine the reasons, or **causes**, something exists or occurs, as well as the results, or **effects**. Record your ideas in the chart below.

Cause	Effect
There was a flash overhead	All of the technology on the street stopped working

PREVIEW VOCABULARY

Key Words and Phrases Read each key word and rate it using this scale: ①I don't know this word or phrase at all. ②I've seen this word or phrase before. ③I know this word or phrase and use it.	Words and Phrases in Context Read to see how the key word or phrase can be used in a sentence.	Definition Write down what you think the word or phrase means. Then use a dictionary to check your definition.	Practice Practice using the key words and phrases by completing the following sentences.
nebulae neb · u · lae (neb ü lī) *noun* ① ② ③	The visible **nebulae** were a blue mist of stars in the sky.		The **nebulae** in outer space might look...
metamorphosis me · ta · mor · pho · sis (me ta môr phō sis) *noun* ① ② ③	The mob went through a **metamorphosis** and stopped fighting when they realized the power was back on.		One animal that might go through a **metamorphosis** is...
knits his brows *idiom* ① ② ③	Alex always **knits his brows** when he is trying to solve a difficult puzzle.		A person might **knits his brows** if...
bum jokes *idiom* ① ② ③	My parents bought a new car when our old car started playing **bum jokes** and wouldn't start.		People don't like **bum jokes** because...
scapegoat scape · goat (skāp´ gōt) *noun* ① ② ③	When my sister lost her homework, she used me as a **scapegoat**. She claimed that I put it in the wrong backpack!		Someone would look for a **scapegoat** if...

Differentiated Instruction: Literacy & Reading Skills

The Monsters Are Due on Maple Street

A Screenplay by Rod Serling

CHARACTERS
NARRATOR
FIGURE ONE
FIGURE TWO

5 **RESIDENTS OF MAPLE STREET**
STEVE BRAND
CHARLIE'S WIFE
MRS. GOODMAN
MRS. BRAND
10 TOMMY
WOMAN
DON MARTIN
SALLY (*Tommy's Mother*)
MAN ONE
15 MAN TWO
PETE VAN HORN
CHARLIE
LES GOODMAN

— ACT 1 —

20 *Fade in on a shot of the night sky. The various nebulae and planet bodies stand out in sharp, sparkling relief, and the camera begins a slow pan across the Heavens.*

NARRATOR'S VOICE. There is a fifth dimension beyond that which is known to man. It is a dimension as vast as space, 25 and as timeless as infinity. It is the middle ground between light and shadow—between science and superstition. And it lies between the pit of man's fears and the summit of his knowledge. This is the dimension of imagination. It is an area which we call The Twilight Zone.

30 *The camera has begun to pan down until it passes the horizon and is on a sign which reads "Maple Street." Pan down*

Build Vocabulary

When you *pan across* something, you slowly shift the view from one place to another. Why would you *pan across* the night sky before starting a television show?

_____

_____

Build Vocabulary

A *dimension* is a place in time and space, and is often associated with a sense of reality. Something that might seem like it cannot happen in this dimension could be said to happen in another dimension. How does knowing that there is a fifth dimension that people don't understand help set up the story in this screenplay?

_____

Culture Note

The Twilight Zone was a popular television show that ran from 1959 to 1964. Each episode was a unique mixture of science fiction, horror, suspense, and surrealism. Today, the expression "the twilight zone" often refers to something that is surreal or strange.

Think and Reflect

The narrator says that monsters will be coming to Maple Street. What do you think the monsters will be like?

_____

_____

until we are shooting down at an angle toward the street below. It's a tree-lined, quiet residential American street, very typical of the small town. The houses have front porches on which people
35 *sit and swing on gliders, conversing across from house to house. Steve Brand polishes his car parked in front of his house. His neighbor,* DON MARTIN, *leans against the fender watching him. A Good Humor man rides a bicycle and is just in the process of stopping to sell some ice cream to a couple of kids. Two women*
40 *gossip on the front lawn. Another man waters his lawn.*

NARRATOR'S VOICE. Maple Street, U.S.A., late summer. A tree-lined little world of front porch gliders, hop scotch, the laughter of children, and the bell of an ice cream vendor.

There is a pause and the camera moves over to a shot of
45 *the Good Humor man and two small boys who are standing alongside, just buying ice cream.*

NARRATOR'S VOICE. At the sound of the roar and the flash of light it will be precisely 6:43 P.M. on Maple Street.

At this moment one of the little boys, TOMMY, *looks up to*
50 *listen to a sound of a tremendous screeching roar from overhead. A flash of light plays on both their faces and then it moves down the street past lawns and porches and rooftops and then disappears.*

Various people leave their porches and stop what they're doing to stare up at the sky. STEVE BRAND, *the man who's been*
55 *polishing his car, now stands there transfixed, staring upwards. He looks at* DON MARTIN, *his neighbor from across the street.*

STEVE. What was that? A meteor?

DON. [*Nods.*] That's what it looked like. I didn't hear any crash though, did you?

60 **STEVE.** [*Shakes his head.*] Nope. I didn't hear anything except a roar.

MRS. BRAND. [*From her porch.*] Steve? What was what?

STEVE. [*Raising his voice and looking toward porch.*] Guess it was a meteor, honey. Came awful close, didn't it?

65   **MRS. BRAND.** Too close for my money! Much too close.

The camera pans across the various porches to people who stand there watching and talking in low tones.

    NARRATOR'S VOICE. Maple Street. Six-forty-four P.M. on a late September evening. [*A pause.*] Maple Street in the last calm
70   and reflective moment…before the monsters came!

The camera slowly pans across the porches again. We see a man screwing a light bulb on a front porch, then getting down off the stool to flick the switch and finding that nothing happens.

Another man is working on an electric power mower. He
75 *plugs in the plug, flicks on the switch of the power mower, off and on, with nothing happening.*

Through the window of a front porch, we see a woman pushing her finger back and forth on the dial hook. Her voice is indistinct and distant, but intelligible and repetitive.

80   **WOMAN.** Operator, operator, something's wrong on the phone, operator!

    MRS. BRAND *comes out on the porch and calls to* STEVE.

    MRS. BRAND. [*Calling.*] Steve, the power's off. I had the soup on the stove and the stove just stopped working.

85   **WOMAN.** Same thing over here. I can't get anybody on the phone either. The phone seems to be dead.

We look down on the street as we hear the voices creep up from below, small, mildly disturbed voices highlighting these kinds of phrases:

90   **VOICES.**

    Electricity's off.

    Phone won't work.

    Can't get a thing on the radio.

    My power mower won't move, won't work at all.

95   Radio's gone dead!

    PETE VAN HORN, *a tall, thin man, is seen standing in front of his house.*

    VAN HORN. I'll cut through the back yard…See if the power's still on on Floral Street. I'll be right back!

100 *He walks past the side of his house and disappears into the back yard.*

The camera pans down slowly until we're looking at ten or eleven people standing around the street and overflowing to the curb and sidewalk. In the background is STEVE BRAND's *car.*

105   **STEVE.** Doesn't make sense. Why should the power go off all of a sudden, and the phone line?

    DON. Maybe some sort of an electrical storm or something.

What time does the flash go overhead?

_____

_____

Analyze Cause and Effect
What are some of the effects of the strange flash of light? Record your answers in your cause-and-effect chart.

Diction List words and phrases that indicate what kind of diction the author uses.

_____

_____

CHARLIE. That don't seem likely. Sky's just as blue as anything. Not a cloud. No lightning. No thunder. No nothing.
110 How could it be a storm?

WOMAN. I can't get a thing on the radio. Not even the portable.

The people again murmur softly in wonderment and question.

CHARLIE. Well, why don't you go downtown and check
115 with the police, though they'll probably think we're crazy or something. A little power failure and right away we get all flustered and everything.

STEVE. It isn't just the power failure, Charlie. If it was, we'd still be able to get a broadcast on the portable.

120 *There's a murmur of reaction to this.* STEVE *looks from face to face and then over to his car.*

STEVE. I'll run downtown. We'll get this all straightened out.

He walks over to the car, gets in it, turns the key. Looking through the open car door, we see the crowd watching him from
125 *the other side.* STEVE *starts the engine. It turns over sluggishly*[1] *and then just stops dead. He tries it again and this time he can't get it to turn over. Then, very slowly and reflectively, he turns the key back to "off" and slowly gets out of the car.*

The people stare at STEVE. *He stands for a moment by the car,*
130 *then walks toward the group.*

STEVE. I don't understand it. It was working fine before...

Don. Out of gas?

STEVE. [*Shakes his head.*] I just had it filled up.

WOMAN. What's it mean?

135 **Charlie.** It's just as if...as if everything had stopped.
[*Then he turns toward* STEVE.] We'd better walk downtown.
[*Another murmur of assent*[2] *at this.*]

---

1. **sluggishly.** Inactively; slowly moving
2. **assent.** Agreement

STEVE. The two of us can go, Charlie. [*He turns to look back at the car.*] It couldn't be the meteor. A meteor couldn't do this.

Think and Reflect

The people of Maple Street are surprised that their telephones, electricity, lawn mowers, stoves, and other machines stop working. How would you react if this happened on your street?

_____

_____

140   He *and* CHARLIE *exchange a look, then they start to walk away from the group.*

We see TOMMY, *a serious-faced fourteen-year-old in spectacles who stands a few feet away from the group. He is halfway between them and the two men, who start to walk down the sidewalk.*

145   **TOMMY.** Mr. Brand…you better not!

STEVE. Why not?

TOMMY. They don't want you to.

STEVE *and* CHARLIE *exchange a grin, and* STEVE *looks back toward the boy.*

150   **STEVE.** Who doesn't want us to?

TOMMY. [*Jerks his head in the general direction of the distant horizon.*] Them!

STEVE. Them?

Charlie. Who are them?

155   **TOMMY.** [*Very intently.*] Whoever was in that thing that came by overhead.

Steve *knits his brows for a moment, cocking his head questioningly. His voice is intense.*

STEVE. What?

160   **TOMMY.** Whoever was in that thing that came over. I don't think they want us to leave here.

STEVE *leaves* CHARLIE *and walks over to the boy. He kneels down in front of him. He forces his voice to remain gentle. He reaches out and holds the boy.*

165   **STEVE.** What do you mean? What are you talking about?

TOMMY. They don't want us to leave. That's why they shut everything off.

STEVE. What makes you say that? Whatever gave you that idea?

170   **WOMAN.** [*From the crowd.*] Now isn't that the craziest thing you ever heard?

TOMMY. [*Persistently but a little intimidated by the crowd.*] It's always that way, in every story I ever read
175 about a ship landing from outer space.

WOMAN. [*To the boy's mother,* SALLY, *who stands on the fringe of the crowd.*] From outer space, yet! Sally, you better get that boy of yours up to
180 bed. He's been reading too many comic books or seeing too many movies or something.

SALLY. Tommy, come over here and stop that kind of talk.

STEVE. Go ahead, Tommy. We'll be right back. And you'll see.
185 That wasn't any ship or anything like it. That was just a…a meteor or something. Likely as not—[*He turns to the group, now trying to weight his words with an optimism he obviously doesn't feel but is desperately trying to instill in himself as well as the others.*] No doubt it did have something to do with all this power failure and
190 the rest of it. Meteors can do some crazy things. Like sunspots.

DON. [*Picking up the cue.*] Sure. That's the kind of thing— like sunspots. They raise Cain[3] with radio reception all over the world. And this thing being so close—why, there's no telling the sort of stuff it can do. [*He wets his lips, smiles nervously.*] Go
195 ahead, Charlie. You and Steve go into town and see if that isn't what's causing it all.

STEVE *and* CHARLIE *again walk away from the group down the sidewalk. The people watch silently.*

TOMMY *stares at them, biting his lips, and finally calling out*
200 *again.*

Think and Reflect

Sunspots are cooler regions on the sun's surface. These areas on the sun have a powerful magnetic field that often interferes with electronic devices, such as radios and television. Why does Steve suggest that the power failure is caused by sunspots?

_____

_____

TOMMY. Mr. Brand!
The two men stop again. TOMMY *takes a step toward them.*

---

3. **raise Cain.** Cause trouble

TOMMY. Mr. Brand…please don't leave here.

STEVE *and* CHARLIE *stop once again and turn toward the*
205 *boy. There's a murmur in the crowd, a murmur of irritation
and concern as if the boy were bringing up fears that shouldn't
be brought up; words which carried with them a strange kind of
validity that came without logic but nonetheless registered and
had meaning and effect. Again we hear a murmur of reaction*
210 *from the crowd.*

TOMMY *is partly frightened and partly defiant as well.*

TOMMY. You might not even be able to get to town. It was
that way in the story. Nobody could leave. Nobody except—

STEVE. Except who?

215 **TOMMY.** Except the people they'd sent down ahead of
them. They looked just like humans. And it wasn't until the ship
landed that—

*The boy suddenly stops again, conscious of the parents staring
at them and of the sudden hush of the crowd.*

220 **SALLY.** [*In a whisper, sensing the antagonism*[4] *of the crowd.*]
TOMMY, please son…honey, don't talk that way—

MAN ONE. That kid shouldn't talk that way…and we
shouldn't stand here listening to him. Why this is the craziest
thing I ever heard of. The kid tells us a comic book plot and
225 here we stand listening—

STEVE *walks toward the camera, stops by the boy.*

STEVE. Go ahead, Tommy. What kind of story was this?
What about the people that they sent out ahead?

TOMMY. That was the way they prepared things for the
230 landing. They sent four people. A mother and a father and two
kids who looked just like humans…but they weren't.

There's another silence as Steve *looks toward the crowd and
then toward* Tommy. *He wears a tight grin.*

STEVE. Well, I guess what we'd better do then is to run a
235 check on the neighborhood and see which ones of us are really
human.

*There's laughter at this, but it's a laughter that comes from a
desperate attempt to lighten the atmosphere. It's a release kind of
laugh. The people look at one another in the middle of their laughter.*

240 **CHARLIE.** There must be somethin' better to do than stand
around makin' bum jokes about it. [*Rubs his jaw nervously.*] I
wonder if Floral Street's got the same deal we got. [*He looks past
the houses.*] Where is Pete Van Horn anyway? Didn't he get
back yet?

---

4. **antagonism.** Hostility; open opposition

Use Reading Skills

Analyze Cause and Effect
What effect do Tommy's words
have on the other residents
of Maple Street? Record your
ideas in your cause-and-effect
chart.

_____

_____

Idiom The expression *no dice* means that something is not possible or likely to happen. Why might Goodman use the phrase instead of saying *no*?

_____

_____

245   *Suddenly there's the sound of a car's engine starting to turn over.*

    We look across the street toward the driveway of LES GOODMAN'S *house. He's at the wheel trying to start the car.*

    SALLY. Can you get it started, Les? [*He gets out of the car,* 250 *shaking his head.*]

    GOODMAN. No dice.

    He walks toward the group. He stops suddenly as behind him, inexplicably and with a noise that inserts itself into the silence, the car engine starts up all by itself. GOODMAN *whirls around to* 255 *stare toward it.*

    The car idles roughly, smoke coming from the exhaust, the frame shaking gently. GOODMAN'S *eyes go wide, and he runs over to his car.*

    The people stare toward the car.

260   **MAN ONE.** He got the car started somehow. He got his car started!

    The camera pans along the faces of the people as they stare, somehow caught up by this revelation and somehow, illogically, wildly, frightened.

265   **WOMAN.** How come his car just up and started like that?

    SALLY. All by itself. He wasn't anywheres near it. It started all by itself.

    Don approaches the group, stops a few feet away to look toward Goodman's *car and then back toward the group.*

270   **DON.** And he never did come out to look at that thing that flew overhead. He wasn't even interested. [*He turns to the faces in the group, his face taut and serious.*] Why? Why didn't he come out with the rest of us to look?

    CHARLIE. He always was an oddball. Him and his whole 275 family. Real oddball.

    DON. What do you say we ask him?

    The group suddenly starts toward the house. In this brief fraction of a moment they take the first step toward performing a metamorphosis[5] that changes people from a group into a 280 *mob. They begin to head purposefully across the street toward the house at the end.* STEVE *stands in front of them. For a moment their fear almost turns their walk into a wild stampede, but* STEVE'S *voice, loud, incisive, and commanding, makes them stop.*

285   **STEVE.** Wait a minute…wait a minute! Let's not be a mob!

---

5. **metamorphosis.** Change in form or nature

The people stop as a group, seem to pause for a moment, and then much more quietly and slowly start to walk across the street. GOODMAN *stands alone facing the people.*

GOODMAN. I just don't understand it. I tried to start it and
290 it wouldn't start. You saw me. All of you saw me.

And now, just as suddenly as the engine started, it stops and there's a long silence that is gradually intruded upon by the frightened murmuring of the people.

GOODMAN. I don't understand. I swear…I don't
295 understand. What's happening?

DON. Maybe you better tell us. Nothing's working on this street. Nothing. No lights, no power, no radio. [*And then meaningfully.*] Nothing except one car—yours!

The people pick this up and now their murmuring becomes
300 *a loud chant filling the air with accusations and demands for action. Two of the men pass Don and head toward* GOODMAN, *who backs away, backing into his car and now at bay.*

GOODMAN. Wait a minute now. You keep your distance—all of you. So I've got a car that starts by itself—well,
305 that's a freak thing, I admit it. But does that make me some kind of a criminal or something? I don't know why the car works—it just does!

This stops the crowd momentarily and now GOODMAN, *still backing away, goes toward his front porch. He goes up the steps*
310 *and then stops to stand facing the mob.*

We see a long shot of STEVE *as he comes through the crowd.*

STEVE. [*Quietly.*] We're all on a monster kick, Les. Seems that the general impression holds that maybe one family isn't what we think they are. Monsters from outer space or
315 something. Different than us. Fifth columnists[6] from the vast beyond. [*He chuckles.*] You know anybody that might fit that description around here on Maple Street?

GOODMAN. What is this, a gag or something? This a practical joke or something?

320 *We see a close-up of the porch light as it suddenly goes out. There's a murmur from the group.*

GOODMAN. Now I suppose that's supposed to incriminate[7] me! The light goes on and off. That really does it, doesn't it? [*He looks around the faces of the people.*] I just don't understand
325 this—[*He wets his lips, looking from face to face.*] Look, you all know me. We've lived here five years. Right in this house. We're

6. **Fifth columnists.** Citizens who support the goals of an invading army
7. **incriminate.** Show proof of involvement in a crime

Build Vocabulary

A *kick* is a temporary idea or activity that someone enjoys. Why does Steve say that the neighborhood is on a monster kick?

_____

_____

Read Aloud

Read lines 229–342 [from "Well, if that's – from the crowd again"] aloud. What is the woman trying to say? Why does she hesitate?

_____

_____

Build Vocabulary

Someone who has *insomnia* has difficulty falling asleep. Why might someone with insomnia look up at the sky?

_____

_____

Note the Facts

How has the street changed since the afternoon when the story began?

_____

_____

no different from any of the rest of you! We're no different at all. Really…this whole thing is just…just weird—

330 [**WOMAN.** Well, if that's the case, Les Goodman, explain why—[*She stops suddenly, clamping her mouth shut.*]
  GOODMAN. [*Softly.*] Explain what?
  STEVE. [*Interjecting.*] Look, let's forget this—
  CHARLIE. [*Overlapping him.*] Go ahead, let her talk. What about it? Explain what?

335 **WOMAN.** [*A little reluctantly.*] Well…sometimes I go to bed late at night. A couple of times…a couple of times I'd come out on the porch and I'd see Mr. Goodman here in the wee hours of the morning standing out in front of his house… looking up at the sky. [*She looks around the circle of faces.*] That's

340 right, looking up at the sky as if…as if he were waiting for something. [*A pause.*] As if he were looking for something.
  There's a murmur of reaction from the crowd again.]
  We cut suddenly to a group shot. As GOODMAN *starts toward them, they back away frightened.*

345 **GOODMAN.** You know really…this is for laughs. You know what I'm guilty of? [*He laughs.*] I'm guilty of insomnia. Now what's the penalty for insomnia? [*At this point the laugh, the humor, leaves his voice.*] Did you hear what I said? I said it was insomnia. [*A pause as he looks around, then shouts.*] I said it

350 was insomnia! You fools. You scared, frightened rabbits, you. You're sick people, do you know that? You're sick people—all of you! And you don't even know what you're starting because let me tell you…let me tell you—this thing you're starting—that should frighten you. As God is my witness…you're letting

355 something begin here that's a nightmare!

— ACT 2 —

  We see a medium shot of the GOODMAN *entry hall at night. On the side table rests an unlit candle.* MRS. GOODMAN *walks into the scene, a glass of milk in hand. She sets the milk down on*

360 *the table, lights the candle with a match from a box on the table, picks up the glass of milk, and starts out of scene.*

  MRS. GOODMAN *comes through her porch door, glass of milk in hand. The entry hall, with table and lit candle, can be seen behind her.*

365 *Outside, the camera slowly pans down the sidewalk, taking in little knots of people who stand around talking in low voices. At the end of each conversation they look toward* LES GOODMAN'S *house. From the various houses we can see candlelight but no electricity, and there's an all-pervading quiet that blankets the*

370 *whole area, disturbed only by the almost whispered voices of the*
people as they stand around. The camera pans over to one group
where CHARLIE *stands. He stares across at* GOODMAN's *house.*

We see a long shot of the house. Two men stand across the
street in almost sentry-like poses. Then we see a medium shot of a
375 *group of people.*

SALLY. [*A little timorously.*[8]] It just doesn't seem right,
though, keeping watch on them. Why…he was right when
he said he was one of our neighbors. Why, I've known Ethel
Goodman ever since they moved in. We've been good friends—

380 CHARLIE. That don't prove a thing. Any guy who'd spend
his time lookin' up at the sky early in the morning—well, there's
something wrong with that kind of person. There's something
that ain't legitimate. Maybe under normal circumstances we
could let it go by, but these aren't normal circumstances. Why,
385 look at this street! Nothin' but candles. Why, it's like goin' back
into the dark ages or somethin'!

Steve *walks down the steps of his porch, walks down the street*
over to LES GOODMAN's *house, and then stops at the foot of the*
steps. GOODMAN *stands there, his wife behind him, very frightened.*

390 GOODMAN. Just stay right where you are, Steve. We don't
want any trouble, but this time if anybody sets foot on my
porch, that's what they're going to get—trouble!

STEVE. Look Les—

GOODMAN. I've already explained to you people. I don't
395 sleep very well at night sometimes. I get up and I take a walk
and I look up at the sky. I look at the stars!

MRS. GOODMAN. That's exactly what he does. Why this
whole thing, it's…it's some kind of madness or something.

STEVE. [*Nods grimly.*] That's exactly what it is—some kind
400 of madness.

CHARLIE'S VOICE. [*Shrill, from across the street.*] You
best watch who you're seen with, Steve! Until we get all this
straightened out, you ain't exactly above suspicion yourself.

STEVE. [*Whirling around toward him.*] Or you, Charlie. Or
405 any of us, it seems. From age eight on up!

WOMAN. What I'd like to know is—what are we gonna do?
Just stand around here all night?

CHARLIE. There's nothin' else we can do! [*He turns back*
looking toward STEVE *and* GOODMAN *again.*] One of 'em'll tip
410 their hand.[9] They got to.

---

8. **timorously.** Shyly
9. **tip their hand.** Expose themselves; accidentally reveal information

STEVE. [*Raising his voice.*] There's something you can do, Charlie. You could go home and keep your mouth shut. You could quit strutting around like a self-appointed hanging judge and just climb into bed and forget it.

415 **CHARLIE.** You sound real anxious to have that happen, Steve. I think we better keep our eye on you too!

DON. [*As if he were taking the bit in his teeth, takes a hesitant step to the front.*] I think everything might as well come out now. [*He turns toward* STEVE.] Your wife's done plenty of
420 talking, Steve, about how odd you are!

CHARLIE. [*Picking this up, his eyes widening.*] Go ahead, tell us what she's said.

We see a long shot of STEVE *as he walks toward them from across the street.*

425 **STEVE.** Go ahead, what's my wife said? Let's get it all out. Let's pick out every idiosyncrasy[10] of every single man, woman, and child on the street. And then we might as well set up some kind of kangaroo court.[11] How about a firing squad at dawn, Charlie, so we can get rid of all the suspects? Narrow them
430 down. Make it easier for you.

DON. There's no need gettin' so upset, Steve. It's just that… well…Myra's talked about how there's been plenty of nights you spent hours down in your basement workin' on some kind of radio or something. Well, none of us have ever seen that radio—

435 *By this time* STEVE *has reached the group. He stands there defiantly close to them.*

CHARLIE. Go ahead, Steve. What kind of "radio set" you workin' on? I never seen it. Neither has anyone else. Who you talk to on that radio set? And who talks to you?

440 **STEVE.** I'm surprised at you, Charlie. How come you're so dense all of a sudden? [*A pause.*] Who do I talk to? I talk to monsters from outer space. I talk to three-headed green men who fly over here in what look like meteors.

445 STEVE's *wife steps down from the porch, bites her lip, calls out.*

MRS. BRAND. Steve! Steve, please. [*Then looking around, frightened, she walks toward the group.*] It's just a ham
450 radio[12] set, that's all. I bought him a

---

10. **idiosyncrasy.** Odd character trait
11. **kangaroo court.** Unjust or unofficial court
12. **ham radio.** Noncommercial two-way radio

Build Vocabulary

Something *dense* is solid and hard to move or get through. What does it mean if you call a person *dense*?

_____

_____

Differentiated Instruction: Literacy & Reading Skills © Carnegie Learning, Inc.

book on it myself. It's just a ham radio set. A lot of people have them. I can show it to you. It's right down in the basement.

STEVE. [*Whirls around toward her.*] Show them nothing! If they want to look inside our house—let them get a search
455 warrant.

CHARLIE. Look, buddy, you can't afford to—

STEVE. [*Interrupting.*] Charlie, don't tell me what I can afford! And stop telling me who's dangerous and who isn't and who's safe and who's a menace. [*He turns to the group and shouts.*] And
460 you're with him, too—all of you! You're standing here all set to crucify—all set to find a scapegoat[13]—all desperate to point some kind of a finger at a neighbor! Well now look, friends, the only thing that's gonna happen is that we'll eat each other up alive—

He stops abruptly as CHARLIE *suddenly grabs his arm.*

465 **CHARLIE.** [*In a hushed voice.*] That's not the only thing that can happen to us.

Cut to a long shot looking down the street. A figure has suddenly materialized in the gloom and in the silence we can hear the clickety-clack of slow, measured footsteps on concrete
470 *as the figure walks slowly toward them. One of the women lets out a stifled cry. The young mother grabs her boy as do a couple of others.*

TOMMY. [*Shouting, frightened.*] It's the monster! It's the monster!

475 *Another woman lets out a wail and the people fall back in a group, staring toward the darkness and the approaching figure.*

We see a medium group shot of the people as they stand in the shadows watching. DON MARTIN *joins them, carrying a shotgun. He holds it up.*

480 **DON.** We may need this.

STEVE. A shotgun? [*He pulls it out of* DON's *hand.*] Good Lord—will anybody think a thought around here? Will you people wise up? What good would a shotgun do against—

Now Charlie *pulls the gun from* Steve's *hand.*

485 **CHARLIE.** No more talk, Steve. You're going to talk us into a grave! You'd let whatever's out there walk right over us, wouldn't yuh? Well, some of us won't!

He swings the gun around to point it toward the sidewalk. The dark figure continues to walk toward them.

490 *The group stands there, fearful, apprehensive, mothers clutching children, men standing in front of wives.* CHARLIE *slowly raises the gun. As the figure gets closer and closer he*

---

13. **scapegoat.** Person, group, or thing that is unfairly blamed

Differentiated Instruction: Literacy & Reading Skills UNIT 7 **167**

Build Vocabulary

Idiom Charlie says that Steve will *talk them into the grave* when they see the figure coming down the street. What does he mean?

_____

_____

suddenly pulls the trigger. The sound of it explodes in the stillness. There is a long angle shot looking down at the figure,
495 *who suddenly lets out a small cry, stumbles forward onto his knees and then falls forward on his face.* DON, CHARLIE, *and* STEVE *race forward over to him.* STEVE *is there first and turns the man over. Now the crowd gathers around them.*

> **Think and Reflect**
>
> Were you surprised that Charlie shoots the gun? Why or why not?
> _____
> _____

500　　**STEVE.** [*Slowly looks up.*] It's Pete Van Horn.

DON. [*In a hushed voice.*] Pete Van Horn! He was just gonna go over to the next block to see if the power was on—

WOMAN. You killed him, Charlie. You shot him dead!

CHARLIE. [*Looks around at the circle of faces, his eyes*
505 *frightened, his face contorted.*] But…but I didn't know who he was. I certainly didn't know who he was. He comes walkin' out of the darkness—how am I supposed to know who he was? [*He grabs* STEVE.] Steve—you know why I shot! How was I supposed to know he wasn't a monster or something? [*He grabs*
510 DON *now.*] We're all scared of the same thing. I was just tryin' to…tryin' to protect my home, that's all! Look, all of you, that's all I was tryin' to do. [*He looks down wildly at the body.*] I didn't know it was somebody we knew! I didn't know—

There's a sudden hush and then an intake of breath. We see a
515 *medium shot of the living room window of* CHARLIE's *house. The window is not lit, but suddenly the house lights come on behind it.*

WOMAN. [*In a very hushed voice.*] Charlie…Charlie…the lights just went on in your house. Why did the lights just go on?

DON. What about it, Charlie? How come you're the only
520 one with lights now?

GOODMAN. That's what I'd like to know. [*A pause as they all stare toward* CHARLIE.]

GOODMAN. You were so quick to kill, Charlie, and you were so quick to tell us who we had to be careful of. Well, maybe you
525 had to kill. Maybe Peter there was trying to tell us something. Maybe he'd found out something and came back to tell us who there was amongst us we should watch out for—Charlie *backs away from the group, his eyes wide with fright.*

CHARLIE. No…no…it's nothing of the sort! I don't know
530 why the lights are on. I swear I don't. Somebody's pulling a gag or something.

Build Vocabulary

Idiom When someone *pulls a gag,* it means the person is playing a practical joke. Why would Charlie suggest that someone might be pulling a gag?

_____

_____

He bumps against STEVE, *who grabs him and whirls him around.*

535 **STEVE.** A gag? A gag? Charlie, there's a dead man on the sidewalk and you killed him! Does this thing look like a gag to you?

CHARLIE breaks away and screams as he runs toward his house.

CHARLIE. No! No! Please!

A man breaks away from the crowd to chase CHARLIE.

540 *We see a long angle shot looking down as the man tackles* CHARLIE *and lands on top of him. The other people start to run toward them.* CHARLIE *is up on his feet, breaks away from the other man's grasp, lands a couple of desperate punches that push the man aside. Then he forces his way, fighting, through the*

545 *crowd to once again break free, jumps up on his front porch. A rock thrown from the group smashes a window alongside of him, the broken glass flying past him. A couple of pieces cut him. He stands there perspiring, rumpled, blood running down from a cut on the cheek. His wife breaks away from the group to throw*

550 *herself into his arms. He buries his face against her. We can see the crowd converging on the porch now.*

Voices.

It must have been him.

He's the one.

555 We got to get Charlie.

Another rock lands on the porch. Now CHARLIE *pushes his wife behind him, facing the group.*

CHARLIE. Look, look I swear to you…it isn't me…but I do know who it is…I swear to you, I do know who it is. I know

560 who the monster is here. I know who it is that doesn't belong. I swear to you I know.

GOODMAN. [*Shouting.*] What are you waiting for?

WOMAN. [*Shouting.*] Come on, Charlie, come on.

MAN ONE. [*Shouting.*] Who is it, Charlie, tell us!

565 **DON.** [*Pushing his way to the front of the crowd.*] All right, Charlie, let's hear it!

CHARLIE'S *eyes dart around wildly.*

CHARLIE. It's…it's…

MAN TWO. [*Screaming.*] Go ahead, Charlie, tell us.

570 **CHARLIE.** It's…it's the kid. It's Tommy. He's the one!

There's a gasp from the crowd as we cut to a shot of SALLY *holding her son* TOMMY. *The boy at first doesn't understand and then, realizing the eyes are all on him, buries his face against his mother.*

Note the Facts

According to Charlie, who is responsible for their problems?

_____

_____

575   **SALLY.** [*Backs away.*] That's crazy! That's crazy! He's a little boy.

    WOMAN. But he knew! He was the only one who knew! He told us all abou t it. Well, how did he know? How could he have known?

580   *The various people take this up and repeat the question aloud.*
    Voices.
    How could he know?
    Who told him?
    Make the kid answer.

585   **DON.** It was Charlie who killed old man Van Horn.

    WOMAN. But it was the kid here who knew what was going to happen all the time. He was the one who knew!

    We see a close-up of STEVE.

    STEVE. Are you all gone crazy? [*Pause as he looks about.*] Stop.

590   *A fist crashes at* STEVE's *face, staggering him back out of the frame of the picture.*

    There are several close camera shots suggesting the coming of violence. A hand fires a rifle. A fist clenches. A hand grabs the hammer from VAN HORN's *body, etc. Meanwhile, we hear the*
595 *following lines.*

    DON. Charlie has to be the one—Where's my rifle—

    WOMAN. Les Goodman's the one. His car started! Let's wreck it.

    MRS. GOODMAN. What about Steve's radio—He's the one
600 that called them—

    MRS. GOODMAN. Smash the radio. Get me a hammer. Get me something.

    STEVE. Stop—Stop—

    CHARLIE. Where's that kid—Let's get him.

605   **MAN ONE.** Get Steve—Get Charlie—They're working together.

    The crowd starts to converge around the mother, who grabs the child and starts to run with him. The crowd starts to follow, at first walking fast,
610 *and then running after him.*

    We see a full shot of the street as suddenly CHARLIE's *lights go off and the lights in another house go on. They stay on for a moment, then from across the street*
615 *other lights go on and then off again.*

    MAN ONE. [*Shouting.*] It isn't the kid…it's Bob Weaver's house.

WOMAN. It isn't Bob Weaver's house. It's Don Martin's place.

CHARLIE. I tell you it's the kid.

620 **DON.** It's Charlie. He's the one.

Think and Reflect

Who or what are the monsters on Maple Street?

_____

_____

We move into a series of close-ups of various people as they shout, accuse, scream, interspersing these shots with shots of houses as the lights go on and off, and then slowly in the middle of this nightmarish morass[14] of sight and sound the camera starts
625 *to pull away, until once again we've reached the opening shot looking at the Maple Street sign from high above.*

The camera continues to move away until we dissolve to a shot looking toward the metal side of a space craft, which sits shrouded in darkness. An open door throws out a beam of light
630 *from the illuminated interior. Two figures silhouetted against the bright lights appear. We get only a vague feeling of form, but nothing more explicit than that.*

Build Vocabulary

Silhouettes are shadowy shapes that make it difficult to make out distinct features. Why might the two figures be silhouetted?

_____

_____

FIGURE ONE. Understand the procedure now? Just stop a few of their machines and radios and telephones and lawn
635 mowers…throw them into darkness for a few hours, and then you just sit back and watch the pattern.

FIGURE TWO. And this pattern is always the same?

FIGURE ONE. With few variations. They pick the most dangerous enemy they can find…and it's themselves. And all
640 we need do is sit back…and watch.

FIGURE TWO. Then I take it this place…this Maple Street…is not unique.

FIGURE ONE. [*Shaking his head.*] By no means. Their world is full of Maple Streets. And we'll go from one to the
645 other and let them destroy themselves. One to the other…one to the other…one to the other—

Now the camera pans up for a shot of the starry sky and over this we hear the NARRATOR'S VOICE.

NARRATOR'S VOICE. The tools of conquest do not neces-
650 sarily come with bombs and explosions and fallout. There are weapons that are simply thoughts, attitudes, prejudices—to be found only in the minds of men. For the record, prejudices

---

14. **morass.** Complicated or bewildering situation

can kill and suspicion can destroy and a thoughtless frightened search for a scapegoat has a fallout all its own for the
655 children…and the children yet unborn. [*A pause.*] And the
pity of it is…that these things cannot be confined to…The
Twilight Zone! ❖

MIRRORS & WINDOWS What would you do if you were a resident of Maple Street? Would it be fair to blame your neighbors for what is going on?

_____

_____

_____

Differentiated Instruction: Literacy & Reading Skills

READING CHECK

Circle the letter of the correct answer.

1. What happens when the flash of light passes over Maple Street?
   A. All of the electronics stop working.
   B. Strangers from out of town arrive in town.
   C. Everyone looks for visitors from outer space.

2. Who is the first person to say that the blackout is caused by people from outer space?
   A. Tommy
   B. Steve
   C. Charlie

3. What happens when Goodman's car starts up by itself?
   A. He uses it to get out of town as quickly as possible.
   B. People accuse him of being responsible for the blackout.
   C. They use the car's power to turn on the street's electricity.

4. Why does Charlie shoot Pete Van Horn?
   A. He doesn't recognize Pete in the shadows.
   B. He thinks Pete is trying to escape.
   C. He hears an odd sound that frightens him.

5. Who is responsible for the strange events on Maple Street?
   A. Tommy
   B. the two figures
   C. the new neighbors

VOCABULARY CHECK

Circle the letter of the correct answer.

1. The *nebulae* are full of stars starting to form. What are *nebulae*?
   A. small stars
   B. clouds of dust
   C. other dimensions

2. The neighbors undergo a *metamorphosis*, and friends become foes. A *metamorphosis* is a
   A. game in which people take sides.
   B. change from one thing to another.
   C. group activity in which people talk together.

3. Ike *knits his brows* whenever he has trouble solving his math homework. This means he is
   A. confused or thinking hard.
   B. unhappy to be working on the problems.
   C. ready to start on his other homework soon.

4. The extra credit is a *bum joke*, because it is even harder than the rest of the test. A *bum joke* is something that is
   A. usually funny to people.
   B. funny only if others tell it.
   C. hardly ever really funny.

5. The people in the crowd want a *scapegoat* for their problems. What does this mean?
   A. They want to see if others have trouble, too.
   B. They want to work everything out together.
   C. They want to find someone they can blame.

ANALYZE LITERATURE: Diction

The author's choice of words and expressions is called **diction**. The diction of a piece can make it sound formal or informal, modern or old-fashioned, and so on. What are some of the words or phrases that make up the diction in "The Monsters Are Due on Maple Street"?

_____

_____

USE READING SKILLS: Cause and Effect

Review the cause-and-effect chart you filled in while reading this story. What are some of the causes? What are the effects of those causes?

_____

_____

BUILD VOCABULARY

Use context clues from each sentence to create definitions for each italicized word or phrase.

1. The strange flash of light was *too close for their money*, leaving the residents of Maple Street alarmed and uncomfortable.

   _____

2. Sally and Tommy stood on the *fringe* of the crowd, toward the back.

   _____

3. There was *no telling* when everything would turn back on again.

   _____

4. People started accusing others of being *oddballs* with strange habits.

   _____

5. The crowd *converged* on Charlie, surrounding him.

   _____

WRITING SKILLS

Think about what would happen if the two figures went down and visited Maple Street. How would they act? How would the residents of Maple Street react to their arrival? Write a short screenplay to describe the scene the way you think it would happen.

Differentiated Instruction: Literacy & Reading Skills

BEFORE READING

page 501

Persephone and Demeter

A Greek Myth retold by Ingri and Edgar Parin d'Aulaire

ABOUT THE STORY

In **"Persephone and Demeter,"** Hades, god of the underworld, falls in love with Persephone, daughter of the harvest goddess, Demeter. Hades knows that Demeter would never agree to a marriage, so he kidnaps the girl, takes her to his kingdom, and makes her his queen. Read this Greek myth and see what happens because of the kidnapping.

MAKE CONNECTIONS

Think about your own relationships. If you loved someone, but you knew that person was leaving, what would you do? Would you let the person go or would you fight for him or her?

_____

_____

_____

_____

ANALYZE LITERATURE: Myth

A **myth** is a traditional story that usually presents supernatural events and that often includes gods and heroes. *Supernatural events* are happenings that cannot be explained by natural law. As you read, look for supernatural events or elements in the story.

USE READING SKILLS: Monitor Comprehension

To **monitor comprehension** means to check your understanding. As you read, ask yourself questions to make sure that you understand what happens in the story. Fill in the first two columns of the chart before you read. Fill in the last column after you read.

What I Know	What I Want to Know	What I Learned
Demeter was the goddess of the harvest	How does she affect the harvest?	If Demeter is sad, nothing grows

PREVIEW VOCABULARY

Key Words and Phrases Read each key word and rate it using this scale: ① I don't know this word or phrase at all. ② I've seen this word or phrase before. ③ I know this word or phrase and use it.	Words and Phrases in Context Read to see how the key word or phrase can be used in a sentence.	Definition Write down what you think the word or phrase means. Then use a dictionary to check your definition.	Practice Practice using the key words and phrases by completing the following sentences.
root (rüt) *verb* ① ② ③	Rabbits **root** around in my garden until they find what they are looking for.		I don't like it when someone **roots** through my…
cleft (kleft) *noun* ① ② ③	The **cleft** in the mountain was difficult to pass.		The **cleft** in the hill is dangerous because…
avenging a · veng · ing (ə venj iŋ) *adjective* ① ② ③	After the father was hurt, the **avenging** sons went looking for the person who harmed their father.		An **avenging** person would…
barren bar · ren (bar än) *adjective* ① ② ③	They cut down the apple tree because it was **barren.**		A **barren** plant doesn't…
radiant ra · di · ant (rā dē ´nt) *adjective* ① ② ③	The diamond ring was **radiant.**		An example of something **radiant** is…
in vain in · vain (in vān) *adverbial phrase* ① ② ③	The dog scratched **in vain** at the door of the empty house.		When you work **in vain,** you feel…

Persephone and Demeter

A Greek Myth retold by Ingri and Edgar Parin d'Aulaire

Persephone grew up on Olympus[1] and her gay[2] laughter rang through the brilliant halls. She was the daughter of Demeter, goddess of the harvest, and her mother loved her so dearly she could not bear to have her out of her sight. When Demeter

5 sat on her golden throne her daughter was always on her lap; when she went down to earth to look after her trees and fields, she took Persephone. Wherever Persephone danced on her light feet, flowers sprang up. She was so lovely and full of grace that even Hades,[3] who saw so little, noticed her and fell in love

10 with her. He wanted her for his queen, but he knew that her mother would never consent to part with her, so he decided to carry her off.

One day as Persephone ran about in the meadow gathering flowers, she strayed away from her mother and

15 the attending nymphs.[4] Suddenly, the ground split open and up from the **yawning** crevice came a dark chariot drawn by black horses. At the reins stood grim Hades. He seized the terrified girl, turned his horses, and plunged back into the ground. A herd of pigs **rooting** in the meadow tumbled

20 into the **cleft**, and Persephone's cries for help died out as the ground closed again as suddenly as it had opened. Up in the field, a little swineherd[5] stood and wept over the pigs he had lost, while Demeter rushed wildly about in the meadow, looking in vain for her daughter, who had vanished without

25 leaving a trace.[6]

With the frightened girl in his arms, Hades raced his snorting horses down away from the sunlit world. Down and down they sped on the dark path to his dismal underground palace. He led weeping Persephone in, seated her beside him

yawn·ing (yô′ niŋ) *adj.,* wide open

root (rüt) *v.,* dig in the ground

cleft (kleft) *n.,* space made when something breaks open

---

1. **Olympus.** Mountain in what is now Thessaly, Greece, where the ancient Greeks believed most gods lived
2. **gay.** Joyful or happy
3. **Hades.** God of the underworld; sometimes the name *Hades* is used for the underworld itself
4. **nymphs.** Minor female goddesses who live in natural spots like forests or trees, rivers, and streams
5. **swineherd.** Person who keeps or tends pigs
6. **without leaving a trace.** Completely disappeared

30 on a throne of black marble, and decked her with gold and precious stones. But the jewels brought her no joy. She wanted no cold stones. She longed for warm sunshine and flowers and her golden-tressed[7] mother.

Think and Reflect

Persephone doesn't care about the jewelry and riches Hades gives her. If you were in Persephone's position, how would you react to the gifts?

_____

_____

35 Dead souls crowded out from cracks and crevices to look at their new queen, while ever more souls came across the Styx[8] and Persephone watched them drink from a spring under dark poplars. It was the spring of Lethe,[9] and those who drank from its waters forgot who they were and what they had done on earth. Rhadamanthus, a judge of the dead, dealt out
40 punishment to the souls of great sinners. They were sentenced to suffer forever under the whips of the **avenging** Erinyes.[10] Heroes were led to the Elysian fields,[11] where they lived happily forever in never-failing light.

Around the palace of Hades there was a garden where
45 whispering poplars and weeping willows grew. They had no flowers and bore no fruit and no birds sang in their branches. There was only one tree in the whole realm of Hades that bore fruit. That was a little pomegranate[12] tree. The gardener of the underworld offered the tempting
50 pomegranates to the queen, but Persephone refused to touch the food of the dead.

Wordlessly she walked through the garden at silent Hades' side and slowly her heart turned to ice.

Above, on earth, Demeter ran about searching for her lost
55 daughter, and all nature grieved with her. Flowers wilted, trees lost their leaves, and the fields grew **barren** and cold. In vain did the plow cut through the icy ground; nothing could sprout and nothing could grow while the goddess of the harvest wept.

---

7. **golden-tressed.** Having golden hair (tresses); blond
8. **Styx.** Main river of the underworld, which surrounds it and separates it from the world of the living
9. **Lethe.** River of forgetfulness
10. **Erinyes.** Three spirits of punishment
11. **Elysian fields.** Paradise
12. **pomegranate.** Round, red fruit with a hard rind

DURING READING

Note the Facts

Who comes out to see Persephone by the river?

_____

_____

a·veng·ing (ə venj´ iŋ) *adj.*, taking revenge or punishing someone for something

Use Reading Skills

Monitor Comprehension
Is there any part of the myth that confuses you? Reread the text to clarify what you don't understand.

_____

_____

bar·ren (ber´ ən) *adj.*, unable to reproduce or bear fruit; desolate

60 People and animals starved and the gods begged Demeter again to bless the earth. But she refused to let anything grow until she had found her daughter.

Bent with grief, Demeter turned into a gray old woman. She returned to the meadow where Persephone had vanished and asked the sun if he had seen what had happened, but he said no, 65 dark clouds had hidden his face that day. She wandered around the meadow and after a while she met a youth whose name was Triptolemus. He told her that his brother, a swineherd, had seen his pigs disappear into the ground and had heard the frightened screams of a girl.

70 Demeter now understood that Hades had kidnapped her daughter, and her grief turned to anger. She called to Zeus[13] and said that she would never again make the earth green if he did not command Hades to return Persephone. Zeus could not let the world perish and he sent Hermes[14] down to 75 Hades, bidding him to let Persephone go. Even Hades had to obey the orders of Zeus, and sadly he said farewell to his queen.

Joyfully, Persephone leaped to her feet, but as she was leaving with Hermes, a hooting laugh came from the garden. 80 There stood the gardener of Hades, grinning. He pointed to a pomegranate from which a few of the kernels were missing. Persephone, lost in thought, had eaten the seeds, he said.

Then dark Hades smiled. He watched Hermes lead Persephone up to the bright world above. He knew that she 85 must return to him, for she had tasted the food of the dead.

When Persephone again appeared on earth, Demeter sprang to her feet with a cry of joy and rushed to greet her daughter. No longer was she a sad old woman, but a **radiant** goddess. Again she blessed her fields and the flowers bloomed anew and 90 the grain ripened.

"Dear child," she said, "never again shall we be parted. Together we shall make all nature bloom." But joy soon was changed to sadness, for Persephone had to admit that she had tasted the food of the dead and must return to Hades. 95 However, Zeus decided that mother and daughter should not be parted forever. He ruled that Persephone had to return to Hades and spend one month in the underworld for each seed she had eaten.

---

13. **Zeus.** King of the Greek gods
14. **Hermes.** Messenger god

Every year, when Persephone left her, Demeter grieved,
100 nothing grew, and there was winter on earth. But as soon as her
daughter's light footsteps were heard, the whole earth burst into
bloom. Spring had come. As long as mother and daughter were
together, the earth was warm and bore fruit.

Demeter was a kind goddess. She did not want mankind to
105 starve during the cold months of winter when Persephone was
away. She lent her chariot, laden[15] with grain, to Triptolemus,
the youth who had helped her to find her lost daughter.
She told him to scatter her golden grain over the world and
teach men how to sow it in spring and reap it in fall and store
110 it away for the long months when again the earth was barren
and cold. ❖

---

15. **laden.** Fully loaded

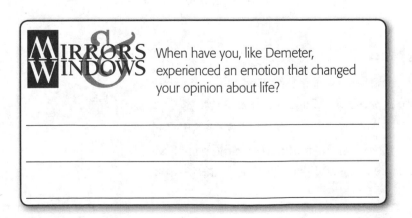

When have you, like Demeter, experienced an emotion that changed your opinion about life?

_____

_____

_____

Analyze Literature

Myth What cycle of nature does this myth explain?

_____

_____

Build Vocabulary

Demeter doesn't want people to *starve*, so she teaches them to grow food. What does *starve* mean?

_____

_____

READING CHECK

Circle the letter of the correct answer.

1. Why does Hades kidnap Persephone?
   A. He knows that Demeter would never agree to let him marry her.
   B. She is a bad person, so he takes her to the underworld.
   C. He is angry at her.

2. What is the one fruit that grows in the gardens of Hades?
   A. weeping willows
   B. poplars
   C. pomegranate

3. Who finally tells Demeter what happens to Persephone?
   A. Triptolemus
   B. Zeus
   C. Hermes

4. Why must Persephone return to the underworld?
   A. She is married to Hades.
   B. She eats a little bit of the pomegranate.
   C. She doesn't miss her mother.

5. Where does Persephone live at the end of the myth?
   A. She lives with Hades.
   B. She lives with Demeter.
   C. She lives in the underworld for part of the year.

VOCABULARY CHECK

Circle the letter of the correct answer.

1. The heard of pigs from the myth is *rooting* in the meadow. What are they doing?
   A. digging
   B. running
   C. falling

2. Why does Hades lead his horses back down into the *cleft* after he kidnaps Persephone?
   A. It is the opening in the earth back to the underworld.
   B. The swineherd directed them there.
   C. He wants to talk to Demeter.

3. According to the myth, bad people are whipped by the *avenging* Erinyes. What does *avenging* mean?
   A. scary
   B. punishing
   C. wise

4. All of nature grew *barren* and cold when Persephone was kidnapped. Which of the following does *not* describe the scene?
   A. Trees lose their leaves and flowers die.
   B. Nothing grows because the ground is like ice.
   C. The earth blooms and bears fruit.

5. When Persephone returns, Demeter is a *radiant* goddess again. What does *radiant* mean?
   A. bright and beautiful
   B. barren and cold
   C. sad and old

ANALYZE LITERATURE: Myth

Remember that a myth usually presents supernatural events. Decide which sentence below is a supernatural event and which one is not. Check the box next to the supernatural event. Then be creative and write two examples of other supernatural events.

❑ The horses decided to trick the farmer when he returned with the pail of oats.

❑ The mother drove the car to the store and back with her child in the car seat.

1. _____

2. _____

USE READING SKILLS: Monitor Comprehension

1. What is it like in the underworld?

   _____

   How is it different than the world above?

   _____

2. According to the myth, what happens to great sinners when they die?

   _____

   What happens to heroes?

   _____

BUILDING LANGUAGE SKILLS: Prepositions

A **preposition** is a word that shows how a word or phrase is related to other words in the sentence. Prepositions often indicate where something is in relation to another object. Complete these sentences with the correct preposition from the box below.

around	beside	down	from	into	on	to

1. Hades takes Persephone _____ to the underworld.

2. Persephone sits _____ Hades _____ a throne of marble.

3. Persephone watches souls drink _____ a spring.

4. There is a garden _____ the palace of Hades.

5. The pigs disappear _____ the ground.

6. A gardener of Hades points _____ a pomegranate.

SPEAKING & LISTENING SKILLS: Persuasive Speech

In the myth, Demeter asks Zeus to help her save her daughter. She tells him that if he doesn't help her, she would never make the earth green again. What else could she say to convince him? Put yourself in Demeter's position and write a short persuasive speech to Zeus on your own paper. You can start with the following: "Zeus, Persephone was taken from me. I need you to help me get her back because…"

BEFORE READING

page 512

The Secret Name of Ra

An Egyptian Myth retold by Geraldine Harris

ABOUT THE STORY

In **"The Secret Name of Ra"** Ra is the god of the sun. He brings life into the world by day with his bright power, and at night he battles a snake in the underworld. Ra is protected from harm because he has a secret name. However, the goddess Isis wants her son, Horus, to become the ruler of the sky. Read the story to learn how Isis betrays Ra.

MAKE CONNECTIONS

Do you have a secret that you don't want to share with anyone?

_____

_____

_____

_____

ANALYZE LITERATURE: Motivation

Motivation is the force that makes a character think, feel, or act in a particular way. Different characters have different motivations, making them act in different ways. In this story, Ra is a god. The gods in stories often act differently than humans because gods have different motivations than humans. As you read, look for the motivations of each of the gods and humans. You will find that in this story, gods and humans sometimes act similarly because they are motivated by similar factors.

USE READING SKILLS: Analyze Cause and Effect

A **cause** is an action or event that makes something else happen. Any action or event that results from a cause is an **effect.** By analyzing causes and effects, you will better understand the plot, characters, and theme of the story. As you read, create a cause-and-effect chart for "The Secret Name of Ra."

Cause	Effect
Isis is jealous of Ra.	She makes a plan to defeat him.

PREVIEW VOCABULARY

Key Words and Phrases Read each key word and rate it using this scale: ①I don't know this word or phrase at all. ②I've seen this word or phrase before. ③I know this word or phrase and use it.	Words and Phrases in Context Read to see how the key word or phrase can be used in a sentence.	Definition Write down what you think the word or phrase means. Then use a dictionary to check your definition.	Practice Practice using the key words and phrases by completing the following sentences.
sole sole (sōl) *adjective* ① ② ③	He was the **sole** singer that night.		The **sole** person in charge is…
exalted ex • alt • ed (ig zōlt´ ed) *adjective* ① ② ③	The **exalted** book was read in classrooms everywhere.		An **exalted** person is…
cunning cun • ning (kʉ´ niŋ) *adjective* ① ② ③	The **cunning** student solved the difficult riddle.		A **cunning** person could…
deity de • i • ty (dē´ə tē) *noun* ① ② ③	Some myths have a water **deity** that lives in the ocean.		A **deity** might…
drivel dri • vel (driv´ əl) *verb* ① ② ③	The old dog **driveled** in his sleep.		Something that might **drivel** is …

The Secret Name of Ra

An Egyptian Myth retold by Geraldine Harris

Ra, the <u>Sole</u> Creator was visible to the people of Egypt as the disc of the sun, but they knew him in many other forms. He could appear as a crowned man, a falcon or a man with a falcon's head and, as the scarab beetle[1] pushes a round ball

5 of dung in front of it, the Egyptians pictured Ra as a scarab pushing the sun across the sky. In caverns deep below the earth were hidden another seventy-five forms of Ra: mysterious beings with mummified bodies[2] and heads consisting of birds or snakes, feathers or flowers. The names of Ra were as numerous

10 as his forms; he was the Shining One, The Hidden One, The Renewer of the Earth, The Wind in the Souls, The <u>Exalted</u> One, but there was one name of the Sun God which had not been spoken since time began. To know this secret name of Ra was to have power over him and over the world that he had created.

15   Isis longed for such a power. She had dreamed that one day she would have a marvellous falcon-headed son called Horus and she wanted the throne of Ra to give to her child. Isis was the Mistress of Magic, wiser than millions of men, but she knew that nothing in creation was powerful enough to harm its

20 creator. Her only chance was to turn the power of Ra against himself and at last Isis thought of a cruel and <u>cunning</u> plan. Every day the Sun God walked through his kingdom, attended by a crowd of spirits and lesser <u>deities</u>, but Ra was growing old. His eyes were dim, his step no longer firm and he had even

25 begun to <u>drivel</u>.
    One morning Isis mingled with a group of minor goddesses and followed behind the King of the Gods. She watched the face of Ra until she saw his saliva drip onto a clod of earth. When she was sure that no-one was taking any notice of her,

30 she scooped up the earth and carried it away. Isis mixed the

---

1. **scarab beetle.** Dung beetle; this insect was held sacred by ancient Egyptians, who saw it as a symbol both of the sun god and of the continued existence of the soul after death.
2. **mummified bodies.** Bodies that have been preserved for burial by removing the internal organs, treating them with special substances, and wrapping them in cloth to keep them from decaying

sole (sōl) *adj.,* only

ex·alt·ed (ig zōlt´ ed) *adj.,* held in high regard

Note the Facts

How does Isis plan to gain Ra's power for her son?

_____

_____

cun·ning (kʉ´ niŋ) *adj.,* clever or tricky

de·i·ty (dē´ə tē) *n.,* god or goddess

driv·el (driv´ əl) *v.,* drool

earth with the saliva of Ra to form clay and modelled a wicked-looking serpent. Through the hours of darkness she whispered spells over the clay serpent as it lay lifeless in her hands. Then the cunning goddess carried it to a crossroads on the route
35 which the Sun God always took. She hid the serpent in the long grass and returned to her palace.

The next day Ra came walking through his kingdom with the spirits and lesser deities crowding behind him. When he approached the crossroads, the spells of Isis began to work and
40 the clay serpent quivered into life. As the Sun God passed, it bit him in the ankle and crumbled back into earth. Ra gave a scream that was heard through all creation.

His jaws chattered and his limbs shook as the poison flooded through him like a rising Nile. "I have been wounded
45 by something deadly," whispered Ra. "I know that in my heart, though my eyes cannot see it. Whatever it was, I, the Lord of Creation, did not make it. I am sure that none of you would have done such a terrible thing to me, but I have never felt such pain! How can this have happened to me? I am the Sole
50 Creator, the child of the watery **abyss**. I am the god with a thousand names, but my secret name was only spoken once, before time began. Then it was hidden in my body so that no-one should ever learn it and be able to work spells against me. Yet as I walked through my kingdom something struck at
55 me and now my heart is on fire and my limbs shake. Send for the Ennead![3] Send for my children! They are wise in magic and their knowledge pierces heaven."

Messengers hurried to the great gods and from the four pillars of the world came the Ennead: Shu and Tefenet, Geb
60 and Nut, Seth and Osiris, Isis and Nephthys. Envoys traveled the land and the sky and the watery abyss to summon all the deities created by Ra. From the marshes came frog-headed Heket, Wadjet the cobra goddess and the fearsome god, crocodile-headed Sobek. From the deserts came fiery Selkis,
65 the scorpion goddess, Anubis the jackal, the guardian of the dead and Nekhbet the vulture goddess. From the cities of the north came warlike Neith, gentle cat-headed Bastet, fierce lion-headed Sekhmet and Ptah the god of crafts. From the cities of the south came Onuris, the divine huntsman
70 and ram-headed Khnum with Anukis his wife and Satis his daughter. Cunning Thoth and wise Seshat, goddess of writing;

---

3. **Ennead.** Literally, a group of nine; in Egyptian mythology, the most ancient group of nine gods

virile Min and snake-headed Renenutet, goddess of the harvest, kindly Meskhenet and monstrous Taweret, goddesses of birth—all of them were summoned to the side of Ra.

Think and Reflect

Ra calls all the gods and goddesses around him when he is hurt. Who would you want to be with you if you were sick?

_____

_____

DURING READING

Note the Facts

What does Isis need to help Ra?

_____

_____

75   The gods and goddesses gathered around the Sun God, weeping and wailing, afraid that he was going to die. Isis stood among them beating her breast and pretending to be as distressed and bewildered as all the other frightened deities.

      "Father of All," she began, "whatever is the matter? Has
80 some snake bitten you? Has some wretched creature dared to strike at his Creator? Few of the gods can compare with me in wisdom and I am the Mistress of Magic. If you will let me help you, I'm sure that I can cure you."

      Ra was grateful to Isis and told her all that had happened.
85 "Now I am colder than water and hotter than fire," complained the Sun God. "My eyes darken. I cannot see the sky and my body is soaked by the sweat of fever."

      "Tell me your full name," said cunning Isis. "Then I can use it in my spells. Without that knowledge the greatest of
90 magicians cannot help you."

      "I am the maker of heaven and earth," said Ra. "I made the heights and the depths, I set horizons at east and west and established the gods in their glory. When I open my eyes it is light; when I close them it is dark. The mighty Nile floods at my
95 command. The gods do not know my true name but I am the maker of time, the giver of festivals. I spark the fire of life. At dawn I rise as Khepri, the scarab and sail across the sky in the Boat of Millions of Years.[4] At noon I blaze in the heavens as Ra and at evening I am Ra-atum, the setting sun."

100   "We know all that," said Isis. "If I am to find a spell to drive out this poison, I will have to use your secret name. Say your name and live."

      "My secret name was given to me so that I could sit at ease," moaned Ra, "and fear no living creature. How can I give
105 it away?"

Use Reading Skills

Analyze Cause and Effect

What happens when Isis tells Ra she needs to know his secret name? What effect does this have on Ra? Write the details in your chart.

Build Vocabulary

Ra's pain becomes _unbearable_, and he tells Isis his secret name. What is something else that is unbearable for Ra?

_____

_____

---

4. **Boat of Millions of Years.** Name often used in Egyptian texts for the boat in which Ra sailed across the sky during the day and through the underworld at night

Ra tells his secret name to Isis, which she will tell Horus. What else does Isis need to tell her son?

_____

_____

Isis said nothing and knelt beside the Sun God while his pain mounted. When it became unbearable, Ra ordered the other gods to stand back while he whispered his secret name to Isis. "Now the power of the secret name has passed from my
110 heart to your heart," said Ra wearily. "In time you can give it to your son, but warn him never to betray the secret!"

Isis nodded and began to chant a great spell that drove the poison out of the limbs of Ra and he rose up stronger than before. The Sun God returned to the Boat of Millions of Years
115 and Isis shouted for joy at the success of her plan. She knew now that one day Horus her son would sit on the throne of Egypt and wield the power of Ra. ✦

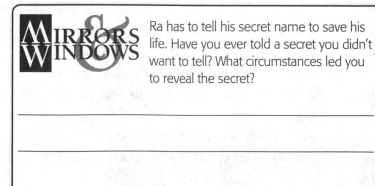

Ra has to tell his secret name to save his life. Have you ever told a secret you didn't want to tell? What circumstances led you to reveal the secret?

_____

_____

_____

READING CHECK

Circle the letter of the correct answer.

1. What does Ra's secret name do?
   A. It helps him move the sun.
   B. It protects him from harm.
   C. It makes him more powerful.

2. What does Isis use to create the snake?
   A. some of Ra's saliva and his power
   B. her own magic and some special clay
   C. water drawn from the great watery abyss

3. Why does Ra call the gods and goddesses to his side?
   A. He is afraid that he is dying.
   B. He wants to figure out who betrayed him.
   C. He doesn't have anyone else to help him.

4. What does Isis ask for?
   A. some of Ra's power
   B. Ra's secret name
   C. magic to cure Ra

5. Why is Isis happy?
   A. She cures Ra of his poison.
   B. She is given strong magic from Ra.
   C. She would be able to give Ra's throne to Horus.

VOCABULARY CHECK

Circle the letter of the correct answer.

1. The *sole* person on the throne is
   A. the oldest person.
   B. the only person.
   C. the first person.

2. Ra is *exalted* because
   A. he is very smart.
   B. he works hard.
   C. he creates everything.

3. Isis is *cunning*, when she acts
   A. cleverly.
   B. jealously.
   C. quickly.

4. Ra is a mighty *deity*, or
   A. god.
   B. human.
   C. creator.

5. Someone who *drivels* is
   A. talking.
   B. drooling.
   C. walking.

ANALYZE LITERATURE: Motivation

What is Isis's motivation for her actions? Does she succeed?

_____

_____

_____

_____

USE READING SKILLS: Analyze Cause and Effect

Review your chart and look at the information you noted. What is one cause that has a significant effect on the entire story?

BUILD VOCABULARY

Complete the following sentences using clues from the text to determine each word's meaning.

1. The *sole* factor that can harm Ra is…

   _____

2. Ra is the *exalted* ruler of everything because…

   _____

3. Isis is *cunning* when she…

   _____

4. One thing a *deity* can do that a human cannot is…

   _____

5. Ra is known to *drivel* because…

   _____

WORK TOGETHER: Reader's Theater

Work in small groups to perform a reader's theater of a section of this story. Decide as a group which section of the story you would like to present. Make sure that there are enough people speaking in that section for everyone in the group to participate. Mark each line with the name or initials of the person who will read that part.

Differentiated Instruction: Literacy & Reading Skills

page E229

Ant and Grasshopper
The Fox and the Crow
The Lion and the Statue

Greek Fables by Aesop

ABOUT THE STORY

In **"Ant and Grasshopper,"** a grasshopper asks an ant for some food during the bitter winter months. In **"The Fox and the Crow,"** a hungry fox tricks a vain crow into giving up a tasty snack. In **"The Lion and the Statue,"** a lion and a man argue about who is mightier. Read the stories to determine what lesson Aesop is trying to teach in each fable.

MAKE CONNECTIONS

Describe one lesson you have learned. How did you learn this lesson?

_____

_____

_____

_____

ANALYZE LITERATURE: Fable

A **fable** is a short story that has a lesson or moral. Fables usually have animals as the main characters, but these animals have human characteristics. As you read each story, write down what lesson or moral is taught in each story.

USE READING SKILLS: Identify Author's Purpose

An author often writes a text for a specific reason. This reason is called the **author's purpose**. When you read a text, you can look for important details that help you determine the author's purpose. Use the chart below to record important details.

Details	Author's Purpose
The wind was keen, and the grasshopper was cold	The author wants us to understand the setting and the characters' reactions to the setting

Differentiated Instruction: Literacy & Reading Skills   © Carnegie Learning, Inc.

PREVIEW VOCABULARY

Key Words and Phrases	Words and Phrases in Context	Definition	Practice
Read each key word and rate it using this scale: ①I don't know this word or phrase at all. ②I've seen this word or phrase before. ③I know this word or phrase and use it.	Read to see how the key word or phrase can be used in a sentence.	Write down what you think the word or phrase means. Then use a dictionary to check your definition.	Practice using the key words and phrases by completing the following sentences.
keen keen (kēn) *adjective* ① ② ③	The wind was **keen** and blew in colder air.		A **keen** remark…
idle i · dle (ī dle) *adjective* ① ② ③	He was **idle** all weekend, enjoying his rest.		The car was **idle** when…
surpass sur · pass (sʉr pas) *verb* ① ② ③	The first team worked to **surpass** their rivals.		If you try to **surpass** something, you…
flatterers flat · ter · ers (flat tʉr ʉrs) *noun* ① ② ③	The **flatterers** told her how much they liked her new dress.		The **flatterers** said that…
overcoming over · coming (ōvʉr kumiŋ) *verb* ① ② ③	The girl was **overcoming** her cold but still sneezed occasionally.		Someone **overcoming** a challenge might…

Ant and Grasshopper

Greek Fables by Aesop

Note the Facts

Why is Ant moving the grain of corn?

_____

_____

Build Vocabulary

Grasshopper says he was not *idle* during the summer. Do you think Ant agrees or disagrees with Grasshopper?

_____

_____

All summer the ant had been working hard, gathering a store of corn for the winter. Grain by grain she had taken it from the fields and stowed it away in a hole in the bank, under a hawthorn bush.

5   One bright, frosty day in winter Grasshopper saw her. She was dragging out a grain of corn to dry it in the sun. The wind was keen, and poor Grasshopper was cold.

"Good morning, Ant," said he. "What a terrible winter it is! I'm half dead with hunger. Please give me just one of your corn

10   grains to eat. I can find nothing, although I've hopped all over the farmyard. There isn't a seed to be found. Spare me a grain, I beg."

"Why haven't you saved anything up?" asked Ant. "I worked hard all through the summer, storing food for the winter. Very glad I am too, for as you say, it's bitterly cold."

15   "I wasn't idle last summer, either," said Grasshopper.

"And what did you do, pray?"

"Why, I spent the time singing," answered Grasshopper. "Every day from dawn till sunset I jumped about or sat in the sun, chirruping to my heart's content."

20

Think and Reflect

Would you help Grasshopper after hearing his story? Why or why not?

_____

"Oh you did, did you?" replied Ant. "Well, since you've sung all summer to keep yourself cheerful, you may dance all winter to keep yourself warm. Not a grain will I give you!"

And she scuttled off into her hole in the bank, while

25   Grasshopper was left cold and hungry. ✤

Analyze Literature

Fable

What lesson is taught in this story?

_____

_____

The Fox and the Crow

Greek Fables by Aesop

A Fox once saw a Crow fly off with a piece of cheese in its beak and settle on a branch of a tree. "That's for me, as I am a Fox," said Master Reynard, and he walked up to the foot of the tree.

"Good day, Mistress Crow," he cried. "How well you are
5 looking today: how glossy your feathers; how bright your eye. I feel sure your voice must surpass that of other birds, just as your figure does; let me hear but one song from you that I may greet you as the Queen of Birds."

The Crow lifted up her head and began to caw her best,
10 but the moment she opened her mouth the piece of cheese fell to the ground, only to be snapped up by Master Fox. "That will do," said he. "That was all I wanted. In exchange for your cheese I will give you a piece of advice for the future—
Do not trust flatterezrs." ❧

The Lion and the Statue

Greek Fables by Aesop

A Man and a Lion were discussing the relative strength of men and lions in general. The Man contended that he and his fellows were stronger than lions by reason of their greater intelligence. "Come now with me," he cried, "and I will soon
5 prove that I am right." So he took him into the public gardens and showed him a statue of Hercules overcoming the Lion and tearing his mouth in two.

"That is all very well," said the Lion, "but proves nothing, for it was a man who made the statue." ❧

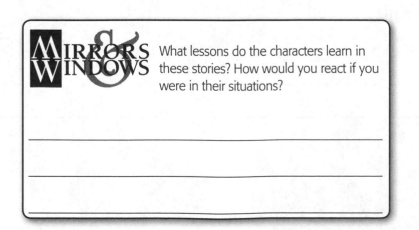

MIRRORS & WINDOWS What lessons do the characters learn in these stories? How would you react if you were in their situations?

_____

_____

Build Vocabulary

Idioms

If someone is *silver tongued*, it means that the person is good at impressing other people with his or her speech. Is Fox silver tongued? Why or why not?

_____

_____

Use Reading Skills

Identify Author's Purpose

We know that fables are used to teach a lesson or a moral. Why did the author italicize the last line of the story? Write your ideas in your author's purpose chart.

Culture Note

In Roman mythology, Hercules is a hero with great strength. In one legend, Hercules is ordered to perform twelve tasks. His first task is to fight the Nemean Lion. He wins the battle, and he wears the skin of the lion as proof of his victory.

READING CHECK

Circle the letter of the correct answer.

1. What does Ant do all summer?
   A. sing songs
   B. sleep all day
   C. gather food

2. Why does Fox talk to Crow?
   A. He wants to see how she is doing.
   B. He wants to get her piece of cheese.
   C. He wants to admire her feathers and songs.

3. What does Fox warn Crow?
   A. She should not trust people who flatter others.
   B. She should not eat the cheese because it is bad.
   C. She should not sit in the tree where others can see her.

4. Why are the man and the lion arguing?
   A. Each thinks he is stronger than the other.
   B. Each thinks the other is a coward in a fight.
   C. Each thinks the statues should be moved somewhere.

5. Why is the lion not impressed by the statue?
   A. It is in the public gardens, not the woods.
   B. It is made by humans, not by any lions.
   C. It has only one lion, but Hercules fought many.

VOCABULARY CHECK

Circle the letter of the correct answer.

1. Wind that is *keen* is
   A. loud and wet.
   B. biting and cold.
   C. gentle and warm.

2. Ant thinks Grasshopper is *idle* because he
   A. plays all summer instead of working.
   B. wants to eat some of her corn and grain.
   C. complains about the bitter cold and wind.

3. Fox says that he thinks Crow *surpassed* all other birds because
   A. she had cheese.
   B. she looked nicer than them.
   C. she opened her mouth to caw.

4. Fox warns Crow of *flatterers*, or people who would
   A. laugh at her.
   B. eat with her.
   C. compliment her.

5. Hercules is o*vercoming* the lion by
   A. defeating it in battle.
   B. standing high above it.
   C. taking it somewhere far away.

ANALYZE LITERATURE: Fable

Which aspects of fables does each story have?

_____

_____

USE READING SKILLS: Identify Author's Purpose

Review your author's purpose chart and look at some of the details you recorded. What is the author's purpose in each fable?

_____

_____

_____

_____

BUILD VOCABULARY

Complete the following sentences using clues from the sentence to determine each word's meaning.

1. The *keen* whistle of a bird…

   _____

2. The workers are often *idle* when the weather is…

   _____

3. I work very hard so that I can *surpass*…

   _____

4. The *flatterers* were telling the movie star…

   _____

5. Although he was shorter than the others, Ken worked on *overcoming*…

   _____

WRITING SKILLS: Writing a Fable

Write your own fable to present to the class. Remember that fables often have animals with human characteristics as the main characters. Think about the lesson or moral you will teach in your story. When you have finished writing your fable, read it aloud to the class.

BEFORE READING

 page E243

Amaterasu

A Japanese Myth retold by Carolyn Swift

ABOUT THE STORY

In **"Amaterasu,"** Susanoo is always complaining. He is god of the sea, but his sister Amaterasu is goddess of the sun, which he thinks is better. Read the myth to see what happens in this difficult relationship between brother and sister.

MAKE CONNECTIONS

How do you react when you feel someone has been unfair to you?

_____

_____

_____

_____

ANALYZE LITERATURE: Characterization

Characterization is the literary techniques writers use to create characters and make them come alive. Writers describe characters in three major ways:

- showing what characters say, do, and think
- showing what other characters say about them
- showing their physical features.

Look for the ways the author describes the characters in this Japanese myth.

USE READING SKILLS: Draw Conclusions

When you **draw conclusions,** you study pieces of information and then decide what that information means. It is helpful to keep track of details from a story, and then decide what conclusions to draw. Record your details and conclusions from the story in the chart below. An example has been done for you.

Details	My Conclusions
After Amaterasu makes daughters, Susanoo says "I can do better than that!" and makes sons.	Susanoo is trying to prove that males are superior to females.

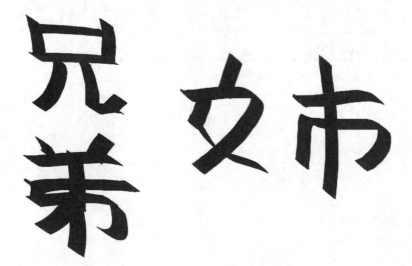

PREVIEW VOCABULARY

Key Words and Phrases Read each key word and rate it using this scale: ①I don't know this word or phrase at all. ②I've seen this word or phrase before. ③I know this word or phrase and use it.	Words and Phrases in Context Read to see how the key word or phrase can be used in a sentence.	Definition Write down what you think the word or phrase means. Then use a dictionary to check your definition.	Practice Practice using the key words and phrases by completing the following sentences.
misery mis • e • ry ('mi zə rē) *noun* ① ② ③	I have such a bad headache; I'm in **misery.**		The opposite of **misery** is…
grumble grum • ble (grʉm′ bəl) *verb* ① ② ③	He **grumbled** a rude response.		People might **grumbled** if they feel…
suspiciously sus • pi • cious • ly (sə 'spi shəs lē) *adverb* ① ② ③	She tasted the new food **suspiciously.**		Someone might act **suspiciously** if…
fondness fond • ness (fän[d] ′ nəs) *noun* ① ② ③	All the children have a **fondness** for that kind of game.		I have a **fondness** for…
rage e • go • tism ('rāj) *noun* ① ② ③	The football player left the field in a **rage.**		Something that might put a person in a **rage** is…

Differentiated Instruction: Literacy & Reading Skills

Amaterasu

A Japanese Myth retold by Carolyn Swift

Back in the mists of time there lived a boy called Susanoo. His father and mother were the first people on earth, but then his father became Lord of the Heavens and his mother Lady of the Underworld.

5   Susanoo himself lived with his brothers and sisters on the bridge which linked heaven and earth, but he was always complaining. He complained about not being able to visit his mother, even though his father explained to him that if he once went to the underworld he would never be able to come back,

10 and he complained even more when his sister Amaterasu was given the jewelled necklace of heaven and made goddess of the sun, while he was given only corals and made god of the sea. Finally his father became sick of his constant moanings and groanings.

15   "I don't want to see your face around Heaven any more," he told him. "You have the whole earth and sea to play around in so there's no need for you to make all our lives a misery up here."

    "Oh, all right," Susanoo **grumbled**, "but first I must say

20 goodbye to Amaterasu."

    So off he stumped to look for her. Being in a bad mood, he shook every mountain he passed so that rocks crashed down the slopes, and he stamped his feet so that the earth quaked. Hearing all the noise, Amaterasu was frightened. She took up

25 her bow and arrow so that, when her younger brother arrived, he found himself facing the drawn bow of a fierce-looking warrior.

    "You can put that thing down," he told her. "I come in peace."

30   "Prove it," she said suspiciously, not taking her eyes off him.

    Susanoo handed her his sword. She took it from him and broke it into three pieces. Then, before he could complain, she blew on them and turned them into three beautiful little girls.

    "One day these three little daughters of mine will bring new

35 life into the world," she told him, "while your sword could only have brought death."

Note the Facts

Who are Susanoo and Amaterasu's parents?

_____

_____

Culture Note

Amaterasu is the sun goddess in the *Shinto* religion of Japan. Japan is called the "land of the rising sun" because the emperor of Japan is said to be a descendant of Amaterasu. This connection to the Amaterasu myth is also displayed in the country's flag, which is a red sun on a white background.

grum·ble (grum´ bəl) *v.*, mumble unhappily

Build Vocabulary

What is Susanoo *grumbling* about?

_____

_____

Why does Susanoo visit
Amaterasu?

_____

_____

Characterization
What characteristics do
Amaterasu and Susanoo show?

_____

_____

Draw Conclusions
What happens when
Amaterasu hides in the cave?
How does this affect the world?
Write the conclusions you can
make in your chart.

"I can do better than that!" Susanoo boasted. "Give me the necklaces you're wearing."

So Amaterasu unclasped the five necklaces and gave them
40 to her brother. Then he blew on them and turned them into five little boys.

"Now I have five sons," he said.

"They were made out of my necklaces so they should be my sons!" Amaterasu snapped.

45 "But your daughters were made from my sword," Susanoo argued.

"That's different!" Amaterasu told him.

At that Susanoo lost his temper. He tore up all the rice fields that Amaterasu had been carefully ripening and caused such
50 destruction that the frightened goddess ran and hid in a cave, blocking the entrance with a large stone.

Think and Reflect

When you are afraid or upset, do you prefer to be alone or with others? What does Amaterasu prefer?

_____

Because Amaterasu was the sun goddess, this meant that the world was suddenly plunged into darkness. Without the sun's heat the land became very cold and nothing grew in field
55 or forest. Worse still, the evil spirits took advantage of the darkness to get up to all sorts of wickedness. It was a disaster. Something had to be done, so all the good spirits gathered together in a dry river bed to try to decide what to do.

"We must tempt Amaterasu to come out of the cave,"
60 said one.

"And block up the entrance the minute she does, so she can't go back into it again," added another.

"But what would tempt her to come out?" asked a third.

"We must put everything she likes most outside," replied
65 the first.

"And what does she like most?" the third asked.

"Seeing her sunny face reflected in the lake," answered a fourth.

"But we can't bring the lake up to the cave!" objected
70 the third.

"Then we must make something that will reflect her face the way the lake does and put that outside the cave," suggested a fifth.

75 "I don't know what we could make that would do that," the third grumbled, "and anyway, how will she know it's there unless we can get her to come out of the cave in the first place?"

At that they all looked thoughtful. No one spoke for a while.

"I know!" the second suddenly shouted in triumph.

80 "She always used to come out every morning as soon as she heard the cock crow. We must get all the cocks to crow outside the cave."

So they all put their heads together to try to think what would reflect the sun like the waters of the lake. After trying all

85 sorts of things in vain, they finally managed to invent a mirror, or looking-glass. This they hung from the branch of a japonica tree[1] immediately opposite the cave and, knowing Amaterasu's **fondness** for jewellery, they hung jewelled necklaces from the other branches.

90 When all was ready, they gathered outside the cave with every cock they could find. First they chanted prayers. Then they gave the signal and all the cocks began to crow. Not satisfied with that, everyone present began to sing and dance, led by the goddess Ama no Uzume[2] doing a tap-dance on an

95 upturned tub.

> **fond·ness** (fän[d]′ nəs) *n.*, affection; having a liking

Build Vocabulary

What does Amaterasu have a *fondness* for?

_____

_____

---

1. **japonica tree.** Any tree, shrub, or plant associated with the Far East
2. **Ama no Uzume.** Goddess of dawn and mirth

How do the gods get Amaterasu to come out of the cave?

_____

_____

Wondering what all the noise was about, Amaterasu peeped out of the cave and at once saw her own face reflected in the mirror. She had never seen a looking-glass before, so she thought the people must have found another sun to replace
100 her and ran from the cave in a rage. The others immediately stretched ropes across the mouth of the cave to stop her from going back into it again, but there was no need. By then she had discovered that it was her own shining face looking back at her. She was delighted by this and by the necklaces, as well
105 as the singing and dancing for, truth to tell, she had begun to feel lonely in her cave. So once more the sun's bright rays lit the earth and the trees and flowers and rice began to grow again in its heat. Then everyone suddenly remembered the cause of all the trouble.
110 "If Susanoo had stayed out of heaven when his father told him to, this would never have happened!" they shouted angrily, and went off in a body to look for him. When they found him, they cut off his pigtail as punishment and threw him out of heaven by force. ✦

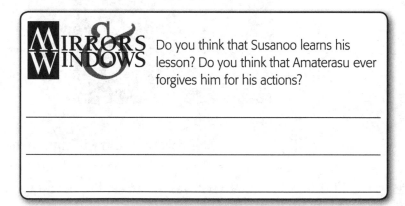

MIRRORS & WINDOWS Do you think that Susanoo learns his lesson? Do you think that Amaterasu ever forgives him for his actions?

_____

_____

_____

READING CHECK

Circle the letter of the correct answer.

1. What is Amaterasu's gift from her father?
   A. a sword
   B. a necklace
   C. a mirror

2. How are the sons of Susanoo created?
   A. He makes them from his sword.
   B. He makes them from Amaterasu's necklace.
   C. He makes them with Amaterasu's help.

3. Why does Amaterasu hide in a cave?
   A. She wants to see her mother.
   B. She wants to be goddess of the sea.
   C. She wants to get away from Susanoo.

4. What do the gods create for Amaterasu?
   A. a lake
   B. a necklace
   C. a mirror

5. What is Susanoo's punishment?
   A. He is thrown from heaven.
   B. He is sent to the underworld.
   C. He is ordered to apologize to Amaterasu.

VOCABULARY CHECK

Circle the letter of the correct answer.

1. Someone who is in *misery* is
   A. very sad.
   B. very tired.
   C. very happy.

2. When Susanoo *grumbles,* he
   A. shouts in anger.
   B. laughs at his sister.
   C. complains under his breath.

3. When Amaterasu *suspiciously* talks to Susanoo, she is
   A. afraid that he is angry at her.
   B. doubtful that he is telling the truth.
   C. angry that he has come to visit her.

4. Amaterasu has a *fondness* for jewelry, meaning
   A. she likes wearing it.
   B. she gives it to her friends.
   C. she thinks it is troublesome.

5. When Amaterasu comes out in a *rage*, she
   A. is in a bad mood.
   B. is afraid of her brother.
   C. is curious about all the noise.

ANALYZE LITERATURE: Characterization

What traits do Amaterasu and Susanoo have in this story? How do they show these traits?

_____

_____

_____

_____

USE READING SKILLS: Draw Conclusions

Review your draw conclusions chart and look at some of the details you noted. What can you conclude from these details?

_____

_____

BUILD VOCABULARY

Complete the following sentences using clues from the text to determine each word's meaning.

1. The earth *quaked* and the ground…

_____

2. Amaterasu *snapped* at her brother by…

_____

3. Although their first efforts were *in vain*, the gods finally…

_____

4. *Truth to tell,* when Amaterasu wasn't happy in the cave…

_____

5. When the gods *went off in a body* to find Susanoo, they…

_____

SPEAKING & LISTENING SKILLS: Narration Versus Speech

Find sections in the text that include both speech and narration. Read the text aloud, changing your voice to show when a character is speaking and when the story is being narrated. Try reading the text in different ways. Think about how each character would sound, and try to read the speech in a way that the character might talk.

English Language Development

Dialect

Every language has a number of different dialects. A **dialect** is a form of language spoken by people of a particular area, time, or group.

People in the United States speak mainly English, but people in California may use the language differently than people across the country in Pennsylvania. They may have their own words, pronunciations, spellings, and grammar.

For example, the word for a carbonated drink is different throughout the United States. Some people say "soda," while others say "coke" or "pop" depending on their regional dialect.

Authors use dialect in a character's dialogue to reflect the way the character would sound when speaking, as with Lester in the story "The 11:59." Sometimes reading dialect aloud helps to clarify the meaning.

The words and phrases from Column A (shown below) are examples of dialect in "The 11:59." Match the dialect form in Column A to the correct Standard English form in Column B.

Column A: Dialect	Column B: Standard English
___ 1. Y'all know Tip	A. It doesn't matter
___ 2. Ain't no way	B. I never did let him forget it
___ 3. Don't matter	C. I didn't make it any better
___ 4. I'm gon' try	D. It keeps perfect train time
___ 5. I didn't make it no better	E. I have come to remind you
___ 6. Keeps perfect train time	F. There is no way
___ 7. Come to remind you	G. Do you all know Tip
___ 8. Never did let him forget it	H. I'm going to try

With a partner, read aloud this excerpt from the story "The 11:59." Then, rewrite the underlined phrases in Standard English.

> "Lester," a young porter asked, "<u>you know anybody who ever heard</u> the whistle of the 11:59 and lived to tell—"
>
> "Not a living soul!"
>
> *Laughter.*
>
> "Well," began one of the men, "<u>wonder will we have to make up berths</u> on *that* train?"
>
> "If it's an overnight trip to heaven, <u>you can best be believing</u> there's bound to be a few of us making up the berths," another answered.
>
> "Shucks," a card player stopped to put in. "They say even up in heaven <u>*we* the ones gon' be</u> keeping all that gold and silver polished."

you know anybody who ever heard:

_____

wonder will we have to make up berths:

_____

you can best be believing:

_____

we the ones gon' be:

_____

Denotation and Connotation

Most words can have two meanings: **denotation** and **connotation**.

Denotation is the dictionary definition of a word, or the true meaning. Some words make you think of positive things, while other words make you think of negative things. **Connotation** refers to whether a word is considered positive or negative.

Sometimes context clues can help to determine whether a word has a positive connotation or a negative connotation. Other times, knowing the denotation of a word can help to determine whether it has a positive or negative connotation.

Review the examples of denotation and connotation below.

- He enjoys talking in front of people because he is <u>confident</u>.

Denotation:	feeling or showing belief in oneself; self-assured
Connotation:	positive

- He enjoys talking in front of people because he is <u>arrogant</u>.

Denotation:	having an exaggerated sense of one's own importance or abilities
Connotation:	negative

Complete the exercise on denotation and connotation with a partner. The sentences in the exercise are from the short story "The Foghorn." Be sure to use a print or online dictionary to identify the denotation of the underlined word. If need be, refer to the story to find more context clues to determine the connotation of the underlined word.

Sentence from "The Foghorn"	Denotation	Connotation
"Something made them swim in and lie in the bay, sort of trembling and staring up at the tower light going red, white, red, white across them so I could see their <u>funny</u> eyes."		This word/phrase makes me think of _____. So, I think it has a _____ _____ connotation.
"The sound of <u>isolation</u>, a viewless sea, a cold night, apartness."		This word/phrase makes me think of _____. So, I think it has a _____ _____ connotation.

"But the next day, unexpectedly, the fog lifted, the sun came out <u>fresh</u>, the sky was as blue as a painting."		This word/phrase makes me think of _____. So, I think it has a _____ _____ connotation.
"It gave a sort of <u>rumble</u>, like a volcano."		This word/phrase makes me think of _____. So, I think it has a _____ _____ connotation.
"The next year they built a new lighthouse, but by that time I had a job in the little town and a wife and a good small warm house that glowed <u>yellow</u> on autumn nights, the doors locked, the chimney puffing smoke."		This word/phrase makes me think of _____. So, I think it has a _____ _____ connotation.

With your partner, find two more sentences from the short story "The Foghorn." One sentence should have a word with a positive connotation and one sentence should have a word with a negative connotation. Then, fill in the chart below. Copy the sentence from the text, underline the word, find the denotation of the word, and indicate whether you believe it has a positive or negative connotation, and why.

Sentence from "The Foghorn"	Denotation	Connotation

Differentiated Instruction: English Language Development

◈ **Uncle Tony's Goat,** page E25　　　　　　　　　**ADVANCED/BRIDGING**

Point of View

Every story contains a point of view. A **point of view** tells the reader about a character's thoughts, opinions, and feelings. The point of view may be from a specific character, or it may be from a narrator outside of the story.

Pair up with a partner and share parts of the story "Uncle Tony's Goat" you did or did not like. How did the narrator's point of view lead you to see things a certain way?

Based on your discussion, take on the point of view of one of the characters (human or animal) and rewrite a section of the story. What did you change from the original story? How is the point of view different? How did you make it different?

After you finish, share it with your partner and explain the reasons behind your changes.

_____

_____

_____

_____

_____

_____

_____

_____

_____

_____

Hollywood and the Pits, page 96   **BEGINNING/EMERGING**

Idioms

An **idiom** is an expression that has a meaning separate from the individual words that make it up.

For example, saying that someone is "on the ball" has nothing to do with being on a ball. Rather, it means that the person is knowledgeable or quick to understand.

Because the words and meanings are not closely related, idioms can be unpredictable and difficult to understand.

In this activity, first illustrate the idioms given on the left side of the chart below. Then, look up the real meaning of the idiom. Finally, illustrate the meaning on the right side of the chart. The first one is done for you.

IDIOM	MEANING
 let the cat out of the bag	 _____ to reveal a secret _____
on the fence	_____
see eye to eye	_____

all ears	_____

Using the bank of idioms below, fill in the sentences from the short story "Hollywood and the Pits." There are more items in the bank than are needed.

Idioms		
speak for myself	miss the boat	give me a hand
made up for lost time	pass for five or six	time flies
have what it takes	break a leg	blow off steam

1. Until I was fifteen, it never occurred to me that one day I wouldn't get parts or that I might not "_____."

2. When I was nine years old, I could _____.

3. But when I turned fifteen, it was as if my body, which hadn't grown for so many years, suddenly _____.

4. She wanted me to _____.

Amigo Brothers, page 117   **INTERMEDIATE/EXPANDING**

Slang

Slang is a kind of informal language. Often, authors use slang to create playfulness in a text or to establish a lively tone. Sometimes, slang is used because informal words capture a meaning better than Standard English. Slang is used mostly in spoken language or in dialogue within a text.

> Example:
> Slang: *What's up?*
> Standard English: *What are you doing?*

Unfamiliar slang can be difficult to understand, but context clues can help to clarify meaning. For example, read this sentence from the short story "Amigo Brothers." The slang word is underlined.

> Antonio glanced at Felix who kept his eyes purposely straight ahead, pausing from time to time to do some fancy leg work while throwing <u>one-twos</u> followed by upper cuts to an imaginary jaw.

The word "throwing" helps to provide context for "one-twos." The rest of the sentence, "followed by upper cuts to an imaginary jaw," also provides context. So, the slang word "one-twos" means punches.

Complete the following activity. Read the sentences from the story "Amigo Brothers" that include the use of slang words. With a partner, use context clues to discuss the definition of the underlined slang word in each sentence. Then, re-write the sentence in Standard English. You can go back to the story for additional context if needed.

1. "Felix got up as fast as he could in his own corner, groggy but <u>still game</u>."

   _____

2. "Walking the streets had not relaxed him, neither had the fight <u>flick</u>."

   _____

3. "Felix decided to <u>split</u> to his aunt's."

   _____

4. "Despite the fact that he was Puerto Rican like them, they eyed him as a stranger to their <u>turf</u>."

   _____

   _____

Now, read the three sentences below that use the slang word "heavy." How is "heavy" used in each sentence? Discuss with your partner, and then write a description of the definition and how it is used in each sentence.

1. "Watch yourself Felix. I hear there's some <u>heavy dudes</u> up in the Bronx."
2. Antonio was spending some <u>heavy time</u> on his rooftop.
3. Whenever they had met in the ring for sparring sessions, it had always been <u>hot and heavy</u>.

_____

_____

_____

_____

_____

Why do you think the author chose to use slang words in both the dialogue and narration in this story? What does that say about the relationship between the reader, narrator, and characters? Write a paragraph exploring these questions.

_____

_____

_____

_____

_____

_____

The White Umbrella, page 131   **ADVANCED/BRIDGING**

Figurative Language

Figurative language helps authors express ideas in a creative way. **Similes** are a type of figurative language that compares two things using the words *like* or *as*. For example, *solid as a rock* or *swims like a fish* are similes.

Here are some examples of similes from the story "The White Umbrella." With a partner, discuss the images that come to mind for these similes. Together, come up with another simile that could describe the mental image.

1. "The umbrella glowed like a scepter on the blue carpet…"

   _____

   _____

2. "I watched as the branches of Miss Crosman's big willow tree started to sway; they had all been trimmed to exactly the same height off the ground, so that they looked beautiful, like hair in the wind."

   _____

   _____

3. "Her face looked dry and crusty, like day-old frosting."

   _____

   _____

Poets also use similes to create mental images—readers get a clear picture of what is being described.

Independently, write a short poem about "The White Umbrella" using at least two similes. You can write about the story's characters, plot, or any specific detail. Your poem does not have to rhyme.

_____

_____

_____

_____

_____

_____

_____

_____

Asking Questions

The author of the story "An American Childhood" describes her experiences of going to the Homewood Library. She was fascinated by the materials she found there.

Libraries are a great resource for research, recreation, and entertainment. They carry hundreds or even thousands of books written by as many individual authors. No matter what interests you, there is bound to be a book on the subject.

Library materials are often divided into sections or categories. Materials are organized according to the content or subject. This makes things easier for visitors to find.

Complete the following activity about library categories.

In small groups, come up with a list of ten categories you would find in a library. Be sure to include resources other than books. Two examples have been provided for you.

Library Subject Categories
mystery books: *The Mystery of the Missing Jewel*
newspapers: *The New York Times*

Now, use this list to write one example that would be found in each category. Write each example to the right of each category. You can use a real title, or you can invent a title, as long as it fits the category. Examples have been provided in the chart above.

What do you think it is like to be an author? Split up into pairs and pretend one person is an author and the other is a reporter interviewing the author. Have the reporter ask at least five questions about the author's work and experience. When you are the reporter, record your questions here. Then, switch roles.

_____

_____

_____

_____

_____

Who is your favorite author? What do you like about his or her writing? What questions would like to ask him or her? Write at least two questions below. If time allows, compare your questions with a partner's questions.

_____

_____

_____

_____

Word Forms

Language is influenced by the world around it and is always changing. Words and phrases that were common one hundred years ago are not necessarily popular or even accepted today. An example of one of these changes is a shift from "gendered" language to "non-gendered" language.

Gendered language reflects one sex (male or female) more than the other. In the past, it has been used in the names of occupations to describe the sex of the person performing the job, such as a *policeman* (masculine) or *policewoman* (feminine). Even the terms *waiter* (masculine) and *waitress* (feminine) are considered gendered language.

With gendered language, the word *man* can refer to people in general when used in words like *mankind*.

In recent years, though, it has become less accepted to use gendered language. Instead we choose to use more gender-neutral words, known as **non-gendered language**. For example, *humankind* now replaces *mankind*. Or, from the example above, *waiter* and *waitress* are now replaced with *server*.

The essay "The Eternal Frontier" was written in a time when it was normal to use gendered language. With a partner, read the text again and find examples of gendered language. Together, decide on non-gendered equivalents that might be used today.

Then, complete the following exercise. Below are more examples of gendered language. With your partner, write gender-neutral equivalents for each term.

Gendered Language	Non-Gendered Equivalent
freshman	
man-made	
the common man	
chairman	
mailman	
foreman	
steward, stewardess	
congressman	

With your partner, discuss the possible reasons behind the shift from gendered to non-gendered language. Why do you think it has changed? Is it an important change? Why or why not? Then, discuss whether gendered language exists in languages other than English. Does it exist in your native language? If so, why might it exist?

Frequently Confused Words

It is easy to see how two words that look alike can be confused for one another.

For example, the words *principal* and *principle* are often confused though they are spelled differently and have two separate meanings.

> The director of Lincoln School was called the *principal*.

> The *principle* reason we were at Lincoln was to become good Americans.

Principal means the head of a school, and *principle* means essential, or extremely important.

Be sure to use the correct word and spelling to convey the meaning of a word. One letter can be the difference between two words with completely different definitions.

Circle the correct word to use in each sentence. Use a print or online dictionary to look up definitions if necessary.

1. The power outage affected/effected hundreds of people.
2. The group's morale/moral was high.
3. The manner/manor was at the end of a winding driveway.
4. Due to inclement weather, the game will be played at a latter/later date.
5. He cannot vote in the election because he is a miner/minor.
6. She advocated for animals to be treated in a humane/human way.

For the words NOT circled in the activity above, write a sentence that shows the correct use for each.

1. _____

2. _____

3. _____

4. _____

5. _____

6. _____

Can you think of other frequently confused words? Do you have a strategy to remember which word is which? Share with a small group some tricks that have worked for you. Use the space below to take notes.

_____

_____

_____

_____

_____

Differentiated Instruction: English Language Development

Prepositional Phrases

A **preposition** is a word that introduces additional information or descriptive information in a sentence.

Review the chart below of common prepositions. Categories like time, place, and direction/movement may help you remember how to identify them.

Prepositions of time:	after, around, at, before, between, during, from, on, until, at, in, from, since, for, during, within
Prepositions of place:	above, across, against, along, among, around, at, behind, below, beneath, beside, between, beyond, by, down, in, inside, into, near, off, on, opposite, out, over, past, through, to, toward, under, underneath
Prepositions of direction/ movement:	at, for, on, to, in, into, onto, between
Other types of prepositions:	by, with, of, for, by, like, as

A preposition cannot stand on its own in a sentence. It is always part of a prepositional phrase.

A **prepositional phrase** is made up of the preposition and the object the preposition describes, along with any related adjectives or adverbs in between.

The object the preposition describes is the noun that follows the preposition.

Here are some examples of prepositional phrases. The preposition is underlined. The object the preposition describes is in bold.

<u>on</u> the same **scale**   <u>at</u> the **center**   <u>from</u> the other **side**

<u>to</u> the **store**   <u>down</u> a long **hallway**   <u>before</u> the next **storm**

Prepositional phrases can act as adjectives or adverbs in a sentence.

- A prepositional phrase that acts as an adjective will answer the question: *Which one?*

    Example: The book <u>with the tattered cover</u> has been read many times.
    Which book? the book with the tattered cover

- A prepositional phrase that acts as an adverb will answer the questions:
  How, when, where, or *why?*

    Example: The balloon drifted <u>up the stairs</u>.
    Where did the balloon drift? up the stairs

Complete the following activity with a partner. Read each sentence carefully. Then for each sentence, write the prepositional phrase. Then write the preposition and the object the preposition describes. Refer back to the chart for support. The first one is done for you.

1. The present inside the big box is mine.

    prepositional phrase: *inside the big box*

    preposition: *inside*

    object of preposition: *the big box*

2. I made a cake for the party.

    prepositional phrase: _____

    preposition:_____

    object of preposition: _____

3. The dolphins were born in captivity.

    prepositional phrase: _____

    preposition:_____

    object of preposition: _____

4. We need to cut the damaged branches in that tree.

    prepositional phrase: _____

    preposition: _____

    object of preposition: _____

5. The tiger crept slowly over the grass.

    prepositional phrase: _____

    preposition: _____

    object of preposition: _____

6. The snow turned the forest into a wonderland.

   prepositional phrase: _____

   preposition: _____

   object of preposition: _____

Read the sentences below. The prepositional phrases are underlined. With your partner, determine whether the prepositional phrase acts as an adjective or an adverb.

1. Tell me the story <u>about the dragon slayer</u>. _____

2. We will order pizza <u>during halftime</u>. _____

3. <u>After breakfast,</u> I will take a bike ride. _____

4. Racing <u>toward the finish line</u>, Sarah realized she just might win. _____

5. I bought the shorts <u>with the blue stripes</u>. _____

The Face of the Deep is Frozen, page 280   **INTERMEDIATE/EXPANDING**

Jargon and Context Clues

Jargon is specialized vocabulary used by people in a particular group or for a specific activity.

People who work in the same profession or industry may use jargon to talk about business. A sport or hobby will have different jargon associated with it that participants will be familiar with and use regularly.

Examples:
- Computer Technician's jargon: operating system, CPU, driver, virus, URL
- Football player's jargon: scramble, blitz, offside, picked off, kickoff

Unfamiliar jargon can be difficult to understand, but context clues can sometimes help to clarify meaning.

The essay "The Face of the Deep is Frozen" includes jargon related to exploration and geological science.

Look at this example from paragraph 3.

"…every year 5,000 to 10,000 icebergs 'calve,' or break off, from the ice sheets into the surrounding ocean."

In this sentence, the word *calve* is defined as *break off*.

Complete the exercise below with a partner. Define the following examples of jargon from the text by looking for context clues. Use a print or online dictionary, or use the vocabulary footnotes in the text if the context does not lead to a clear understanding.

berg (paragraph 1):	
stores (paragraph 7):	
cache (paragraph 10):	
erodes (paragraph 3):	
expedition (paragraph 8):	
floes (paragraph 1):	

Have a discussion with your partner and answer these questions:

- How is jargon different from slang or dialect?
- What effect does the use of jargon have on the text?
- When have you come across jargon you had never heard before? What was this like? How did you learn the meaning of the jargon?
- What kind of jargon do you know? Think about a hobby, sport, or game you like, and the jargon you might use. Write one paragraph using at least three examples of jargon. Try to include context clues for each example of jargon. Be sure to use complete sentences.

_____

_____

_____

_____

_____

_____

_____

Make a separate vocabulary list defining each example of jargon you used in your paragraph. Then, exchange paragraphs with a partner and see what jargon you can define using context clues before checking your vocabulary lists.

Compound Words/Art Activity

A **compound word** is a word made of two smaller words that are joined together. Both words keep their meaning and contribute to the new word to form one idea. Dividing a compound word into its two parts can help clarify its meaning.

Below are a few examples of compound words.

fireproof	fire + proof
gateway	gate + way
thunderstorm	thunder + storm

Complete the following exercise. Look at the examples of compound words from the article "Astonishing Animals." Divide each compound word into its word parts. Then, write your own definition of the compound word. Be sure to include the part of speech. Use a print or online dictionary to check your definition and make corrections as needed. The first one is done for you.

Compound word	Parts	Definition
anglerfish	angler + fish	*noun*: a fish with a body part that resembles a fishing pole which it uses to lure prey
overbite		
extraordinary		
fisherman		
widespread		
supersensitive		
deepwater		

What other compound words do you know? Come up with a list of ten compound words. These words may be in English or in your native language. When you finish, compare your list with a partner. If time allows, illustrate your two favorite compound words from your list.

_____   _____

_____   _____

_____   _____

_____   _____

_____   _____

Hyphenated Words

Sometimes, authors use hyphens between words. A **hyphen** (-) joins words together. This means that all of the words connected to a hyphen contribute to a larger, combined word meaning.

When an author uses hyphens between words that come before a noun, the hyphenated word is known as a **compound adjective**. A compound adjective, like a regular adjective, describes the noun. A compound adjective gives very specific details about a noun.

A compound adjective can be made from a variety of words and parts of speech.

Compound Adjective	Words in the Compound Adjective	Explanation	Meaning
a world-famous artist	noun and adjective: *world* and *famous*	The noun *world* and the adjective *famous* modify the noun *artist*. What kind of artist? a *world-famous* artist	known throughout the world
a pale-blue scarf	adjective and adjective: *pale* and *blue*	Both of the adjectives *pale* and *blue* modify the noun *scarf*. What kind of scarf? a *pale-blue* scarf	extremely light blue
a family-owned business	noun and verb (past participle): *family* and *owned*	The noun *family* and the past participle verb *owned* modify the noun *business*. What kind of business? a *family-owned* business	business owned by a particular family

TIP: *If you aren't sure whether two words need a hyphen, imagine the word "and" between them.*

Does the sentence make sense using the word "and" between the two words? If so, then it probably doesn't need a hyphen. If the sentence doesn't make sense using the word "and," then the two words probably need a hyphen between them.

Try this out with the examples above.

Differentiated Instruction: English Language Development

Authors also use hyphens to combine two nouns in an unusual way.

In the poem "Feel Like a Bird," May Swenson combines two nouns to create original and unusual words. For example, Swenson creates the following words by combining two nouns:

- star-toes
- finger-beak

Complete the following exercise with a partner. Read each sentence carefully. Then, circle the noun that the underlined words are describing. Determine whether a hyphen is needed between the underlined words. If the words need a hyphen, insert the hyphens where needed. Refer back to the chart for support.

1. The <u>play group</u> of toddlers enjoyed the <u>sugar free</u> juice served after recess.

2. A <u>chestnut brown</u> rabbit darted out from behind a <u>large old</u> tree.

3. Underneath the <u>star speckled</u> sky, the moon was shining brightly.

4. The <u>hot sticky</u> greenhouse reminded her of a tropical rainforest.

5. Before he even realized it, a <u>multi colored</u> lizard crawled onto his <u>short sleeve</u> shirt.

6. The art teacher mixed two paints to make a pretty <u>ocean blue</u> shade of teal.

7. The movie theater in town plays <u>old classic</u> movies on Sunday afternoons.

8. She ordered a <u>three cheese</u> pizza for her <u>pirate party</u> sleepover.

If time allows, identify the hyphenated words in "Feel Like a Bird" with your partner. Discuss the meanings of each hyphenated word.

Formal and Informal Language

Formal language is used when writing or speaking to someone other than a close friend or family member. For example, when you write an essay for school, you use formal language.

Informal language is a relaxed way of talking to someone. Typically, informal language includes slang words, contractions, or other shortened word forms. Most people use informal language when they talk to close contacts, such as a brother or a best friend.

The poem "Mother to Son" is an example of informal language. The line "So, boy, don't you turn back" offers advice from a mother to a son in a relaxed and familiar way.

It is important to remember that formal language and informal language are aimed at different audiences. They also have different tones.

Compare formal language and informal language in the chart below.

Formal Language	Informal Language
• Standard English often with polite language; less personal	• Casual, friendly language; personal
• Used to communicate with people you might not be familiar with and/or hold in high respect, such as teachers, principals, bosses, police officers, firefighters	• Used to communicate with people you are familiar with and/or are comfortable around, such as friends, family, close relatives
• Does not include first-person pronouns (I, We, Us)	• Often includes first-person pronouns (I, We, Us)
• Does not include figurative language; consists of very clear and precise language	• Could include figurative language, sayings, or idioms

Complete the following exercise. Read the example in the left column. Then, place a checkmark next to the type of language that should be used. Use the chart above for support.

Example	Formal Language	Informal Language
1. A letter to your Town Councilwoman about creating a new park		
2. A blog post to your aunt about getting together for a family reunion		
3. A text message to your brother about baseball practice		
4. A report for your science class about ecosystems		
5. A note left for your friend about hanging out after school		

Imagine you need to write an e-mail to two different audiences about the same topic. You will need to use formal language in one of your e-mails and informal language in the other. Choose a topic that can be used in both e-mails. Make sure to identify your target audience at the beginning of each e-mail.

After you write your e-mails, read them to a partner. Have your partner guess the kind of language used in each e-mail. Ask your partner to explain how he or she identified the type of language used.

_____

_____

_____

_____

_____

Multiple-Meaning Words

Some words have more than one meaning. These words are called **multiple-meaning words**. Because they have more than one meaning, readers rely on context clues to figure out the meaning of these words.

Example: *The scorching desert is no place to desert a friend.*

Desert is a multiple-meaning word. The first meaning in the sentence relates to a hot, arid place. The second meaning in the sentence relates to leaving someone behind.

Multiple-meaning words may sound the same or may have different pronunciations. Some are different parts of speech, while others are the same part of speech.

Review the multiple-meaning words from the poem "How to Eat a Poem." Circle the correct meaning used in the poem.

Multiple-Meaning Word from "How to Eat a Poem"	Meaning #1	Meaning #2
pick	verb: grab or take hold of	noun: the act of choosing something
run	verb: move at a fast pace	verb: flow or drip
core	noun: the tough center of a fruit	noun: the central or most important part of something
pit	noun: a large hole in the ground	noun: a hard seed in a fruit
seed	verb: sow or plant things in an area of land	noun: a small object that produces more plants
skin	noun: the outer covering on a human	noun: the peel of a vegetable or a fruit

Many times, multiple-meaning words have more than two meanings—they may have three or four or five meanings. It is the reader's job to determine the exact meaning of a multiple-meaning word.

Write a short poem using at least four multiple-meaning words. Then, find a partner and exchange poems. Have your partner identify the multiple-meaning words in your poem and determine the exact word meaning.

_____

_____

_____

_____

_____

_____

_____

_____

Occupations

An **occupation** is a job or a profession. It is the line of work a person performs. An occupation can be very challenging, yet extremely rewarding.

The poem "Ancestors" is about occupations our earlier relatives may have had. An **ancestor** is a family member who was born long before you. Your grandparents, great-grandparents, and great-great grandparents are examples of your ancestors. Read the following stanza from the poem "Ancestors."

> My own ancestor
> (research reveals)
> was a swineherd
> who tended the pigs
> in the Royal Pigstye
> and slept in the mud
> among the hogs.

Think about the occupations your current family members have had. Ask yourself the following questions, then discuss with a partner:

- What kinds of jobs have they had?
- What kinds of tasks were involved with each occupation?
- How might these occupations have shaped your current family members?
- Do you think your ancestors were influenced by their occupations? Why or why not?

Complete the activity below. Look at the image in the left column. Identify the occupation in the right column. Make notes about your conclusions. The first one is done for you.

I think this image represents the following occupation:
a bus driver

Here's why I think that:

- The lady is wearing a seat belt and is behind a steering wheel.
- She is wearing a safety vest.
- There is a machine that takes money and radio equipment, and I've seen these on city buses.

This occupation might shape a person because
a bus driver meets new people everyday.

I think this image represents the following occupation:

_____

Here's why I think that:

- _____

- _____

- _____

This occupation might shape a person because

_____

I think this image represents the following occupation:

_____

Here's why I think that:

- _____

- _____

- _____

This occupation might shape a person because

_____

I think this image represents the following occupation:

_____

Here's why I think that:

- _____

- _____

- _____

This occupation might shape a person because

_____

With a partner, read the statements below. Based on these clues, try to identify the occupation being described. Use resources, such as a print or online dictionary or the Internet, to help if you are unsure of a word.

1. My occupation has existed for many, many years in nearly every culture.

_____

2. I use a furnace, a hammer, an anvil, and a chisel.

_____

3. I have an apprentice who helps me and who I teach.

_____

4. I make objects from different kinds of metal, like iron or steel.

_____

5. My occupation still exists today and there are schools that teach people how to do this.

_____

6. I have made simple things, such as nails, and I have made elaborate things, such as weapons and armor.

_____

Imagine you have found out that your ancestor had this occupation. How do you think this occupation may have shaped your ancestors? How might knowing this information shape or change you? Take turns with your partner sharing your thoughts. Be sure to justify your opinions.

 **Money Order,** page E183   **INTERMEDIATE/EXPANDING**

Infinitive Phrases

Infinitive phrases consist of the word *to* and the base word of a verb. For example, *to jump* is an infinitive phrase.

Look at the examples of infinitive phrases from the poem "Money Order." Notice how each infinitive phrase has the word *to* and a verb. The verb is underlined in the infinitive phrases.

- to <u>save</u> some money
- to <u>send</u> to cousins
- to <u>buy</u> a color TV

Infinitive phrases can function as nouns, adjectives, or adverbs. Review the chart below to see different examples of infinitive phrases. Notice how the infinitive phrases modify words differently.

Infinitive Phrase as a Noun	Infinitive Phrase as an Adjective	Infinitive Phrase as an Adverb
<u>To smile</u> is happiness. Noun, Subject: *To smile* is the subject	I have too much work <u>to do</u>. Adjective: *to do* modifies the noun *work*	He agreed <u>to take</u> the trash out after dinner. Adverb: *to take* describes what was *agreed* (verb)
The girl refuses <u>to smile</u>. Noun, Direct Object: *to smile* describes what is happening to *the girl* (noun)	She has several invitations <u>to write</u>. Adjective: *to write* modifies the noun *invitations*	The cat meowed at the owner <u>to show</u> it was hungry. Adverb: *to show* describes why it *meowed* (verb)

When an infinitive phrase is a noun, it can be either a subject or a direct object.

The subject of a sentence is the main part of a sentence. The rest of the sentence hinges on the subject. In the example above, "is happiness" hinges on the subject "To smile."

The direct object of a sentence describes how or what a person or thing receives the action of the verb. In the example above, "to smile" is the direct object for the verb "refuses." *Think: Refuses to do what? Refuses to smile.*

Complete the activities below. Use the examples of infinitive phrases from the poem "Money Order" and the chart above for support.

Infinitive Phrases as Nouns

Underline the infinitive phrase in each sentence. Then, determine whether the infinitive phrase is a subject or a direct object, and place a circle around the correct one.

1. The fisherman lured the fish to come by the shore.   SUBJECT   DIRECT OBJECT
2. To solve a problem is a great achievement.   SUBJECT   DIRECT OBJECT
3. The waiter told us to sit in the booth.   SUBJECT   DIRECT OBJECT

Infinitive Phrases as Adjectives

Underline the infinitive phrase in each sentence. Then, place a circle around the noun each infinitive phrase modifies.

1. He made chicken noodle soup to eat.
2. My neighbor brought over some of his vegetables to share.
3. The museum will have a pottery exhibit to set up.

Infinitive Phrases as Adverbs

Write the correct infinitive phrase in each blank.

1. I continued practicing my song even though the dog was barking.

   I continued _____ my song even though the dog was barking.

2. We camped outside in the tent enjoying the warm weather.

   We camped outside in the tent _____ the warm weather.

3. The boy started playing soccer when he was five years old.

   The boy started _____ soccer when he was five years old.

Cultural Heritage and Traditions

Consider the things that make you who you are: values you were brought up having, traditions, customs, or beliefs you have learned from your family, and events from your native home. All of these things are part of your **cultural heritage**.

Lorna Dee Cervantes, the author of the poem "Refugee Ship," discusses her cultural heritage in the poem. She also talks about her life in the United States.

Think of the traditions you and your family have. Is there a tradition from your past experiences that is now different being in the United States?

Choose one tradition to share with your classmates. In small groups, take turns discussing your family traditions. Answer the following questions:

- How did the tradition start?
- What are some important parts of your tradition?
- Has the tradition changed since you and your family moved to the United States? If so, how?
- How is your tradition part of your cultural heritage and part of your present life in the United States?

In small groups, discuss how the poem "Refugee Ship," relates to your own cultural heritage and traditions. Write a paragraph to justify your opinions.

_____

_____

_____

_____

_____

_____

_____

A Defenseless Creature, page 417   **BEGINNING/EMERGING**

Idiomatic Expressions

An **idiomatic expression** is a phrase that consists of an idiom. An **idiom** is an expression that has a meaning separate from the individual words that make it up. Although idioms can be confusing, authors use idioms to convey meaning through imagery. When a person reads an idiom, he or she imagines the meaning and how it applies to the author's message.

Review the following idiomatic expressions from the play "A Defenseless Creature."

Idiomatic Expression	Meaning
grates on his nerves	annoys someone
lose my mind	become crazy
making headway	making progress
man of your word	person who can be trusted
sink/sank in	become/became
make head or tail out of	understand at all
skin and bones	very thin

Write a sentence using each of the idiomatic expressions above. Use the play and the chart above for reference.

1. _____

2. _____

3. _____

4. _____

5. _____

6. _____

7. _____

Compare sentences with a partner. Then, discuss why the author might have included idiomatic expressions. What effect does it have on the audience?

Work with your partner to write a short play. Choose four idiomatic expressions from the bank below to use in your play. Be sure to use the idiom correctly. If you need help understanding the phrase, use a dictionary or ask your teacher.

Idiomatic Expression	Meaning
pack it in	stop an activity
spill the beans	let out a secret
keep an eye out	stay aware to notice something
feeling blue	feeling sad
not rocket science	not difficult
cut to the chase	get to the main point
butterflies in your stomach	nervous or anxious
piece of cake	very easy
sick as a dog	very ill
out of the blue	unexpectedly
woke up on the wrong side of the bed	is extremely grumpy
bite your tongue	do not say anything
back to the drawing board	start all over again
wild goose chase	a hopeless situation
bad apple	a person that behaves badly
hit the hay	go to bed

Then, exchange plays with other pairs and act them out. Circle the idiomatic expressions in the play and be sure to act them out the clearly.

A Christmas Carol: Scrooge and Marley, page 429   **INTERMEDIATE/EXPANDING**

Formal Archaic Language

Sometimes, language in older texts can be difficult to understand. The language might be outdated, or archaic (pronounced *ar-kay-ick*). **Archaic language** is language that is no longer used. Most old-fashioned language is also formal.

Charles Dickens published the original play *A Christmas Carol* in 1843. The story was set in the 1800s.

In Israel Horovitz's play "A Christmas Carol: Scrooge and Marley," see "The Time of the Play" description on page 431—the play is set in 1843. The author uses formal archaic language because of the time period.

Archaic language typically contains sentences with strange structures. For example, Marley states on page 439:

> "How is it that I appear before you in a shape that you can see, I may not tell."

In modern language, this sentence might "translate" into something like this:

> "I'm not sure how you can see me since I look like this."

With a partner, "translate" the following sentences from the play. First, identify the formal archaic language. Then, rewrite the sentence in modern, easily understood language. Remember to use context clues to determine the meanings of difficult words.

1. It is required of every man that the spirit within him should walk around among his fellow-men, and travel far and wide; and if that spirit goes not forth in life, it is condemned to do so after death. (page 438)

   _____

   _____

   _____

2. I will, but don't be hard upon me. (page 439)

   _____

3. Without their visits, you cannot hope to shun the path I tread. (page 439)

   _____

4. I pray go in ahead of me. (page 453)

_____

5. Sit ye down before the fire, my dear, and have a warm, Lord bless ye! (page 454)

_____

6. 'Tis I! (page 454)

_____

7. Mark my words, Ebenezer Scrooge. (page 457)

_____

8. The time is drawing near! (page 458)

_____

Affixes

Affixes are word parts that give clues to word meanings. They can come at the beginning of words (called **prefixes**), or they can come at word endings (called **suffixes**). Usually, affixes are two to four letters long.

Affixes attach to root words. **Root words** are the building blocks from which larger words can be made.

Some verb endings are considered suffixes. For example, *-s*, *-ed*, and *-ing* are considered to be suffixes.

Review the chart below.

Common Affixes: Prefixes	Meaning	Example
un-, dis-, non-	not	**un**spoken, **dis**like, **non**sense
pre-	before	**pre**heat
re-	again	**re**union
trans-	across	**trans**port
semi-	half; partly	**semi**pro
Common Affixes: Suffixes	**Meaning**	**Example**
-ful	full of	skill**ful**
-en	made of	gold**en**
-able, -ible	is; can be	enjoy**able**, revers**ible**
-ion, -tion, -ation	act; process	precis**ion**, creat**ion**, communic**ation**
-less	without	bone**less**

Look at the prefixes used in each sentence. Circle the correct word based on the prefix meaning and the context clues.

1. We can buy **pre**cut/**un**cut carrots at the store to save time by not having to cut them when we get home.

2. I am going to **trans**fer/**re**fer money from my savings account to my checking account today because I need to buy a gift for my friend.

3. By the time people arrived, the chairs were in a **re**circle/**semi**circle facing the podium and the guest speaker.

4. I **un**stated/**re**stated my idea in a different way so that my friends could hear it again.

Look at the words with affixes from the play "Let Me Hear You Whisper." Rewrite
each root word on the left using the new affix provided. Some words might need an
additional letter added, depending on the affix used. Use a print or online dictionary
to check your spelling and to determine the meaning of each new word. The first one is
done for you.

1. recommend**ation**   **-able**   _____recommend**able**: can be recommended or praised_____

2. prefer**s**   **-ence**   _____

3. recept**ion**   **-ive**   _____

4. equip**ment**   **-er**   _____

5. **im**planting   **trans-**   _____

6. **en**danger   **-ous**   _____

7. revolution**ized**   **-ist**   _____

8. **sub**marines   **trans-**   _____

9. **un**question**ing**   **-able**   _____

10. **dis**charg**ed**   **re-**   _____

Types of Pronouns

In the story "Tsali of the Cherokees," you read many different pronouns. Authors use **pronouns** to refer to nouns already mentioned. If an author were to use a person's name in every sentence, the story would sound clumsy and repetitive. Pronouns add variety to the flow of a story.

The charts below show common pronouns. Notice that the personal and possessive pronouns have a singular version and a plural version.

Personal Pronouns (subjective)	Singular		Plural	
	I		we	
	you		you	
	he/she/it		they	
Personal Pronouns (objective)				
	me		us	
	you		you	
	him/her/it		them	
Possessive Pronouns				
	mine		ours	
	yours		yours	
	his/hers/its		theirs	
Demonstrative	this		these	
	that		those	
Indefinite	anything	something		nothing
	anybody	somebody		nobody
	anyone	someone		no one

Look at the examples from the story "Tsali of the Cherokees." The pronouns are underlined.

- "My husband's father worked this place, and <u>his</u> father before <u>him</u>." (page 525)
- The Cherokees were tired and cold and hungry, but <u>they</u> were silent. (page 526)
- "What are <u>you</u> going to do with <u>us</u>?" Tsali demanded. (page 527)

Read the sentences from the story "Tsali of the Cherokees." Place a circle around the pronouns in the sentence. Then, write the types of pronouns used. Some sentences may have more than one pronoun. The first one is done for you.

1. "(You) will have to go soon," said one white preacher to Tsali. (page 523)

   You = Personal Pronoun

2. "My sons are my partners, as I was my father's." (page 524)

   _____

3. "I have my family and we all have our good health." (page 524)

   _____

   _____

4. She gave him his father's old squirrel gun, and he sneaked his own blowgun and darts and slid out the back of the house. (page 526)

   _____

   _____

   _____

   _____

5. "If you shoot, shoot us both," she ordered. (page 527)

   _____

   _____

   _____

Read each sentence. Fill in each blank using the type of pronoun listed. Use the charts to help you determine the correct pronoun.

1. _____ play in the park with my friends. (personal pronoun, subjective)

2. It took _____ twenty minutes to hike the trail. (personal pronoun, objective)

3. This book is _____. (possessive pronoun)

4. _____ sandwiches are for after school. (demonstrative)

5. We went to the mall today and _____ was there. (indefinite)

Now, think about your native language. Does your native language have different pronouns when referring to male or female? Does your native language have different pronouns for formal language or informal language?

Draw connections between your native language and the English language. Discuss with your teacher the connections you have identified.

Multiple-Meaning Words

As you already know, some words have more than one meaning. These words are called **multiple-meaning words**. Because they have more than one meaning, readers rely on context clues to figure out the meaning of these words.

The word *great* is a multiple-meaning word and it is used in a variety of ways in the folk tale "We Are All One." While in casual conversation, *great* usually means "really good" or "fantastic," it has other meanings, which can be slightly or very different.

Match the following phrases with the correct meaning of the word *great*.

____ 1. the pain was so great   a. noble

____ 2. a great city   b. huge

____ 3. the great emperor Yü   c. terrible

____ 4. the great flood   d. valuable

____ 5. a great reward   e. major

Read the multiple-meaning words from the folk tale in the chart below. Write two to three sentences for each multiple-meaning word. Be sure to use a different meaning in each sentence. Also, make sure to include enough context clues to help the reader determine the correct meaning.

Multiple-Meaning Word from "We Are All One"	
cure	1. _____ 2. _____ 3. _____
slipping	1. _____ 2. _____ 3. _____
shade	1. _____ 2. _____ 3. _____

flood	1. _____ 2. _____ 3. _____
fresh	1. _____ 2. _____ 3. _____
back	1. _____ 2. _____ 3. _____
temple	1. _____ 2. _____ 3. _____
call	1. _____ 2. _____ 3. _____
sharp	1. _____ 2. _____ 3. _____
rest	1. _____ 2. _____ 3. _____

If time allows, work with a partner and point out the context clues. Be sure to explain how the context clues help the reader determine the correct word meaning.

Phaëthon, Son of Apollo, page 539　　　　　　　　　**ADVANCED/BRIDGING**

Formal Language

Myths, such as "Phaëthon, Son of Apollo," typically include **formal language**. It is a way for authors to express ideas using Standard English. Formal language has a specific grammar style and tone.

Informal language is a more relaxed way of communicating ideas. Sometimes it is called "natural language" because it represents how we normally talk.

Formal Language	Informal Language
• newspaper article • encyclopedia entry	• social media post • phone call to a friend

Most people don't speak the same way that "Phaëthon, Son of Apollo" is written—which is perfectly fine. However, it is important to know the differences between formal and informal language, and how to use each type of language.

Read the sentences from the Greek myth "Phaëthon, Son of Apollo." Rewrite the formal language into informal language. You can use more than one sentence to rewrite the language. The first one is done for you.

1. "Phaëthon loved to boast of his divine father as he saw the golden chariot riding high through the air."

   Phaëthon loved to brag about his dad, who was a god, He was totally bragging when he checked out the golden chariot flying way up there in the sky.

2. "Up the steep hill and the bright steps climbed Phaëthon, passing unafraid through the silver doors, and stood in the presence of the sun."

   _____

   _____

3. "When the father saw that nothing else would satisfy the boy, he bade the Hours bring forth his chariot and yoke the horses."

   _____

   _____

4. "As soon as the horses felt that there was no hand controlling them, they soared up, up with fiery speed into the heavens till the earth grew pale and cold beneath them."

_____

_____

5. "Then the horses dropped down, more swiftly than a falling stone, flinging themselves madly from side to side in panic because they were masterless."

_____

_____

Complete the chart below. Review the three texts you have read from this unit. Identify the kind of language used in each text by putting a check mark in the appropriate column. You may find that a text has both types of language. Then, include examples of the language used and explain how you know the type of language.

	Text from this Unit	Formal Language	Informal Language	Examples of Language Used
1.				• • • I know the text includes _____ language because_____ _____.
2.				• • • I know the text includes _____ language because_____ _____.
3.				• • • I know the text includes _____ language because_____ _____.

Differentiated Instruction: English Language Development

Foundational Literacy Skills

Lesson 1: Vowel Sounds

The English alphabet has 26 letters. The letters *a, e, i, o,* and *u* are the **vowels**. Sometimes *y* can sound like a vowel, too. All the other letters are the **consonants.**

The vowels and consonants represent all the different sounds, or **phonemes**, in the English language. Consonant sounds, such as /t/, /p/, and /l/, are made by touching the teeth, lips, or tongue together. Vowel sounds, such as /a/ and /o/, are made with the mouth and throat open. The teeth, lips, and tongue do not touch. The sound is made by the shape of the mouth and throat as the air flows through it.

🔊 Short sounds	🔊 Long sounds	🔊 Other sounds
/a/ pan, sap	/ā/ mate, sail	/ô/ or, raw, author
/e/ bet, sell	/ē/ be, deep	/u̇/ soot, foot, put
/i/ kit, lip	/ī/ my, ice	/ou/ out, now
/o/, /ä/ lot, star	/ō/ so, boat	/oi/ toy, boil
/u/ up, scrub	/ü/ tune, crew	/ə/ tractor, even

Short, Long, and R-Controlled Vowel Sounds

There are only five vowels in English, but there are more than twice as many vowel sounds. This is because every vowel can make more than one sound. Each vowel has a short sound and a long sound. When a vowel has a long sound, it "says its name." For example, the *a* in *mate* sounds like the letter A. The letter *y* can also sound like a short /i/ (system), a long /ī/ (my) or a long /ē/ (surely).

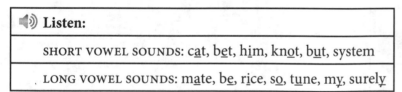

🔊 **Listen:**

SHORT VOWEL SOUNDS: c**a**t, b**e**t, h**i**m, kn**o**t, b**u**t, syst**e**m

LONG VOWEL SOUNDS: m**a**te, b**e**, r**i**ce, s**o**, t**u**ne, m**y**, surel**y**

When a vowel is followed by the letter *r*, it has a weaker sound because it is controlled by the *r*.

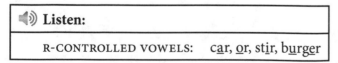

🔊 **Listen:**

R-CONTROLLED VOWELS: c**ar**, **or**, st**ir**, b**ur**ge**r**

Vowels can also sound like other vowels. Sometimes the letter *a* can sound like a short /o/—notice how *father* rhymes with *bother*! The letter *o* sounds like a long /ü/ in words like *lose* and *pool*. The many different ways to spell vowel sounds can make reading and spelling in English very tricky.

Vowel Teams

In English, two vowels often team up to create one vowel sound. These vowel teams are called **digraphs.** The consonants *y* and *w* often appear in vowel teams. The letter *y* can follow a vowel to make the sounds /ā/ and /oi/ (**bay**, **boy**). The letter *w* can team up with vowels to make the sounds /ô/, /ü/, and /ou/ (**raw**, **crew**, **cow**).

Here are some examples of digraphs that create long vowel sounds:

🔊 **Listen:**	
Long /ā/:	ai, ay, ei, ey (<u>ai</u>m, pl<u>ay</u>, v<u>ei</u>n, ob<u>ey</u>)
Long /ē/:	ee, ea, ie, (s<u>ee</u>n, b<u>ea</u>d, n<u>ie</u>ce)
Long /ī/:	ie, uy (t<u>ie</u>, b<u>uy</u>)
Long /ō/:	oa, oe, ow (b<u>oa</u>t, t<u>oe</u>, sh<u>ow</u>)
Long /ü/:	oo, ou, ui, ue, ew (b<u>oo</u>t, gr<u>ou</u>p, s<u>ui</u>t, cl<u>ue</u>, fl<u>ew</u>)

The sounds /ou/ and /oi/ are **diphthongs.** That is, they contain two vowel sounds in one. They begin with one vowel sound and end with another.

🔊 **Listen:**	
ou, ow	f<u>ou</u>nd, bl<u>ou</u>se, c<u>ow</u>, cr<u>ow</u>d
oi, oy	b<u>oi</u>l, s<u>oi</u>l, b<u>oy</u>s, t<u>oy</u>

Some vowel teams can make more than one sound. There are at least three ways to pronounce the vowel team *ea*:

🔊 **Listen:**	
Long /ē/:	b<u>ea</u>d
Short /e/:	h<u>ea</u>d, pl<u>ea</u>sant
R-controlled /e/:	w<u>ea</u>r, b<u>ea</u>r

The team *oo* has a long sound and a short sound. The long *oo* sound is a long /ü/. The short *oo* is like the *u* in *put*.

🔊 **Listen:**	
Long *oo*:	sp<u>oo</u>n, f<u>oo</u>d
Short *oo*:	l<u>oo</u>k, f<u>oo</u>t, b<u>oo</u>k

Differentiated Instruction: Foundational Literacy Skills

PRACTICE

Exercise 1: Silent *e*

When a word ends in a silent *e*, it usually has a long vowel sound. Create new words by adding the letter *e* to the words listed below. Notice how the silent *e* changes the short vowel sound into a long vowel sound. Write a sentence using each new word.

> Example   pal___
> pale
> Her face went <u>pale</u> when she heard the news.

1. sham
2. grim
3. cod
4. them
5. cur

Exercise 2: Vowel Teams

When two vowels combine in English, the first one usually makes a long vowel sound, while the second one is silent. In other words, "When two vowels go walking, the first does the talking." However, there are many exceptions. Read the words below. Which ones follow the pattern? Which ones do not?

aim	tie	group
play	buy	suit
obey	boat	flew
seen	show	clue
niece	boot	

Exercise 3: Word Pairs

Read the following word pairs aloud to yourself, being sure to pronounce each word clearly. Then, listen to the audio and choose the word you hear.

1. sheep / ship 🔊
2. tail / tile 🔊
3. coat / court 🔊
4. caught / cot 🔊
5. feel / fell 🔊
6. rum / room 🔊

Exercise 4: Tongue Twister

Try the following tongue twister to practice different vowel sounds!

Betty Botter bought a bit of butter;	It will make my batter bitter
"But," she said, "this butter's bitter!	But a bit of better butter
If I put it in my batter	Will make my batter better."

Lesson 2: Consonant Sounds

The consonants include all the letters of the alphabet other than the vowels *a*, *e*, *i*, *o*, and *u*. Consonant sounds are made by touching the tongue, lips, or teeth together. When pronouncing the consonants in English, you should feel a puff of air as the sound is forced through the tongue, lips, or teeth.

Here is a list of consonant sounds in English:

Consonant Sounds					
🔊 /b/	but, cub	🔊 /l/	lip, pull	🔊 /t/	tip, cut
/ch/	child, patch	/m/	man, lamb	/th/	thank, forth
/d/	doll, cod	/n/	not, can	/th/	there, that
/f/	fall, cuff	/ŋ/	sing, ink	/v/	very, cove
/g/	girl, hug	/p/	pull, up	/w/	wet, twin
/h/	hope, ham	/r/	ram, core	/y/	your, yard
/j/	jam, fudge	/s/	sip, miss	/z/	zip
/k/	kid, pick	/sh/	ship, lotion	/zh/	pleasure, vision

Repeat the consonant sounds on your own. Try holding a sheet of paper in front of your mouth as you say each word. A puff of air should escape your mouth as you say each consonant, causing the paper to move slightly.

Consonants with More Than One Sound

Some consonants make more than one sound. The consonants c, q, and x make the sounds shown below:

🔊 Listen:
c can have a soft sound like /s/ if it is followed by e, i, or y (cell, city, icy), or a hard sound like /k/ if it is followed by a, o, or u (cap, cone, culture).
q combines with u to make the sound /kw/ (as in quack) or /k/ (as in unique).
g can have a soft sound like /j/ if it comes before e, i, or y (gem, giant, gym).
s can have a sound like /z/ at the end of a word (is, rose).
x can sound like /ks/ (as in next) or, rarely, /z/ (as in xylophone).

Consonant Blends

Consonants often blend together to make a sound. For instance, the letters *c* and *k* combine to make one sound in words like *click* and *pick*. Other consonant blends, such as *sh* and *st*, make two sounds, but they are blended together so that one sound runs into the other.

Consonant blends that appear at the beginning of many words include *ch, sh, st, th, gh, str, sk, bl, cl, fl, gl, pl, br, cr, dr, fr, gr, pr, tr, thr, phr,* and *shr*.

Blends that appear at the ends of words include *ct, ft, ld, lp, lt, mp, nd, nk, nt, pt, rd, rk, sk, sp,* and *st*.

PRACTICE

Exercise 1: Soft and Hard Consonant Sounds

Read the following vocabulary words from your textbook aloud. Which words have the soft g sound, /j/? Which words have a hard g sound, /g/? Which words do not fit in either group?

genteel	kindling	fledglings
gilded	legible	poignant
dangle	egotism	thoroughfare

Words with Soft g sound	Words with Hard g sound	Neither

Exercise 2: *Sh* sound

The following words all contain the sound /sh/. However, they use different letters to spell the sound. Sort them into groups according to the way they are spelled. How many different ways did you find to spell the sound /sh/?

ashamed	mission	special
commercial	nation	sugar
dish	patient	tissue
initial	shell	unsure

Exercise 3: Word Pairs

Read the following word pairs aloud to yourself, being sure to pronounce each word clearly. Then, listen to the audio and choose the word you hear.

1. ring / rink 🔊
2. steam / stream 🔊
3. wit / with 🔊
4. mats / match 🔊
5. plant / plank 🔊

Exercise 4: Think About It

Consonant and vowel sounds are not the same in every language. For instance, the *th* sound in English does not exist in many languages, so English language learners sometimes find it difficult to pronounce. The vowel *œ* in French, found in the word *œuvre* ("artwork"), is difficult for English speakers to pronounce because this vowel sound does not exist in English.

If you speak a language other than English, can you think of a consonant or vowel sound that an English speaker might find difficult to pronounce? Try teaching this sound to someone. How difficult or easy is it to master a new phoneme?

Differentiated Instruction: Foundational Literacy Skills

Lesson 3: Breaking Words into Syllables

A **syllable** is a word part that contains a single vowel sound. Read each of the following words aloud, listening for the vowel sound in each syllable:

One syllable: soap
Two syllables: tea-cher
Three syllables: pres-i-dent
Four syllables: li-brar-i-an
Five syllables: cu-ri-os-i-ty

Breaking new words into their syllables can help you read and spell them correctly. To break a word into its syllables, first break off any prefixes or suffixes (pre-school, quick-ly). Divide compound words into separate parts (house-hold, book-shelf). Next, look for the pattern of vowels (V) and consonants (C) in the word. Follow these rules:

1. **VC/CV and VC/CCCV Rule:** If a word has two or more consonants in the middle, you should usually divide after the first consonant (hap-pen, an-swer, ob-struct). However, consonant blends such as *ch*, *sh*, *th*, *gh*, *sk*, or *ck* should not be divided. Break the word before or after the blend (ba-sket, tick-et).

2. **V/CV Rule:** If a word has one consonant in the middle, divide before the consonant (re-ject). However, if the vowel sound is short, divide after the consonant (lev-er).

3. **V/V Rule:** Two vowels together in a word should be split if they are sounded separately (li-on, sci-ence). Do not separate vowel teams that work together to make one sound (bear, vein).

4. **VC + Silent *e* Rule:** When a vowel is followed by a consonant and silent *e* (VC + *e*), the silent *e* must be kept in the same syllable. It causes the vowel to have its long sound. (Examples e-<u>rase</u>, ig-<u>nite</u>.)

5. **C + -*le* Rule:** When the suffix –*le* appears at the end of the word, it forms a syllable with the consonant or consonant blend that comes before it. (Examples ti-<u>tle</u>, chu-<u>ckle</u>, bub-<u>ble</u>.)

6. **C + -*ed* Rule:** The suffix –*ed* forms a separate syllable when it follows *d* or *t* (wad-<u>ded</u>, chan-<u>ted</u>). Otherwise, it does not form a new syllable (walked, stopped).

PRACTICE

Exercise 1: VC/CV

The following words have the pattern VCCV, VCCCV, or VCCCCV. Divide each word into its syllables, being careful not to separate consonant blends.

EXAMPLE   muddy
                 mud / dy

1. victim   _____

2. toughest   _____

3. chatterbox   _____

4. wicker   _____

5. instruct   _____

6. monstrous   _____

7. bumblebee   _____

8. necklace   _____

Exercise 2: Vowel Sounds and Syllables

Read each word aloud, paying attention to the vowel sound you hear in the first syllable. Then, choose the correct way to divide the word into syllables.

_____ 1. native
        a. na-tive   b. nat-ive

_____ 2. desert
        a. de-sert   b. des-ert

_____ 3. acrobat
        a. a-cro-bat   b. ac-ro-bat

_____ 4. robot
        a. ro-bot   b. rob-ot

_____ 5. event
        a. e-vent   b. ev-ent

Exercise 3: Consonant + -le

Read aloud the following consonant + -le syllables. Then, match the syllables to create words ending in -le:

       -ble   -cle   -dle   -gle   -tle

1. rus-_____

2. rub-_____

3. mus-_____

4. strug-_____

5. mud-_____

Exercise 4: Syllables with -ed

Divide the following words into syllables. If the word cannot be divided, tell why.

1. riot   _____

2. beam   _____

3. stopped   _____

4. drive   _____

5. anticipated _____

Lesson 4: Syllables and Stress

English is a stress-timed language. This means that certain words and syllables receive more stress, or emphasis, than others. The stressed syllables are longer, while the unstressed syllables are shorter. Learning how to use stress correctly can give you a more natural rhythm when speaking English.

Many English words have stress on the first syllable of the word. If a word has a prefix, however, the second syllable is usually stressed instead.

EXAMPLE   decorate   dec′ o rate
              redecorate   re dec′ o rate

Longer words often have a primary and a secondary stress. In the following word, the syllable with the primary stress is capitalized.

EXAMPLE   syllabification syl lab′ i fi CA′ tion

When a stressed syllable ends in a vowel, that vowel has a long sound. If the stressed syllable ends in a vowel plus a consonant, the vowel will have a short sound because it is cut short by the consonant.

LONG SOUND   il lu′ mi nate
              com po′ sure
              ex cla ma′ tion

SHORT SOUND   sed′ i ment
              viv′ id
              tem′ po ra ry

The vowels in unstressed syllables often make a weak, indistinct sound, called a schwa (ə). Notice how the vowels in these examples have a clear sound when they are stressed, but a schwa sound in unstressed syllables.

EXAMPLES   liver   (liv′ ər)
              actor   (act′ ər)
              olive   (ol′ əv)
              opal   (o′ pəl)

PRACTICE

Exercise 1: Mark Stressed Syllables

Divide each word into syllables. Mark the stressed syllables with an accent mark (').
Write a schwa (ə) for the vowel sounds that have a schwa sound.

1. intolerable   _____

2. tolerate   _____

3. understanding   _____

4. standpoint   _____

5. cursor   _____

Exercise 2: Stress and Meaning

In English, stress can be changed to emphasize important ideas in a sentence. Notice
how a change in stress changes the meaning of the sentence. What is being emphasized
in each example?

> Do you beLIEVE me?
> Do YOU believe me?
> Do you believe ME?
> DO you believe me?

Exercise 3: Just for Fun

Write the names of five of your friends, classmates, or family members. Divide each
name into syllables and use accent marks to mark stressed syllables.

EXAMPLE   Tab' i tha

Lesson 5: Meaningful Word Parts: Prefixes and Suffixes

Many words in English are made up of meaningful parts. These meaningful word parts, or **morphemes**, include prefixes and suffixes. They are added to the beginning or the end of a word to change its meaning.

A **prefix** is a word part that attaches to the beginning of a word.

EXAMPLES   re- (meaning "again")
re- + play = replay, meaning "play again"
pre- (meaning "before")
pre- + judge = prejudge, meaning "to judge beforehand"

Negative prefixes change a word's meaning to its opposite. Common negative prefixes include dis-, un-, and in-. The prefix in- changes its spelling to il-, im-, or ir- when it comes before a word beginning with *l*, *m*, or *r*.

EXAMPLES   <u>dis</u>order, <u>un</u>real, <u>in</u>valid, <u>il</u>legal, <u>ir</u>regular

A **suffix** attaches to the end of a word. If the word ends in silent *e* and the suffix begins with a vowel, the silent *e* is usually dropped. If the word ends in *y*, it is sometimes changed to an *i* before adding the suffix.

EXAMPLES   -able or -ible (meaning "able to be")   believable
-ful (meaning "full of")   joyful
-less (meaning "without")   hopeless
-ness (meaning "state of being")   happiness
-ous (meaning "possessing the qualities of")   famous

PRACTICE

Exercise 1: Negative Prefixes

Change each word to its opposite by adding a negative prefix from the list below. You will use each prefix only once.

dis- un- in- il- im- ir-

1. ___justice

2. ___responsible

3. ___agree

4. ___possible

5. ___logical

6. ____mobile

Exercise 2: Adding Suffixes

Complete the sentences in a logical way by adding a suffix to the base word. Drop the silent *e* if necessary.

-able/-ible -ful -less -ous

1. The puppy was absolutely <u>adore</u>_____.

2. The explorers were very <u>adventure</u>_____.

3. Don't make a <u>care</u>_____ mistake!

4. We admired the <u>grace</u>_____ dancers.

5. This hat is <u>reverse</u>_____; I can wear it inside out.

Exercise 3: Guess the Meaning

Break each word apart, identifying its prefix, suffix, and base word. Guess the meaning of each word based on its prefix and/or suffix. Then, use the word in a sentence.

> EXAMPLE   unrecognizable
> un- + recognize + -able

Unrecognizable means "not able to be recognized."

The teacher was <u>unrecognizable</u> in her witch costume.

1. aimless _____

_____

2. rechargeable _____

_____

3. unavoidable _____

_____

4. melodious _____

_____

5. presoak _____

_____

Lesson 6: Meaningful Word Parts: Base Words and Word Roots

Many words in English are made up of word parts from older languages, especially Greek and Latin. Knowing the meaning of these **word roots** can help you increase your vocabulary.

Unlike **base words**, word roots cannot stand alone. They must be combined with other meaningful word parts, including prefixes, suffixes, and other word roots. Following are some common word roots found in many English words.

Greek Word Roots

astr	star
bio	life
graph, graphy	write, writing
logy	study of
meter/metr	measure of
phon	sound
psych	mind; soul
scop/scope	to see
tele	far off
therm	heat

Latin Word Roots

aud	to hear
vis	to see
port	to carry
rupt	to break
scrib	to write
spect	to watch or look
struct	to build

Common Prefixes and Suffixes Used with Word Roots

con-, sym-	together
de-	opposite; remove; reduce
dis-	not
in-	not; in; within
inter-	between; among
trans-	across
-ion/-tion	action or process

PRACTICE

Exercise 1: Break It Down

Break each word down into its morphemes, or word parts. Give the meaning of the word root and any prefixes or suffixes. Then, tell the meaning of the whole word based on its parts. You may use a dictionary to check your answers.

1. interrupt
2. transport
3. telescope
4. audition
5. thermography
6. astrology
7. symphony

Exercise 2: Which Word?

Which word fits in each sentence? Explain how you used your knowledge of word roots to find the answer.

1. The kind lady was known for her (beneficent/malignant) deeds.

2. The spaceship could travel to far-off places using (thermography/teleportation).

3. The earthquake caused a (structure/rupture) in the ground.

4. (Phonology/Graphology) is the study of sound.

5. (Biography/Biology) is the study of life on earth.

Exercise 3: Word Families

Find three or more words in English that contain each of the following roots.

1. vis _____

2. logy _____

3. aud _____

4. phon _____

5. scop _____

LITERARY CREDITS

"A Day's Wait" from *The Short Stories of Ernest Hemingway.* Copyright 1933 by Charles Scribner's Sons. Copyright renewed 1961 by Mary Hemingway. Reprinted with permission of Scribner, a Division of Simon & Schuster.

"The War of the Wall" from *Deep Sightings and Rescue Missions* by Toni Cade Bambara, copyright © 1996 by The Estate of Toni Cade Bambara. Used by permission of Pantheon Books a division of Random House, Inc.

"The Green Mamba" from *Going Solo* by Roald Dahl. Copyright © 1986 by Roald Dahl. Reprinted by permission of Farrar, Straus, and Giroux, LLC.

"The Courage That My Mother Had" by Edna St. Vincent Millay from *Collected Poems.* Copyright © 1954, 1982 by Norma Millay Ellis. Reprinted by permission of Elizabeth Barnett, Literary Executor, the Millay Society.

"Antaeus" by Borden Deal. Reprinted by permission of Ashley Matin Moss.

"Names/Nombres" by Julia Alvarez from *Nuestro,* March 1985. Reprinted by permission of Susan Bergholz Literary Services.

"Fish Cheeks" by Amy Tan. Copyright © 1989 by Amy Tan. First appeared in *Seventeen* Magazine. Reprinted by permission of the author and the Sandra Dijkstra Literary Agency.

"Roberto Clemente: A Bittersweet Memoir" from *Great Latin Sport Figures* by Jerry Izenberg. Reprinted by permission of the author.

"Madam C.J. Walker" from *One More River to Cross: The Stories of Twelve Black Americans* by Jim Haskins. Copyright © by Jim Haskins. Reprinted by permission of Scholastic Inc.

"I'm Nobody! Who are you?" by Emily Dickinson. Reprinted by permission of the publishers and the Trustees of Amherst College from The Poems of Emily Dickinson, Ralph W. Franklin, ed., Cambridge, Mass.: The Belknap Press of Harvard University Press, Copyright © 1998 by the President and Fellows of Harvard College. Copyright © 1951, 1955, 1979, 1983 by the President and Fellows of Harvard College.

"Monsters Are Due on Maple Street" by Rod Sterling. Reprinted by permission of the Rode Sterling Trust.

"Persephone and Demeter" from *D'Aulaires Book of Greek Myths* by Ingri & Edgar Parin D'Aulaire, copyright © 1962 by Ingri and Edgar Parin D'Aulaire. Used by permission of Random House Children's Books, a division of Random House, Inc.

"The Secret Name of Ra" from *Gods and Pharaohs from Egyptian Mythology* retold by Geraldine Harris Pinch. Reprinted by permissions of author.

"The Lion and the Statue" from *The Fables of Aesop* by Joseph Jacobs. Reprinted with the permission of Simon & Schuster Books for Young Readers, an imprint of Simon & Schuster Children's Publishing Division from *The Fables of Aesop: Selected, Told Anew and Their History Traced* by Joseph Jacobs. Copyright © 1964 Macmillan Publishing Company.

"Amaterasu" from *World Myths and Tales* by Carolyn Swift. Reprinted by permission of Poolbeg Press Ltd.

PHOTO CREDITS